Facing a Pandemic

Facing a Pandemic

The African Church and the Crisis of HIV/AIDS

Elias K. Bongmba

BAYLOR UNIVERSITY PRESS

Scripture quotations are from the New Revised Standard Version Bible, copyright 1989, Division of Christian Education of the National Council of the Churches of Christ in the United States of America. Used by permission. All rights reserved.

Cover Design by Stephanie Blumenthal
Cover Image by AP Images / Themba Hadebe. Used with permission.

Library of Congress Cataloging-in-Publication Data

Bongmba, Elias Kifon, 1953-
  Facing a pandemic : the African church and the crisis of HIV/AIDS / Elias K. Bongmba.
      p. cm.
  Includes bibliographical references and index.
  ISBN 978-1-932792-82-9 (pbk. : alk. paper)
  1. AIDS (Disease)--Africa--Religious aspects--Christianity. 2. HIV infections--Africa--Religious aspects--Christianity. I. Title.

  RA643.86.A35B6698 2007
  362.196'97920096--dc22
                                                2007007088

Printed in the United States of America on acid-free paper with a minimum of 30% pcw content.

Dedicated to

Dr. Helen Marie Schmidt
Dr. Deiter Lemke
Dr. Julie Stone
Dr. Pius Tih
Dr. Thomas Welty
Dr. Edith Welty
Mrs. Beatrice Bongmba

Individuals who have dedicated their lives to fighting
HIV/AIDS in the Cameroon Baptist Convention

Contents

Preface

The Christian churches in Africa, alongside other faith traditions, have a pandemic in their midst. It is not going away soon. In the pages that follow, I offer theological reflections on the pandemic based on the claim that humanity has the *imago dei*, and suggest ways the church must scale up its fight against HIV/AIDS.

This book has been in the making for several years. My research and interviews have been conducted mostly in Cameroon. I have traveled to Cameroon every year since 1994 and I have seen the devastating effects of HIV/AIDS on individuals, families, and communities. I have talked with families, pastors, doctors, health care professionals, and politicians. I have had the opportunity of doing focused research among youths in the Bamenda urban area and talked with pastors about the crisis facing youth today. In addition to this fieldwork, I have carried out an extensive library research on HIV/AIDS in Africa and followed the work of several organizations involved with African HIV/AIDS relief. This study is a result of these efforts to understand what the community can do in response to the devastation that has come to human community and seems likely to stay for a while.

Several people have supported my research over the years and I want to recognize them here. First, I thank the Dean of Humanities at Rice University for a Mosle Research Grant for the summer of 2003 and for the dean's summer travel grants for the same period. In Cameroon, I am indebted to all the youths who spoke to me about their lives. I also express my gratitude for the insights received in my conversations with the following people in Cameroon: Dr. Helen Marie Schmidt, formerly of Banso Baptist Hospital; Professor Pius Tih, director of the medical board of the Cameroon Baptist Convention; Dr. Julie Stone; Mrs. Beatrice Bongmba; and Mr. Richard Nji, assistant to the director of the medical board of the Cameroon Baptist Convention. His lordship, Most Reverend Dr. Paul Verdzekov, archbishop of Bamenda was very generous with his time during the summer of 2003. I also interviewed the following members of the clergy: Rev. Hans Dibbie of the Full Gospel Church in Bamenda; Pastor Divine Azeh Ndaksa and Ngeh Martin of the Cameroon Baptist Convention in Nkwen; Rev. Daniel Mbiwan of the Full Gospel Church in Bamenda; Rev. Bernard Eta of Revivalist End Time Ministries in Bamenda; Rev. Yufenyui, Catholic education secretary in Bamenda; Rev. Jo Set Aji Mvo of the Presbyterian Church Center in Ntamulung; Rev. Akih Abraham, Presbyterian youth pastor for the Northwest Province; Father George Ngwa, of Catholic Youth Services, Mankon; and Father Tatah H. Mbuy. I also express my appreciation to my sister Caroline Bongmba Nfor and her husband Mr. Ernest Nfor for their hospitality to me every time I have visited Bamenda.

I am grateful to the library staff of Fondren Library at Rice University for their services in helping me locate reading materials and especially to the interlibrary loan staff for finding documents I needed in a timely manner. My colleague Anthony Pinn of the Department of Religious Studies read parts of the manuscript and offered useful suggestions. I also want to express my appreciation to the members of the Donga Mantung, division of Cameroon AIDS committee in the United States, for the conversations we have had concerning HIV/AIDS in our district in Cameroon. I thank the many Cameroonians who have shared their views and comments about HIV/AIDS with me.

Early drafts of the book were presented at South Main Baptist Church in Houston, Texas in the summer of 2005. Parts of chapter 2 were presented at the conference on "Jesus and Healing" at the University of Kwazulu-Natal Pietermaritzburg in October 2004. I thank Professor Jonathan Draper, the organizer, and the Department of Religious Studies at the University of Kwazulu-Natal and the University of Oslo, who jointly hosted the conference, for inviting me to participate. Sections of chapter 4 grew out of my participation in the Ford Foundation "Altering Nature Project" at Rice University. I want to thank Baruch Broady and Gerald McKenny for inviting me to serve on the advisory board of that project. I also express my appreciation to my colleagues on the legal and economic team of that project, Mary Anderlik, Les Rothenberg, Margaret Byrne, and Nancy Dubler for allowing me to use some of the material from that project in chapter. 4. A section of chapter 4 was also presented at the medical ethics section of the American Academy of Religion meeting in Philadelphia, November 19, 2005. I presented chapter 2 and chapter 5 at the Institute of Ethiopian studies at Addis Ababa University in May of 2006. I thank Dr. Mousumi Roy Chowdhury for inviting me to give the lectures. Sections of chapter 3 were presented at the

Caribbean Philosophical Association meeting in Montreal, July 3, 2006 and at the American Academy of Religion meeting in Washington D.C., November 20, 2006. I thank Professor Allen F. Roberts, director of the Department of World Arts and Culture, UCLA, for inviting me.

I would like to thank Dr. Carey Newman, the editorial director at Baylor University Press for his interest and encouragement of this project. I also thank Diane Smith, the production manager, who has worked with me to get this book through the production process. I thank the anonymous reviewers who have read this manuscript and given me valuable insights. The book is better because of their critical feedback.

Finally, I thank my partner Odelia Yuh Bongmba for her support and for stimulating conversations about HIV/AIDS and public responsibility in Cameroon. I also thank Christian Ndzi Bongmba for his constant support; and Donald Bongmba, Dino Bongmba, and Doug Bongmba for their patience, because in working on this project I was not always available when they wanted my attention. While all of these and the numerous authors whose work has provided inspiration and challenged my thoughts have contributed significantly to this book, I take responsibility for the manuscript.

Elias K. Bongmba
Houston, 2006

Introduction

The HIV/AIDS pandemic that has struck the global community has brought fear, shame, stigmatization, discrimination, isolation, economic hardships, illness, pain, despair, and death. In this book, I will use the theological motif *imago dei* to rethink the obligations and responsibilities of Christian churches in Africa in a day of HIV/AIDS. I use the term church to refer in general to the Christian tradition in Africa: the historic churches, the so-called mainline churches and their denominations, as well as the African-initiated churches (AIC). My reflections draw from and remain within the Christian tradition, which H. T. Englehart has argued

> lives in the revisionary hope of recasting the past of the moral and social vision shaped by the Enlightenment and defined by the dominant spirit of the twenty-first century. This Christianity affirms at its core a theology rooted in discursive reflections-cum-critical interpretive appreciations of the Bible as one text among others, all guided by an embrace of the moral [visions] of our age.[1]

I am motivated by the fact that is now clear that the HIV/AIDS pandemic is not a mishap taking place out there in the "world" while the church and its members are shielded and protected and can sing, "under his wings, what a refuge in sorrow! How the heart yearningly turns to his rest! Often when earth has no balm for my healing, there I find comfort and there I am blest."[2] HIV/AIDS is decimating the African church one member at a time. This disease continues to elude all attempts at treatment in

1

areas where treatment is available. The church is part of a rich human story and cannot merely stand by and watch HIV/AIDS continue to kill.

My reflections are drawn from research in Cameroon from 2001–2006 and from a sustained theological reflection and interpretation of the church's response to the crisis in many different parts of Africa. Cameroon has been the focus of this study for several reasons. Some researchers continue to claim that the HIV virus might have first jumped from a monkey to a human being in Cameroon, a view many Cameroonians reject. I do not pursue this question here because that is not my primary concern, although I believe that an investigation of the origins of a virus like HIV/AIDS could give us clues to new forms of therapies. I have followed the work and interacted with members of the Cameroon Baptist Convention Health Board. At the beginning of the pandemic, the level of seroprevalence in Cameroon was low, but neglect and denial has caused the rates to go up; the Cameroon Baptist Convention Health Board has shown remarkable leadership in dealing with the HIV/AIDS crisis.

I agree with Alexander Irwin and his colleagues, who argue: "there is nothing intrinsically African about the key factors driving the spread of HIV/AIDS—above all poverty, socioeconomic inequality, instability and armed conflict, and the disempowerment of marginalized groups."[3] I seek neither to unmask something uniquely African about the HIV/AIDS crisis nor to conceal its reality.[4] I offer no united African response because each community must come to terms with the disease, but I do believe African communities can learn from each other. My purpose is to highlight a theological perspective that communities should take into consideration as they use various forms of discourse and narrative to scale up the fight. HIV/AIDS is not, as some would have it, a disease spread from a few "highly sexually active female prostitutes to males."[5] It is a complex disease that has affected people in all sectors of society and calls for a multifaceted understanding and response because it has increased our perception of vulnerability as a human community.[6] I argue that the theological motif, the *imago dei* (the image of God), should be employed by the Christian church as it fights HIV/AIDS alongside other communities. The *imago dei* provides an opening to discuss what it means to be human and to have dignity and rights. I do not imply that the Christian view of personhood precedes other views on this subject, or that it is the only valid way of conceptualizing and organizing community response to HIV/AIDS. Rather, I call on Christian churches to use this motif as a basis for a broad-based conversation with other communities. Theological ideas that are brought to the table in an open manner can influence other views. As Lisa Sowle Cahill has argued: "social practices and policy outcomes are more likely to reflect respect for all human lives . . . if religious thinkers represent these values while engaging with others in the practical negotiation of solutions to problems."[7]

I do not think that the idea that humanity is created in the image of God privileges human beings above other creatures; instead, it calls humanity to recognize the profound ethical responsibility we owe to those who suffer in our world. As human beings, we share the world with other beings and the relationship between human beings and the divine being does not diminish the other beings, and certainly does not diminish God's relationship to the other beings.[8] Furthermore, I do not use *imago dei* to dismiss other views about humanity and I do not claim that this concept *alone* would solve all problems. However, I am convinced that Christian churches could achieve more success in the fight against HIV/AIDS and other diseases if they advance their perspective—a perspective grounded in the *imago dei*—in respectful dialogue with other traditions.

Other people who fight against HIV/AIDS do not use the language of creation, but subscribe to an evolutionary account of human society and the inhabited order. I see no reason to address this issue here because a non-creationist view of life is a valid viewpoint of how the world can be accounted for. I am aware that because they are limited, Christian symbols do not always clarify our doubts about the world. I recognize that many subscribe to the view that humanity evolved from lower forms and I do not address that here. I only argue that the tradition that the Christian church has inherited proclaims that God and humanity share the same image and act as collaborators in governing the created order. Therefore, the church has an obligation to do something about the threat to the *imago dei* by HIV/AIDS.[9]

I employ the *imago dei* as a mediating concept in the same way theologians have used "middle axioms" to articulate a theological praxis in interdisciplinary contexts with proposals that are open to debate and amendment.[10] The position I take in this book is one among many combative strategies which the Christian community could adapt. An approach rooted in the *imago dei* could help the wider community see HIV/AIDS as a disease that spreads and thrives in conditions of inequality and other forms of socioeconomic marginalization, deprivation, and discrimination. Such an approach, combining abstinence campaigns with other broad intervention strategies, could work better than one-dimensional schemes.

During the first two decades of the HIV/AIDS pandemic, religious leaders and medical experts have tended to focus on sexual behaviors that have put people at risk. While this has called attention to one of the main ways in which HIV/AIDS is transmitted in Africa, it is important that churches

and religious communities continue their fight against the disease by carrying out a broad conversation and exploring intervention strategies that identify the social and economic conditions that create and perpetuate risk
situations. Such an approach would probe cultural praxis and seek ways of
introducing modifications to particular cultural norms and practices that
might pose a threat to some members of the community. This should be
done with care because the battle is against a disease and not against culture
as such, although it might be necessary to dismantle cultural practices that
pose a threat, or could likely place some one at risk.[11] The battle against
HIV/AIDS would be strengthened if communities examined and modified
ways of being-in-the-world that compromise human health and human
flourishing. Therefore, where research reveals that cultural practices contribute to the risk factors identified by medical experts and social scientists,
the church should employ its most powerful weapon, the voice of persua-
sion, to help people reconfigure those practices in order to save lives.
Cultural norms and practices are often established or developed over a long
period to enhance life and when aspects of culture pose a danger to human
well being and flourishing, it might be prudent to modify that practice and
reconfigure to fulfill its role in society.

In Cameroon people in religious communities have repeatedly asked why
they have to face this disease. They wonder what God wants to teach them
through this disease. Many people who follow news about the disease and
know that people are succumbing to HIV/AIDS in other places in Africa, ask
if God cares about Africa at all? A large section of the population in the
Northwest Province of Cameroon knows that this is a global disease, but they
still wonder why Africa has so many HIV/AIDS cases. The Wimbum people
have a saying: *Nyu iki fan yang fa mshep*, meaning, "When God gives a disease he also gives the cure" (or literally, "gives the medicine"). Yet the
Wimbum have found out that if HIV/AIDS is what they consider *yang Nyu*,
then God has not yet given the cure. This is a difficult concession for some
Christians in Africa where Pentecostal preachers have recently claimed that
they can heal all kinds of illnesses, including HIV/AIDS. (Such claims
inspired President Frederick Chiluba of Zambia to visit the Pentecostal congregation, Church of All Nations Synagogue in Lagos Nigeria, pastored by
Prophet T. B. Joshua on November 12, 2000.[12]) The question for those who
do not share this vision of spectacular, miraculous healing is: If God is going
to give a cure, why is God waiting for so many to die before bringing the cure?

When I visit in the Wimbum community, I avoid talking about *yang
Nyu* in discussion about HIV/AIDS because there is a strong temptation to
interpret this disease in a punitive light. The expression *yang Nyu* in the eyes

of some Christians means God has inflicted people with AIDS in order to punish the present generation for its promiscuity. This perspective, while not foreign or strange in a context where the cosmology also teaches that God or the ancestors often punish people who have failed to live up to their obligations, calls for a deeper reflection to avoid the view that HIV/AIDS is a punishment from God. My own view is that HIV/AIDS could be called by the Wimbum people *yang Nyu,* to mean something close to the idea of vulnerability to viruses and other disease-causing agents. Suffering brought by those conditions is part of the natural order and in that sense one could refer to HIV/AIDS as a "natural" disease and not mean that it is an illness imposed on the human family by an angry God. Therefore, we are dealing with an illness that should first be seen as a natural illness because the body has succumbed to disease-causing agents.

HIV/AIDS has created new opportunities for the church in Africa. It has opened up a space for caring, compassion, creative thinking, collaboration, and combat. To think creatively, the church must employ new tools to inquire about what it means to be human in the context of an illness that has no cure and resists treatment even where it is available. The task of thinking about our common humanity in a world of HIV/AIDS is too great for the church to claim that it can do it alone. The church must come out of its shell and collaborate with other communities of discourse to address this pressing issue. Karl Barth once conveyed the public nature of the church very aptly:

> The Church is not a snail that carries its little house on its back and is so well off in it, that only now and then it sticks out its feelers, and then thinks that the 'claim of publicity' has been satisfied. . . Christianity is . . . an out-and-out 'worldly' thing open to all humanity.[13]

Finally, the church cannot stand by and expect others to take action to protect the most vulnerable in its midst. Acting in care and compassion calls for a combat intended to remove situations that continually compromise human dignity. All of these efforts involve breaking the conspiracy of silence that surrounds HIV/AIDS today.[14] Breaking the silence also includes the deployment of an ethic that motivates an intersubjective engagement through which members of faith communities would desire to bring relief and human flourishing to people living with HIV/AIDS.

Christians in Africa need to prioritize the personal and to work with members of their communities to build strong intersubjective bonds, strengthening members to serve each other as individuals, but working as a community to enhance a broad communal response to HIV/AIDS and its devastating effects.[15] The *imago dei* is a useful concept because it affirms human dignity at both the individual and communal levels. By embracing this concept the church could pursue an intersubjective approach to the pandemic without negating either an individualist or communitarian ethos. HIV/AIDS demonstrates human interconnectedness and reminds the human community that we should avoid thoughts, actions, behavior, and policies that could compromise that interconnection. Although the HIV virus infects, grows, thrives, and destroys the immune system of individuals, these invidiuals are known to us as children, siblings, spouses, friends, fellow members of the faith community, and members of a professional, political, or social community.

Although it attacks one person at a time, HIV/AIDS is a public disease that disrupts families and communities. The fact that it afflicts many people in Africa through the privacy of the sexual act does not negate the sociopolitical character of the AIDS crisis. The structural connections of the human community present intersubjective claims upon members of all communities as they struggle to defeat HIV/AIDS.[16] The rate at which people are losing the battle to HIV/AIDS can only be compared to a massive military campaign which has targeted civilians. The transactions that bring about the infection—whether it is a sexual act, medical procedure, drug use, or mother to child transmission—are all intersubjective. Communities pursuing an intersubjective approach must balance individual privacy with the public good; individual responsibility with communal obligations to protect life. I am not directly concerned here with *micro level* ethics that focuses strictly on special relations like that of a doctor and patient. I am interested in ethical issues at the meso-level where communal concerns are articulated.[17] I will explore the implications of the *imago dei* for a comprehensive response to HIV/AIDS at the personal, communal, professional, national, and international level.[18] The church in Africa reaches millions of people on a weekly basis, and it has an obligation to offer valuable information for the public who may not have access to television or newspapers.[19]

I discuss sexuality in the context of the HIV/AIDS pandemic but chose not to engage in speculation about the private lives of people living with HIV/AIDS. HIV/AIDS has forced scholars to generate new and highly problematic literature on African sexuality. My goal is not to evaluate the merits of each claim but to discuss sexuality in the context of a crisis that is taking millions of lives. In doing that, I will work with some generalizations without holding them up to scrutiny. Scholarly generalizations often err, but the hope here is that these generalizations can be applied to issues and situations that offer prospects for preventing the spread of HIV/AIDS.

Finally, my reflections are a limited exercise in theology and ethics. This is not the first effort in this regard on HIV/AIDS. What is different now is the growing realization that HIV/AIDS might be with the church for a long time. The Christian community needs to contribute vigorously to the debate on the fight against HIV/AIDS. S. Heald has argued:

> biomedical models of the disease have been so much to the forefront that other understandings have been subdued . . . as a product of ignorance or of outmoded traditional views by those primarily involved in the AIDS field, both by government personnel and western AIDS specialists. The language of AIDS is the language of western science and policy. All programmes in Africa, whether medical or social, have been dominated by the WHO, and more recently UNAIDS, as well as USAID and other western-based NOGs.[20]

I am sympathetic to what Heald argues, and think that the African church needs to continue its fight against the disease in collaboration with other groups who are waging a war against HIV/AIDS. The medical community will continue to deepen our understanding of the disease, but churches at the local, denominational, and ecumenical levels have a vested interest in exploring the broader social context in which HIV/AIDS occurs and in working out new intervention strategies.

The argument will proceed in the following manner. In chapter 1, I discuss the HIV/AIDS pandemic in Africa and argue that HIV/AIDS offers challenges to the church and public policy that must be addressed in a comprehensive program to combat the disease. In chapter 2, I argue that the theological motif, the *imago dei*, provides a basis for the church to scale up its fight against HIV/AIDS. The image of God mandates an ethic of love and compassion for people living with HIV/AIDS. Furthermore, the *imago dei* invites a prophetic critique of the social environment in which HIV/AIDS thrives. In chapter 3, I make a case for virtue ethics as an individual and social practice that strengthens the *imago dei*, to experience the good and to flourish. In chapter 4, I argue that the idea of a suffering *imago dei* invites a bold pastoral ministry at the local, denominational, and ecumenical levels of the church. At all levels, the church's obligations include facing the challenges posed by the complexity of human sexuality, combating the epidemic of violence against women and children, and promoting a praxis that would restructure its social services to address the social conditions that create risk situations and provide a climate for the spread of the HIV virus. In chapter 5 I argue that the idea of globalization is an ethical

proposition that invites (and indeed obligates) the international community
to work to combat HIV/AIDS. I go on to discuss the church's obligations to
people living with HIV/AIDS in the global era, arguing that the church
should join the campaign for universal access to health care and work with
other organizations in vaccine development and drug trials. I conclude the
book by inviting the international community to reflect on the dialectic of
responsibility and obligation in response to HIV/AIDS.

Chapter 1

Background to HIV/AIDS in Africa

"We want to apologise for not doing what we should have done and doing what we should not have done."

—Archbishop Benjamin Nzimbi of Kenya[1]

HIV/AIDS in Popular and Academic Discourse

The human immunodeficiency virus (HIV) that causes Acquired Immune Deficiency Syndrome (AIDS) first came to public notice in 1981. In 1983 researchers identified the following modes of transmission: sexual intercourse (various forms); exposure to blood products; parent to child transmission, especially during childbirth; and intravenous drug use.[2] HIV/AIDS has continued to spread: a contributor to an online discussion of Cameroon issues recently described the pandemic as "our weapons of mass destruction." The analogy reflects the view that long neglect of the disease has allowed it to become a deadly force. As Helen Singer Kaplan, director of the Human Sexuality Program at the New York Hospital-Cornell Medical Center, has said: "In this age of AIDS there is a real danger that the world as we know it might end not with a nuclear bang but with the whimpers of dying AIDS patients."[3] Only two other epidemics have been as deadly as HIV/AIDS. The influenza epidemic of 1918 reportedly killed 25 million people, and The Black Death in the fourteenth century killed about one-third of the population in Europe between 1347 and 1350.[4] President Clinton declared HIV/AIDS a security

9

threat to the industrial world and the Commonwealth heads of states called HIV/AIDS a global emergency. However, for Africans, HIV/AIDS is a human catastrophe that could decimate the productive generation.

In December 2005 the Joint United Nations Programme on HIV/AIDS (UNAIDS) estimated that about 38.6 million people live with HIV/AIDS around the world. Of this number, 38 million are adults, 17.5 million are women, and 2.3 million are children under the age of 15, with 2.1 million of them living in sub-Saharan Africa. In 2005 alone, 4.1 million people were infected with the HIV virus. In Africa it is estimated that about 24.5 million people live with HIV/AIDS. Two thirds or 64 percent of the people living with HIV/AIDS worldwide are in sub-Saharan Africa, which has only 10 percent of the world's population, and 2 million of them are children under the age of 15. About 2.8 million people died from HIV-related illnesses in 2005.[5] In Africa, where there are over 24 million people living with HIV/ AIDS, the numbers are growing in countries like Madagascar and Swaziland, but declining in Uganda. An estimated 2.7 million people are infected yearly and about 2 million deaths are linked to the AIDS complex. The rate of infection has "intensified," especially in southern Africa where one in three people who are infected live. The rate of prevalence among pregnant women is estimated to be at 20 percent.[6] It is estimated that 43 percent living with HIV are in the southern African region.

In other parts of the world, about 8.3 million people live with HIV/AIDS in Asia, 930,000 of whom were infected in 2005. The epidemic is spreading quickly in India, where there are now 5.2 million infected with the virus. In East Asia about 870,000 people are infected. Further, 1.3 million are infected in Eastern Europe and Central Asia, 80 percent of them under the age of 30. Other areas that have been affected seriously are Estonia, Latvia, the Russian Federation, and Ukraine where drug use is the main source of transmission. In Latin America, there are an estimated 1.6 million people living with HIV/AIDS, and in the Caribbean, about 430,000. About 1.6 million people are living with HIV/AIDS in high-income countries. In North Africa and the Middle East, there are 480,000 people living with HIV.

UNAIDS has stated that HIV/AIDS is not an "African epidemic" because the disease has different characteristics in the region. In six countries, the level of prevalence is 2 percent, but in six other countries, it is 20 percent, while the level of prevalence in Botswana and Swaziland could be as high as 35 percent. In all regions in Africa, women and children are at greater risk than are men. There are about thirteen infected women for every ten infected men, and the ratio of young women to men living with HIV is as high as twenty to ten in South Africa and forty-five to ten in Kenya and Mali.

When HIV/AIDS became a global disease, African leaders played ostrich and said that it was a gay disease found only in the West and Africans did not have to worry because there were no gays and lesbians in Africa. However, African countries were rudely awakened to the reality that HIV/AIDS had affected all sectors of the society, and was transmitted mostly through hetero-sexual contact. In 2002 the Nigerian health minister Eyitayo Lambo reported that the disease had killed 2.3 million Nigerians and 3.8 million others were infected with the HIV virus. Experts project that Nigeria will have 10 to 15 million cases and Ethiopia in the Horn of Africa will have 7 to 10 million cases by 2010.[7] In South Africa, HIV/AIDS is now the number one killer. A report by the Medical Research Council claims: "Projections show that, with-out treatment to prevent AIDS, deaths can be expected to grow, within the next 10 years, to more than double the number of deaths due to all other causes, resulting in 5 to 7 million cumulative AIDS deaths in South Africa by 2010."[8] In Harare Zimbabwe, about 240 people die every day from AIDS-related illnesses.[9] Africa has been colonized again, this time by a lethal disease.

The fact that HIV/AIDS is transmitted in Africa mostly through hetero-sexual contact has created stigmatization, discrimination, and complicated prevention strategies, making it difficult to come up with a comprehensive plan to combat the disease. In the second decade of HIV/AIDS, it is clear that there is a definite relationship between social, economic, and political realities and the spread of the virus.[10] HIV/AIDS in Africa should be studied broadly and responses to the pandemic developed by implementing strategies that would redress the socio-structural imbalance and violence that has gripped the continent.

Media coverage of HIV/AIDS in Africa and other parts of the world has sensationalized it and tended to assign blame to certain segments of the soci-ety, perpetuating labels like "gay disease," "white man's disease," and " the African disease."[11] Elsewhere Catherine Raissiguier reports that she was shocked to see graffiti on a wall in Paris declaring *Islam = Sida* (Islam equals AIDS).[12] (Raissiguier has pointed out that in some places in France the term Islam refers to undesirable immigrants who come mainly from sub-Saharan Africa and the Maghreb and are seen as invaders and a threat to everything French.) For many people HIV/AIDS remains what they call "deadly syn-drome," "killer disease," "disease with no cure," and "unexplained new plague."[13] However, I must state two things; first, HIV/AIDS does not nec-essarily spell death, although it offers a challenging life. Second, HIV/AIDS invites all in the global community to rethink what it means to be human.

HIV/AIDS has created new medical politics. First, since Africa is the epicenter of HIV/AIDS, she is now at the center of a new politics of representation and the rest of the world has had the false impression that they do not need to worry about the disease. To many who have shared the Afro-pessimists thesis, HIV/AIDS further confirms the view that the continent is dying and might not save itself. However, one must not conjure up images of a dark continent, lands of epidemic, and endemic problems and claim that the rest of the world is better.[14] It is unfortunately the case that this deadly disease is now spreading in places like China, Thailand, and India. It is indeed a global disease.

Second, Africa is involved in the politics of HIV/AIDS in a direct way because some people speculate that HIV/AIDS originated in Cameroon. Jean Goens in *De la Syphilis au Sida* locates the source in Africa because tests have been conducted on tissue preserved from the 1950s and 1960s of people who died of diseases with AIDS-like symptoms. One of the persons who died of these diseases might have contracted it in Africa, where a small outbreak of similar disease was reported in the 1970s.[15] There is speculation that it might have originated in an African monkey, or a malaria experiment that missed the mark.[16] These speculations have cast a negative image in the minds of many people about Africa. HIV/AIDS has also been racialized by people who claim that the disease will cleanse some parts of the world of the black population. A satirist in South African proclaimed: "AIDS will succeed where apartheid failed."[17] The racialization of HIV/AIDS gives the false hope to non-blacks that they do not need to worry about HIV/AIDS. Killer diseases have always originated from somewhere and the stigma attached to Africa is not new. During the Black Death some people blamed Jews for the disease.

Phillip Winn has addressed the question of origins under what he calls personal and metaphysical-mythical responsibility.[18] According to Winn, when people identify someone as the source of the transmission, they typically name a friend, companion, lover, or someone with whom they have shared drugs or had contact.[19] However, in some of the literature in which someone discusses the source of infection, the answers are less clear.[20] Sometimes the origin of the infection is attributed to a mythic person, such as a mysterious *femme fatale* who deliberately spreads the infection. In the late 1900s, for example, *radio trotoir* in Yaoundé, Cameroon created a femme fatale figure and passed on rumors that a real individual, a beautiful nurse who was infected with the HIV virus decided to have sexual relations with everyone who asked her for a date. Those who spread the rumors also claimed that she seduced high profile individuals and kept a list of all her partners. When she developed clinical AIDS and her health deteriorated, she made the list public, causing great panic among her lovers in Yaoundé. There are also cases of what we might call *l'homme fatale*. In Yaoundé, stories also circulated about top military and security officers who continued to engage in unsafe sexual activity after they found out that they were HIV-positive. Two of them acted in a vindictive manner, seducing and having unprotected sexual relations with young female professionals. When rumors spread about the medical condition of one of the officers, his partners were alarmed and many of them panicked.[21]

People have also advanced abstract or metaphysical explanations for the origin of AIDS, explanations often grounded in religious and scientific narratives. Winn has pointed out that one of the greatest abstractions in the literature is the view of Africa as a "land of the virus." In a play for Radio Canada titled "Deuil," Haitian writer Michel Philip has one of the characters portray Africa as the source of a deadly virus that killed many and frightened many doctors. This disease moved to Haiti because many of its citizens went to work in the Democratic Republic in the 1970s and contracted the virus while there.[22] Leonard Horowitz argues that Africa's role in the history of HIV/AIDS might be circumstantial, that the disease might actually have originated from American biological weapons, or bad vaccines distributed by the World Health Organization (WHO).[23]

Many Africans have their own theories about the origin of the disease. In my village, Ntumbaw, in the Northwest Province of Cameroon, some elders speculated that HIV/AIDS was a sexually transmitted disease passed on from Fulani women only to non-Fulani men who had sexual contact with them. They also claimed if a man was infected as a result of having sexual contact with a Fulani woman, only a Fulani healer could treat him. There is nothing in the literature that supports this speculation.[24] However, it is important to trace the genesis of a mystery virus like HIV. Careful documentation will hopefully shed light on the nature of the virus, its early history, its dormant years, transportation to different parts of the world, and the conditions under which it has survived, mutated, as well as when and how it took its deadly turn. Regardless of what position a person takes on the origin of the disease, or the source of individual infection, known, or unknown, the impact of HIV/AIDS is catastrophic and the millions of people living with HIV/AIDS demand our attention and action.

The Epidemiology of HIV/AIDS

Central to the task of epidemiology when a disease affects a specific population are these questions: who is affected, where is the disease concentrated, when did it begin, and why has that population been affected or why is it spreading in that particular region and affecting the people it is affecting. Epidemiologists often work to identify risk groups, risk factors, and ways of managing and reducing the identified risk factors through effective intervention programs.[25] Researchers have identified two main types of HIV, which they designate HIV 1 and HIV 2. The difference between the two types is that HIV 2, found mostly in West Africa, is not transmitted easily and that it takes longer for someone infected with HIV 2 to experience the complications of the virus. HIV 1 has three subclassifications known as Group M, Group N, and Group O. The last group is very rare; researchers identified it in Cameroon in 1998. Most people who are infected with HIV around the world have the Group M type, of which there are about nine different subtypes.[26]

The earliest studies of HIV/AIDS identified the primary risk groups as gay men, intravenous drug users, truck drivers, sex workers, and people who have multiple sex partners. Researchers pointed out that HIV spread followed three patterns around the world. The first pattern was the one found in North America, Western Europe, South America, Australia, and New Zealand where the virus was first detected in gay and bisexual people and intravenous drug users. Researchers speculated that HIV might have been introduced into these areas in the early 1970s. The second pattern was found mostly in the Caribbean, Africa, and Latin America where it was believed that the virus spread mostly among heterosexual people. The third pattern was found in Asia, the Middle East, and Eastern Europe. Early studies in these areas indicated that the virus might have been introduced to the region in the 1980s. The significant shift in the last several years is that the spread of the virus has slowed down in the United States and Western European countries, but has increased significantly in Africa.

The first epidemiological study of HIV/AIDS that appeared in *Morbidity and Mortality Weekly Report* described it as a mysterious condition manifested as a skin disease.[27] Since 1987, UNAIDS and the WHO have given good descriptions of the disease as well as regular epidemiological data which have enabled the public to follow the development of HIV/AIDS "as it happens"—if one can afford to be that flippant about the contemporaneity of the statistics on global AIDS. Experts continue to study the spread of the disease because the statistics do not give us the complete picture. Ann Larson has argued that since national governments, which are reticent of bad publicity, authorize and supervise the gathering of statistics, what we have is not the full picture.[28] Most of the estimates come from statistics gathered at antenatal clinics and from documentation of opportunistic infections associated with HIV infection such as frequent cough, diarrhea, frequent bouts of malaria, and tuberculosis; such estimates could be misleading.[29] Whatever their limitations,however, they provide a general picture of the disease and enable caregivers to plan prevention and treatment campaigns.

In addition to the risk groups already mentioned, some early epidemiological studies also identified Africans, Haitians, adolescent women, widows, orphans, minorities in the United States (especially African American women), people who have same-sex relations, and military personnel. These studies also identified risk factors and risk behavior.[30] Isolating risk groups has always been problematic. Some religious groups have blamed the gay community for spreading HIV/AIDS despite the fact that in many places in Africa, the virus has spread mostly through heterosexual sex. In Western Kenya, the Luo community became the subject of a nationwide conversation and ridicule when statistics indicated that 28.8 percent of HIV/AIDS cases in Kenya were found in the Nyanza region. People focused on the Luo people because in that community widows take part in rites that require sexual relations with another man to "cleanse" her after her husband has died. Health experts have long suspected that such rites might be contributing to the spread of HIV/AIDS. The focus on widowhood rites created a sensation in the media. In March 2001 the Kenyan *Daily Nation* reported that widows were forced into the "traumatizing and barbaric sexual cleansing rites" with an inheritor. The widows "who had buried their husbands a few days earlier, were locked up, tied with ropes and forced into sex with the hired man after refusing to be inherited."[31] This particular act is indeed brutal and criminal. Isolating such risk groups, however, often gives the rest of the population a false sense of security, implying that if one avoided sexual contact with a member of the risk group, he or she would not be at risk.[32] For example, in Tanzania, people thought that young people who engaged in recreational sexual activity were mostly responsible for the spread of HIV/AIDS; therefore if they avoided sex with anyone in that group they could not become infected or spread HIV/AIDS. These three examples point to some of the problems of that have arisen because of the emphasis on specific risk groups in the study of HIV/AIDS.[33]

Furthermore, the "risk groups" approach has focused mainly on sexual behavior, and has suggested interventions emphasizing mainly the modification of such behavior. Although sexual contact is one of the primary modes of transmission, the HIV virus thrives in a sociopolitical world and subculture where economic and social marginalization is rampant. The Joint United Nations Programme on AIDS (UNAIDS), World Health Organization (WHO), United Nations Children's Fund (UNICEF), United Nations Population Fund (UNFPA), United Nations Development Fund for Women (UNIFEM), the World Bank, non-governmental organizations, faith-based organizations, and HIV/AIDS activists around the world have highlighted the political dimension of the HIV/AIDS pandemic, but this has not slowed down the spread of the virus because prevention campaigns have emphasized sexuality almost exclusively. Solomon Benatar has argued:

> Failure to recognize the pervasive social, economic, behavioral and political aspect of HIV/AIDS—both in terms of its origins and its control—is self-defeating. The complexity of the scientific endeavour required to understand the pathobiology of the disease and to develop appropriate treatment and vaccines is more than matched by the complexity of understanding and dealing with the social underpinnings of HIV/AIDS and other plagues locally and globally.[34]

In sum, epidemiological studies privileging biomedical approaches with emphasis on risk groups have led to prevention strategies that stress sexual behavior modification: "Knowledge, Attitudes, and Practices" (KAP); "Abstain, Be Faithful, Use a Condom" (ABC); and "Zero grazing." But sexuality must be understood in a broad context in which social domination creates what Akeroyd has described as marginal situations increasing the risk of HIV transmission, and in which "the sexualization of work" has created an epidemic of sexual violence occurring in the name of sexual favors.[35] Researchers have focused on sexual behavior since it is one of the direct modes of transmission. Emphasizing sexual activity alone, however, might have fostered false hope that if human beings could simply control their sexual appetites, all would be well. As a result, many churches and governments have ignored the social world of HIV/AIDS and the social institutions that ought to provide care to people living with HIV/AIDS.

The Social Dimensions of HIV/AIDS

Social scientists and humanists working in Africa have carried the inquiry beyond the analysis of identifiable risk groups to assessment of risk behavior, risk situations, and vulnerable groups. The idea of vulnerability is especially important because gender biases have made women and young girls especially vulnerable to HIV/AIDS.[36] Interdisciplinary scholarship and policy studies that analyze the social, economic, and political dynamics within a specific area offer a better perspective of the pandemic and open more doors to strategic interventions and global action against the disease.[37]

While HIV/AIDS is almost always transmitted individually, overarching societal realities shape social relationships in ways that facilitate the transmission of the virus. Social and economic marginalization, for example, has given rise to sex work. It is a mistake for communities to demonize sex workers if they cannot change the social and economic culture that promotes commercial sex as a livelihood for the disadvantaged. Focusing on this larger social world would enable AIDS activists, public policy analysts, religious groups, and the international community to get past sociocultural stereotypes and rethink ineffective prevention methods.[38] A broad social perspective demands reforms that will in turn create opportunities for many more people to work and support themselves economically. Since heterosexual intercourse is the major path of transmission in Africa, scholars studying sexuality in Africa ought to probe the structural imbalance between men and women that promotes problematic sexual relationships.[39]

When HIV/AIDS hit Africa, urbanization played a role in the spread of the disease. Urban areas in Africa outgrew their resources and the economic decline of the late 1970s imposed restrictions on state spending on social resource, weakening the ability of the state to meet the social needs of the people.[40] Poverty, economic destitution, and economic marginalization in urban centers such as Lagos, Kinshasa, Johannesburg, Yaoundé, and Nairobi provide a climate for risky sexual behavior. Eliya Msiyaphazi Zulu and others describe conditions that give rise to risky behavior in Nairobi:

> The urban setting is one in which prostitution, multiple sexual partnerships, and teenage pregnancy are common. . . . Evidence . . . shows that women living in the slums are driven by poverty and deprivation to engage in risky behaviours that include multiple sexual partnerships. . . . Unemployment and inadequate wages among the employed restrict slum residents' ability to meet personal needs and familial obligations. As other economic options run out, economic desperation pushes women to rely on sexual relations to obtain sufficient money for rent, school children's clothing, and other basic necessities, and many of them maximize the number of sexual partners they have in order to increase their economic security.[41]

African young people in urban settings start sexual activity at an early age and typically have multiple partners. "Young women (aged 15–24) and married women in slums are 6.4 and 3.7 times more likely to have multiple sexual partners than their non-slum counterparts."[42] Although education may delay the start of sexual intercourse, it does not significantly affect the number of sexual partners one is likely to have. The sad irony is that for many people in Africa, urban settings provide the only opportunity to find jobs. Poor government planning has neglected rural development and concentrated industry in urban centers. In Cameroon, young people no longer see agriculture as an important aspect of economic development as they did in the past when the government encouraged the green revolution. In the Northwest Province of Cameroon, youths have moved to towns like Nkambe, Kumbo, and Bamenda, leaving the poor, rural districts of Donga Mantung, Mentchum, and Momo Divisions. Most of the educated people and elites of these divisions have already moved to urban centers, beginning with civil servants, teachers, and employees in private sector establishments such as church hospitals, health clinics, and schools. In the urban centers, unscrupulous property owners sometimes extort female tenants. Commercial sex is linked to economic hardship, which creates relations of dependence between young females and older men.[43] During the Structural Adjustment Program, sugar daddies in cities like Yaoundé and Douala exploited many students. Some of the students engaged in these relationships for money to purchase status symbols like cell phones. While these young women are not sex workers, they routinely exchange sex for their needs. Unfortunately, the growth of urban centers continues at an alarming pace. The UN projects that by 2016, a large segment of the population in Africa will be urban dwellers and by 2025, about half of the population in the developing countries will live in urban areas.[44]

In addition to the overall pattern of urbanization, transient labor migrations also create a climate for the spread of HIV/AIDS.[45] Men who work away from home and family often engage in new sexual liaisons where sex work is prevalent. Once infected under these circumstances they are likely to infect their wives and other sex partners.[46] Overall, it is economic difficulties that continue to fuel the spread of HIV/AIDS. Poor conditions have increased the number of people engaged in commercial sex and made it difficult for them to get treatment for sexually transmitted diseases, thus leaving them vulnerable to infections. Colonial and postcolonial economic systems have created a culture that leaves women vulnerable to abuse and domination. So, although sexual activity is responsible for most of the transmission, prevention campaigns that focus mainly on individual responsibility such as abstinence, fidelity, and condom use, without addressing these larger social issues, are not sufficient.

The Impact of HIV/AIDS in Africa

How has HIV/AIDS changed the face of Africa? First, it has created an AIDS generation.[47] Many of the youths of Africa, born since 1980, have been orphaned by the disease. The virus has made its way to every country on the continent, and affected all segments of society. Many of the youths today have grown up hearing about the disease and many of them have been affected because they know someone who is living with HIV/AIDS, or has died from the disease.

Second, although HIV/AIDS has affected every sector of African society, the hardest hit have been women and children. And it is no longer a matter of one or two populations at risk: civil servants, schoolteachers, members of the military, hospital workers, high-profile artists, academics, high-level government workers, and people engaged in public policy or close relatives of their families have all been affected by HIV/AIDS. In 2005 President Robert Mugabe of Zimbabwe admitted that two members of his cabinet died of AIDS-related complications. Although HIV/AIDS is the quintessential equal opportunity affliction, the most productive members of the community have been affected severely.

Third, HIV/AIDS has dealt a severe blow to the economy, stalled economic development, and slowed down economic recovery in Africa. HIV/AIDS is decimating capacity-building efforts across the board. At the personal and family level, many people have lost the only family member who earned an income from his or her job. It is difficult in the midst of the pandemic to calculate the effects of HIV/AIDS on the African economy , but those effects are severe. It was estimated that the gross domestic product of Kenya in 2005 would be reduced by 15 percent over what it would have been without HIV/AIDS.[48] Africa will see a decline in production in all areas, including the crucial agricultural sector. The loss to individual families and communities is enormous but the loss of long-term productive capacity remains incalculable. Some are calling the social space decimated by HIV/AIDS as killing fields. Others, who argue that the monumental problem has resulted from neglect, call it a slow genocide or holocaust eliminating the most productive members of the society and leaving devastation never seen in the past.[49] HIV/AIDS has undercut the human potential of Africa.

The cost of treating HIV/AIDS is a burden both to families and to African states. Few people have medical insurance and the insurance companies now require applicants to take an AIDS test to demonstrate that they are not infected with the virus. It is estimated that an AIDS patient in Nairobi spends about KES 27,000 ($365) during the course of his or her life. This is an enormous amount of money for some people in Kenya who do not have the economic means. The cost of treating AIDS patients takes away resources from the treatment of other infectious diseases and public health programs. Shorter and Onyancha estimate that preventive and treatment programs of the National AIDS and STD Control Program in Kenya could cost several billion U.S. dollars.[50] HIV/AIDS has imposed an incalculable financial burden on families who now have to provide care for widows and orphans, many of them living with HIV/AIDS. Extended families often help to carry the financial burden of HIV/AIDS. This follows the tradition of solidarity and hospitality, values that reflect and depend on large extended family systems. The magnitude of the crisis is challenging the extended family system, which has almost collapsed in some communities due to deaths from HIV/AIDS.

One entire family in the Wimbum area of the Northwest Province has nearly disappeared, because most of the adults in the family between age 25 and 50 have lost the battle with HIV/AIDS. When I met with the only surviving male member of one of the families in Bamenda, he expressed his grief and burden to me.[51] He believed that his relatives had succumbed from the practice of witchcraft that was prevalent in the family. He accused the head of the family of being a witch and responsible for all of the deaths in his family. Some of the few surviving relatives, however, said that their relatives died from HIV-related complications. In many families, the children who survive their parents fend for themselves under the care of a young girl who assumes the role of parent. Young girls who take care of families are often exposed to vicious individuals who exploit them for sex, a situation that perpetuates the vicious cycle already established by HIV/AIDS.

Fourth, HIV/AIDS has heightened human suffering. People who develop full-blown AIDS endure prolonged illness brought about by opportunistic infections. They suffer pain and agony for a long time before they die, as do their loved ones. Children suffer mental anguish as they see their parents wither away. Some of them have no time to absorb the pain and grief because they have to support the rest of the family. Their friends, typically, are going through a similar experience. The world of their elders is fragile instead of secure; they see their teachers also get sick and die. All around them is a cycle of illness, pain, and death.

Fifth, the HIV/AIDS crisis has affected the community at a personal and spiritual level. At a personal level, HIV/AIDS has challenged our understanding of human sexuality in ways that are difficult to comprehend. It has called our attention again to the interrelationship between love, sex, and death. Phillip Winn has argued: "As an incurable, largely sexually transmitted, and frequently fatal infection, AIDS holds a particularly fertile grip on the imagination; so much so that it is now a cliché to invoke the trinity of great human and literary themes—love, sex, and death—in any summation of the disease's significance."[52] HIV/AIDS comes to us through the most intimate dimension of life that has been ritualized and structured to celebrate our humanity. Coming of age and taking one's place in society in some ways celebrates the sexual dimension of our being. It is for that reason that sexuality is ritualized and regularized in many communities. But sexual initiation has now become a path of death for many people in the African community. Accepting the reality that love, sex and death are tied up together in HIV/AIDS should not be seen as clichéd. Nor does it make one a puritan or indicated that one is in denial of his or her sexuality.

HIV/AIDS has refocused attention on the link between *eros* and *thanatos*.[53] As such it has complicated and compromised human desire, testing normative conceptions of love and lovemaking to their limits. Until the human family stops the spread of the virus, the link between sex and death might remain a grim reality. Musa Dube has argued that with HIV/AIDS, humanity is at war and the enemy is all around us. "It is everywhere—between men and women, boys and girls, husbands and wives. It is in the beds of our intimacy—in the best moments of our lives. When we kiss and make love, the enemy is there. It is now in our veins, in our blood, in our cells, in our fluids, in our minds. HIV/AIDS makes love drag us to death."[54] Of course, when women lack social parity with men and are victimized by unwanted or violent sexual overture, the linkage between love and death is not theoretical, but reflects a social reality that calls for close consideration. Scholars who study Africa rightly criticize media misrepresentation of popular reaction in the Democratic Republic of the Congo, where people sometimes called SIDA (AIDS), "Syndrome imaginaire pour décourager les amoureux," because at a deeper level, that statement could also be read as a critique of the political regime that lacked credibility. Yet, the pandemic is far from imaginary, and continues to force Africans to think carefully about the relationship between love, sex, and death. In this, the Christian leaders should offer guidance.

Church leaders should, however, avoid an Augustinian approach, which posits rejection of sex as the only way to flee death. Augustine links his account of the fall to sex because after the fall, "humans beings are no longer able to control what Augustine calls the 'shameful' parts of the body: the sexual organs. Adam and Eve's disobedience is thus 'the origin of death in us, and we bear in our members, and in our vitiated nature, the striving of the flesh, or indeed, its victory.' "[55] Elsewhere, Augustine argues that male orgasm can make one lose the godlike capability of reasoning. Sex in this sense is an intimation of death.[56] Augustine epitomizes what Carter Heyward has described as "the sex-as-sin obsession which characterizes Christianity [and] has produced a repressive, guilt-inducing sexual ethic which, in turn, generates a pornographic culture of eruptive sexual violence."[57]

Further, human desire and sexuality ought to be celebrated within the limits of reason. This Kantian language does not signal a new rational theory of sex, but points to the fact that sexual desires which constitute an integral part of our humanity can be made meaningful if they are seen as life enhancing. Beverley Clark has argued that humans "are open to both relationship and reflection: and it is through reflection on the aspects of ordinary human life—the reality and necessity of sexual intercourse and the inevitability of death—that we can arrive at this conclusion." [58] The question for church leaders is how to conceive of human desire in the light of HIV/AIDS. Plato's *Symposium* presents us with different voices that praise love. In this classic text, both Socrates and Diotima praise spiritual love because it is superior to physical love. [59] In the speeches each makes in praise of love, it is clear that love can be an exercise of freedom and choice. Such freedom of choice in love is needed in context where love has become a nightmare for many people.

HIV/AIDS and its Challenges to the Church in Africa

On June 14, 2004 the Ecumenical News Service of the World Council of Churches reported: "Church leaders from 39 African countries, meeting in Nairobi, have declared an all out war against AIDS and poverty, two problems threatening to annihilate the continent's population. 'Africa has sounded a distress call to reverse depopulation of her people by the HIV/AIDS pandemic,' members of the All Africa Conference of Churches said in a statement at the end of a three-day summit." [60] The HIV/AIDS pandemic has touched all religious groups, brought fear and shame, and raised disturbing questions about sickness, healing, death, and divine power. Initially, conservative religious groups around the world proclaimed HIV/AIDS as a divine judgment on this generation for its sins. In 1982, The Reverend Billy Graham said: "We have the Pill. We have conquered venereal disease with penicillin. But then along comes Herpes Simplex II. Nature itself lashes back when we go against God." [61] The Reverend Jerry Falwell was more direct when he declared that HIV/AIDS was a punishment from God for sin, especially homosexuality: "AIDS is a lethal judgment of God on America for endorsing this vulgar, perverted and reprobate lifestyle." [62] Other religious leaders have rejected the view that HIV/AIDS was a punishment for sin. The Anglican Archbishop of Cape Town, the Most Reverend Njongonkulu Ndungane said: "We need to shout from the rooftops that AIDS is not God's punishment of the wicked. It is a virus and not a sin, and the stigma that society has created around the epidemic is causing people to die instead of living positively."[63] At the United Nations Special General Assembly on HIV/AIDS, faith-based organizations argued that HIV/AIDS spreads in the context of poverty that has affected women and children disproportionately.[64] These organizations pledged to fight against the disease, expressed regret that they may have contributed to discrimination against those affected by HIV/AIDS, and offered to work with governments and the UN to address the problems.[65]

By the end of the 1980s, it became clear that the growing HIV/AIDS crisis was affecting church members and church leaders. African Christians faced the grim reality that HIV/AIDS was no longer a strange disease that targeted only sex workers and gay men. Church leaders were also forced to acknowledge that "Christian women start sexual activity significantly earlier than both Muslim women and those who subscribe to traditional religions."[66]

Once they became engaged, churches responded in a remarkable way, given the limited resources they were working with. In Uganda, Kenya, Botswana and South Africa, churches collaborated with faith-based organizations and non-governmental organizations to begin an assault on HIV/AIDS. In Kenya, the Catholic secretariat started a ministry among people living with HIV/AIDS and the National Council of Churches started its program to fight HIV/AIDS in 1989. The Christian Health Association of Kenya, which has a network of more than 15 hospitals, 32 health centers, and an estimated 183 dispensaries, embarked on a campaign to inform the population about the disease by distributing literature on the HIV virus.[67]

In Cameroon, the government signed an agreement with several faith-based organizations in 2001 to work together with the National AIDS Control Committee to fight the spread of the disease. In 2002, the government also provided funding to certain denominational ministries to facilitate their work on HIV/AIDS.[68] Cameroon churches and denominations have conducted seminars to educate the people on HIV/AIDS. The Cameroon Baptist Convention focused on education in local schools and communities, using evangelistic teams, and organized rallies where youths were warned about the danger of the disease. The youth departments promoted the ABC project and encouraged youths to make chastity pledges. The medical board handles the bulk of work on HIV/AIDS in the Cameroon Baptist Convention. Under the director of medical services, Dr. Pius Tih and physicians Dr. Dieter Lemke, Dr. Helen Marie Schmidt, and Dr. Julie Stone, staff members are trained to do testing and counseling. Church leaders now recognize HIV/AIDS as a disease like any other. Dr. Anne Daban of the Catholic health services in the Archdiocese of Yaoundé stated this clearly: "Since we consider HIV/AIDS as any other disease, Catholic health services have recognized the urgent need to break the silence surrounding HIV/AIDS in our churches and congregations to provide prevention measures, care, counseling, support and advocacy." [69] However, many people still believe that since HIV/AIDS is contracted mainly through sexual intercourse, the people living with HIV/AIDS have committed sinful acts. It is this view that brings feelings of shame, stigma, and discrimination.

Response to HIV/AIDS by the church in Africa has not been without conflicts and controversies. First, conservative religious voices continue to declare that HIV/AIDS is a punishment from God for sin. This has created a culture of shame and silence. Second, the Christian community has engaged in a vicious debate on the promotion and use of condoms to promote safe sex. Catholic bishops in Southern Africa have lashed out at condoms as "the heart of evil," arguing that they promote promiscuity. In an article in *Modern Theology*, African theologian Emmanuel Katongole criticized the "condomization of Africa" in a piece that reflected the critical stance some church leaders have taken for a long time on the promotion of the use of condoms in Africa. [70]

I am convinced that the African church has erred on the issue of condoms and wasted valuable time and energy. Public health officials and supporters of condoms agree that abstinence is the only "safe sex" option. However, using condoms along with other prevention methods is an effective method of preventing new infections. Effective distribution of condoms contributed to the Ugandan success story in fighting HIV/AIDS. In April 2004, the journal *Science* carried an article in which the authors argued that abstinence was largely responsible for the decline of new cases in Uganda. [71] The prevention campaign that worked so well in Uganda was called ABC, where A stood for Abstinence, B for "Be faithful" and C for Condoms. The campaign was supported by most organizations including the WHO and UNAIDS, but social conservatives opposed the condoms part of the campaign on grounds that it would promote sexual promiscuity. Dr. David Serwadda, who has worked on HIV/AIDS research for many years in Uganda, has said that condoms played a key role in reducing the rate of infection:

> As a physician who has been involved in Uganda's response to AIDS for 20 years, I fear that one small part of what led to Uganda's success—promoting sexual abstinence [and faithfulness]—is being overemphasized in policy debates. While abstinence has played an important role in Uganda, it has not been a magic bullet . . . abstinence is not always possible for people at risk. [72]

The strategy th at has worked well so far includes promoting the use of condoms, encouraging youths to delay sexual intercourse, and emphasizing monogamous relationships. Studies by Marie Laga, Michel Alary, Peter Piot, and others indicate that effective condom use also contributed to the decline of HIV transmission in the Democratic Republic of Congo.[73]

The Christian community needs to deal with the reality of human sexuality. One young woman who has decided to remain a virgin told me in Bamenda in the summer of 2003, "the young people of today think that they have to enjoy their life, and it is not right for the older generation to deprive them of this opportunity."[74] This desire to experience sex as part of a full life runs contrary to church teaching and cultural norms, but it is a reality that the church has to face and address. It cannot be said that condoms promote sexual relations outside marriage, because such activity already exists.

Opponents of condoms also argue that the very idea of condoms introduces guilt into adult relationships. Some contend that condoms can and do often fail; there is also a misconception that a condom could remain in a woman's vagina and cause sterility. Others argue that using a condom during sexual intercourse is unnatural. Early in the debate on condoms in Africa, opponents of condoms received a boost from Pope John Paul II when he spoke out against condoms on a visit to Kinshasa, probably in response to suggestions by the Catholic Archdiocese of Kinshasa that those who could not abstain from sex should use a condom.

The anti-condom position has failed to recognize that the effective use of condoms could save lives. This debate continues within the African church because Archbishop Orlando Antonini, the Vatican nuncio to Zambia, has reiterated the church's prohibition of condoms by saying that they are a false solution to the burning issue of HIV/AIDS in Africa.[75] This anti-condom campaign has weakened a UNICEF campaign in Tanzania. Brooke Grundfest Schoepf, who rightly categorized HIV/AIDS as major development issue, drafted the guidelines for that campaign.[76]

At the beginning of the fight against HIV/AIDS in Uganda, evangelical and conservative Christians influenced President Museveni to reject condoms. Museveni changed his mind after Cuban President Fidel Castro told him that about one third of the Ugandan officers who were sent to Cuba for training tested positive for the HIV virus.[77] However, Musevini backtracked on condoms. Addressing a plenary session of the fifteenth International AIDS Conference in Bangkok on July 13, 2004, Museveni shocked the world by rejecting condoms and arguing that abstinence was the most important factor in the drop of the rate of HIV prevalence from 30 percent to 6 percent. Museveni argued: "I am against plans by those who want to 'condomise' the world by telling us that it holds the ultimate solution."[78] He called condoms an improvisation, not a solution, and stated that men typically do not wear condoms correctly or sometimes just forget to wear them. Museveni accused Europeans of fueling the spread of AIDS in Africa by advocating "ideologically based monogamy." He also took an anti-evangelical position when he argued that urging people whose marriages have failed to stay together would force one of the partners to seek sex elsewhere and fuel the spread of the virus. He called for a new approach to African marriages that would consider "home-grown solutions." He also called on researchers to be open to herbal medicine. He commended President Bush for allocating $15 billion to fight AIDS in Africa.

One could argue that Museveni, as a born again Christian, never accepted condoms as a means of preventing HIV/AIDS. The irony is that most researchers and health specialists also consider condoms an improvisation. The only difference is that while health experts believe that if condoms are used correctly they could save lives, Museveni thinks that using condoms promotes promiscuity. Museveni's assertion that African men are often drunk when they have sex (a suspect generalization) cannot be taken to prove the ineffectiveness of condoms in the fight against the spread of the virus. The problem is with alcoholism itself, since it impairs people from making responsible decisions about safe sex. Therefore, part of the campaign for safe sex ought to include education about the effect of alcohol on decision-making.

Museveni claims incorrectly that people are "condomising" Africa. The manufacturers of condoms may have a vested interested in promoting condoms, but AIDS activists have no financial stake in encouraging irresponsible sexual behavior. They only argue that if people choose to have sexual intercourse, they should practice safe sex by using a protective device like a condom. Museveni also confuses monogamous relationships with monogamous marriages. HIV/AIDS activists discourage multiple partners, married or not. One wonders what the "home-grown solutions" are since we have entered the third decade of HIV/AIDS and so far the rate of prevalence in most countries have gone up, except for Uganda, where researchers argue that effective use of condoms along with death from HIV complications, has reduced the rate of prevalence. Museveni rolled back the clock in the fight against HIV/AIDS in his Bangkok speech. Many suspect that he changed his mind to attract part of the $15 billion in American President George Bush's Emergency Plan for AIDS Relief (PEPFAR), since the Bush administration is heavily influenced by conservative religious groups who prefer abstinence above other HIV/AIDS prevention strategies.[79]

Is there a middle ground between supporters of condom use and those who oppose them? Some Catholic moral theologians have supported use of condoms as prophylactics to prevent the spread of disease and to save life. The idea that a condom could serve a prophylactic function should be seen in the context of U.S. Catholic bishop's perspectives on HIV/AIDS. *The bishop's conference has issued two proclamations on AIDS: The Many Faces of AIDS: A Gospel Response, and Called to Compassion and Responsibility: A Response to the HIV/ADIS Crisis.*[80] These documents make several claims. First, AIDS is a human disease that demands response from the scientific and medical communities. Second, the Christian community has the responsibility of reaching out to those suffering from the disease. Third, AIDS calls for an understanding of human sexuality, and promotion of behavior that takes into consideration the teaching of the Catholic church on sexuality. Fourth, discrimination against infected persons is unjustified and indeed immoral. Fifth, society needs to develop educational programs to address the disease. Sixth, those who are already infected ought to live responsibly and avoid infecting others. It is in this context that the Catholic bishops' statement argues that if an infected person cannot "act without bringing harm to others" then a health-care worker may advise the infected person to use prophylactics. In addition, the documents call for testing for the HIV virus and recommend that those who are infected should not be removed from insurance coverage. They also call for the government to provide adequate funding to take care of those who are infected, arguing that the fight against HIV will only be effective if society addresses poverty, oppression, and alienation.

These documents remain controversial because the bishops rejected safe sex practices that involved the use of condoms. They called on people to practice chastity and to avoid intravenous drug use.[81] Their follow up publication, *Called to Compassion and Responsibility*, emphasized compassion, integrity, responsibility, social justice, prayer, and conversion. This document was more progressive because the Bishop's stretched our understanding of prayer and conversion by calling on people to turn away from ignorance and intolerance. It also addressed a variety of issues such as testing and confidentiality, research, public policy, discrimination, counseling and care for people who are suffering from the disease.

Since sexual abstinence is a desirable but a difficult proposition, the Christian church has a moral obligation to recognize the role that effective use of condoms could play in this dangerous time of HIV/AIDS, especially in protecting the most vulnerable. That reality was spelled out at the 2004 International AIDS Conference in Bangkok by U.S. congresswoman Barbara Lee, who argued that for many women and young girls "abstaining from sex often times is not a choice, and therefore, [the] only hope of preventing HIV infection is the use of condoms."[82] For Lee, emphasizing abstinence at a time when five million people are infected with the HIV virus each year is inhumane and irresponsible.

While the church's position on abstinence is laudable and prescribes the best prevention against infection, prevention campaigns that reject condoms are callous, deceitful, and immoral in light of the dangers that many people face today in Africa. Human beings are sexual beings who engage in sexual activity outside the boundaries recognized by the Christian tradition. I would argue that the church should continue to teach abstinence but in the context of this catastrophe, the church, which advocates and preaches a message of life, ought to encourage those who cannot abstain to protect themselves. Urging sexually active people to use a condom is an act of compassion that could protect the human being who is created in the image of God.

As the African church moves into the future, I think its leaders have an obligation to listen to the voices of women theologians in Africa. The Circle of Concerned African Women Theologians took up the challenge of HIV/AIDS at one of their conferences in August 2002 in Addis Ababa. They discussed "Sex: Stigma and HIV/AIDS: African Women Challenging Religion, Culture and Social Practices."[83] The Circle defines HIV/AIDS as a critical gender issue because more women than men live with HIV/AIDS in Africa. Some of the youngest victims of HIV/AIDS are girls as young as 11, infected through acts of sexual violence. African women are at risk because of physiological differences between men and women, sociocultural and economic factors, the fact that men prefer dry sex, practices that range from female genital cutting and sewing, widowhood rites and inheritance, the practice of polygamy, and a general cultural disposition for men to have many sexual partners.[84] Circle members criticize positions that encourage women to give in to all of their husbands' sexual demands, especially if they suspect their husbands of having extramarital affairs. They call on African churches to read the Bible and to enact a spiritual and social ministry that is attuned to gender differences and promotes the emancipation of women.

HIV/AIDS Offers Challenges to Public Policy

The social world created by HIV/AIDS challenges status quo public policy and calls for new priorities in Africa today. HIV/AIDS is the greatest threat to the political, economic, and social stability of African countries because it is causing the *polis* to disintegrate at an unprecedented rate. This tragedy could have been avoided if African governments had acted on time but as the following examples show, they did not. First, in South Africa, political leaders from the apartheid and post-apartheid state knew about the destructive force of AIDS but delayed taking direct action against it.[85] A government minister during the time of apartheid said of HIV/AIDS: "it is a disease which is going to shake Africa to its foundation."[86] But the apartheid regime established an advisory group on HIV/AIDS and limited the scope of its work to white areas. Given the legacy of apartheid, Nelson Mandela pointed out that blacks did not trust the South African government in dealing with the crisis.[87] The racist attempt by the apartheid regime to use HIV/AIDS as a lethal weapon was revealed during the Truth and Reconciliation Commission hearings by two applicants for amnesty who confessed that they recruited HIV-positive individuals to spread the disease in some black areas.[88]

The government's failure to act in South Africa is astounding because in the early 1990s over fifty publications in various disciplines provided epidemiological as well as sociopolitical studies of HIV/AIDS in South Africa, giving enough information to prompt the authorities to take action. This was only the beginning of a publication phenomenon that opened the floodgates of interdisciplinary studies of AIDS in South Africa.[89] That is why President Thabo Mbeki's statements on HIV/AIDS have shocked many people in South Africa. Adam Sitze has argued that although both apartheid policy and Mbeki policy toward HIV/AIDS constitute denialism, the root of the problem today lies in the fact that "the sovereign power to let die . . . was not sufficiently dissolved with the transfer of power in 1994."[90] Sitze suggests that one noteworthy trend in the post-apartheid era is the new form of resistance against public policy mounted especially by Zackie Achmat's refusal to take antiretroviral drugs until those drugs were available to poor people in South Africa.

Nigeria reported its first case of HIV/AIDS in 1986, and, although the government established the National AIDS/STD Control Program (NASCP) in 1987, it did not provide sufficient funds for the agency to do its work. It took the government several years to take action after conducting its first seroprevalence survey in 1991.[91] African leaders imitated President Ronald Reagan's silence on HIV/AIDS.[92] Thus, a World Council of Churches study indicates that the first case of HIV/AIDS was reported in Cameroon in 1986 but the government waited ten years before it created an AIDS control program in the ministry of public health. After its creation in 1996, the AIDS control program was plagued by lack of funds and poor coordination between government agencies.[93] In 1986 the rate of prevalence for Cameroon was 0.5 percent. By delaying action that rate grew to 3 percent in 2003, with about 75 percent of all cases found among people in the

20–39 age bracket, although infection rates among the 15–39-year-olds was on the rise.[94] Political silence clearly contributed to the spread of HIV/AIDS in Cameroon and the Central African region. Other factors include cultural silence, poverty, political instability, taboos on discussion about sex, stigmatization, discrimination, gender inequality, lack of education (especially for young girls who marry early), global economic inequities, and negative effects of structural adjustment to the economy.

In 2001 the Cameroon government collaborated with non-governmental organizations, faith-based organizations, and international donor agencies to launch an aggressive program situating HIV/AIDS as a big factor in poverty and economic and social development. The government has distributed funds to various organizations and churches to help fight the disease. The program has focused on testing, counseling, the highly effective prevention of mother-to-child-transmission, and distribution of antiretroviral drugs.[95]

In Kenya, "it was felt that any talk about HIV/AIDS was a gratuitous criticism of Kenya and its ruling authorities. For this reason, little or no publicity was given to the AIDS pandemic or to the response of the Kenya government in the early years."[96] Preserving the image of the country in the early stages of the disease has proven a costly exercise. The Kenyan government eventually declared HIV/AIDS a national disaster in 1997, and followed that declaration with official guidelines in *The Sessional Paper No. 4 on AIDS in Kenya.*

HIV/AIDS is the single most devastating crisis to affect the political community in Africa and calls for radical action. First, African governments need to come to terms with the fact that they are dealing with a catastrophe of enormous proportions. Denial and silence, which Jonathan Mann described as the third epidemic (the first being HIV infection, the second being clinical AIDS), allowed the virus to spread uncontrollably.[97] The pandemic escalated while the postcolonial state was facing economic hardships and external and internal critics blamed African states for bad governance and abuse of human rights. Some African leaders were silent about HIV/AIDS to protect the image of their countries. The conspiracy of silence is not completely broken. Kris Peterson has pointed out that as recently as 2003, the local government of Badagry in Nigeria still denied that AIDS exists.[98] Conspiracy theories abound about the human invention of AIDS. The most controversial statement on HIV/AIDS has come from one of the continent's most prominent politicians, South African President Thabo Mbeki. Mbeki has stated that he does not think the HIV virus causes AIDS. At one level, it is clear that Mbeki was not denying the reality of the virus, but only questioning if the HIV virus causes the condition AIDS. It is not difficult to figure out why the intellectually inquisitive and ideological astute South African president took these positions, although I disagree with many of his views and pronouncements on HIV/AIDS.   Mbeki was not always a skeptic on HIV/AIDS; as deputy president, he supported research funding for the controversial drug Virodene that was developed by researchers at the University of Pretoria. Some scholars touted Virodene as a major breakthrough in HIV/AIDS research, but the Medicines Control Council of South Africa did not support it because other studies indicated that Diethylformamide, one of the active ingredients used in the drug, caused damage to the DNA and liver in humans. Mbeki on his part argued that providing treatment to those suffering from HIV/AIDS was a moral obligation that required funding of the Virodene research. He took this position before engaging the global HIV/AIDS economics that was marked vicious competition between researchers, pharmaceutical companies, and states whose economies stood to benefit from the marketing of new drugs. Mbeki's views changed during negotiations with big pharmaceutical companies, especially when he realized that even the U.S. government supported big pharmaceutical companies in violation of the provisions of the WTO over Trade Related Aspects of Intellectual Property Rights, (TIPPS). Mbeki was also disappointed with the political and economic machinations of the pharmaceutical companies that were marketing ARVs. But the most important thing that changed his thinking on HIV/AIDS was the fact that he was exposed to, and he believed, the arguments presented by HIH/AIDS dissenters in popular literature and on the internet.

Mbeki called for further research on established positions that HIV causes AIDS; he questioned the usefulness of ARVs, which he stated several times, were toxic. He sent a letter to world leaders in which he called these positions into question, but also called for careful study and open debate on the science of HIV/AIDS because the majority views and the epidemiology of HIV/AIDS often failed to take into account the social conditions under which the disease spread and the particular context of South Africa where sociopolitical realities were shaped by apartheid. While these were all compelling issues, I do not think that as a leader of a country where millions of people were infected with the HIV virus, it was prudent for President Mbeki to engage in these debates and take sides without examining all the evidence on grounds that he wanted to stimulate a healthy scientific debate.[99]

If he wanted to stimulate debate in the scientific community, he could have opened debate on a number of issues that would have kept them busy for a long time. Mbeki has contributed significantly to the revival of Africa by championing the African Renaissance, and the New Partnership for African Development (NEPAD). However, he has missed the renaissance on HIV/AIDS. He entered the game of debating HIV/AIDS on the side of the playing ground that belongs to the medical and scientific community. As a strong supporter of his renaissance project, I ought to confess that it is difficult to estimate the damage done by the speculation of President Mbeki on whether HIV virus causes clinical AIDS. (It is mind-boggling also that his former deputy Jacob Zuma thinks that one can have unprotected sex with someone who is HIV-positive and then simply shower to minimize the risk of infection.)

Mbeki has also questioned claims that the drug Nevirapine stops mother to child transmission of HIV/AIDS. Here again he ought to leave the technical and medical debates to the scientific community (and there is a very robust scientific and medical community in South Africa). I do not imply that politicians should not debate issues about the HIV/AIDS pandemic. The irony is that Mbeki is doing the right thing by engaging in a debate and dialogue when other leaders have remained silent. I am convinced that the African community will take a big leap forward in the fight against HIV/AIDS based on what politicians think, say, and do. However, they must think, say, and do the right thing. They do not need to "reinvent the wheel" by questioning well-established scientific findings. African states need strong leaders who will domesticate the HIV/AIDS crisis and then work with the international community to stop new infections and provide treatment for people living with HIV/AIDS. Such leadership could start by addressing the social imbalance that has created a permanent underclass in Africa.

Second, African governments should scale up their actions against HIV/AIDS by implementing and sustaining their own projects. When denial gave way to acknowledgment of a new reality in the 1980s, the Kenyan government established the National AIDS Committee and an AIDS secretariat in 1985. The National AIDS and STDs Control Programme (NASCOP), was created to focus the fight against HIV/AIDS. Working with international organizations the Kenyan government used these institutions to establish five-year action plans called Medium Term Plans (MTP). The costs for the education campaigns were projected at $10 million in 1992 and $13 million in 1996. The Kenyan government received a World Bank grant of $40 million to fight HIV/AIDS for about three years.[100] NASCOP mobilized workers to sensitize about 90 percent of the population on two ways of preventing AIDS through safe sex practices. The program included distribution of 170 million condoms by 1996, with a goal of achieving 100 percent condom use by sex workers, teachers, and security forces. The National AIDS Committee also launched an education program to teach 90 percent of the traditional healers to use safe procedures. Their goal was to reduce HIV/AIDS prevalence by 2.5 percent by their target date of 1996.

Aylward Shorter and Edwin Onyancha call this an overly ambitious project and argue that the government could have accomplished more by focusing on "sexual promiscuity, which is currently rife among adolescents and young adults."[101] While irresponsible sexual behavior is a great threat to public health, the Kenyan government's plan was nonetheless bold and visionary; one can only wish that it had covered all aspects of the pandemic by addressing systemic marginalization and violence that has created risk situations for many people. The plan of action preferred by Shorter and Onyancha would have been a one-dimensional strategy with emphasis on sexual issues at the expense of broad social interventions. If the fight against HIV/AIDS is going to succeed, bold initiatives must include long-term multi-sectoral approaches and must be fully funded with local as well as donor agency monies.

Third, the fight against HIV/AIDS demands courageous leadership. African states need leadership at the presidential, ministerial, and regional levels to fight against HIV/AIDS on all fronts. Addressing delegates at the opening session of the fifteenth International AIDS Conference in Bangkok, United Nations Secretary General Kofi Annan reiterated that the fight against HIV/AIDS demands effective government leadership because HIV/AIDS is a health crisis and a threat to human development. Annan called for world leaders to support the campaign for treatment and for prevention of new infections, and to use their positions to empower women and girls to protect themselves. I am convinced that, in Africa especially, leaders should act decisively to reverse cultural norms that continue to place the lives of so many women at risk.

The new political praxis in an age of HIV/AIDS calls for more than World AIDS Day speeches. It calls for the kind of open dialogue modeled by the early Museveni who talked openly about HIV/AIDS and encouraged people to protect themselves and participate in voluntary testing and counseling. Recently, nine parliamentarians in Zimbabwe volunteered and took the test for HIV virus through the program of Populations Services International (PSI) at the New Voluntary Counseling and Testing (VCT). They took this step to encourage people to do the same and find out about their HIV status, hoping to reduce the stigma and fears many in the public have about HIV tests. The largest VCT network in Africa has been established in Zimbabwe with funding from the United States Agency for

International Development (USAID) and the British Department for International Development (DFID).[102]

Fourth, public policy makers should rebuild and restructure public health systems that are in shambles. Health-care systems in many African countries are nothing more than a massive bureaucracy that no longer meets the needs of the people. Daniel J. Smith has argued: "by most accounts Nigeria's overall public health infrastructure is in disarray, unable to provide basic primary health-care service, much less cope with the tremendous burdens of a burgeoning AIDS epidemic."[103] HIV/AIDS has taxed what remains of the health-care system in African countries to capacity. During the 1980s African countries joined the WHO in working toward "health for all by the 2000." However, the millennium ushered in something more like death for all. The priorities are clear. In some countries religious institutions continue to offer health care to many people in the wake of the collapse of public health-care systems. But many health-care workers who are employed by the government operate their own private clinics and divert patients to those clinics where they charge exorbitant fees. Fighting HIV/AIDS requires the mobilization of the health-care systems and responsible leadership that rewards health-care workers so that they will not abandon their responsibility in search of a better income.

Fifth, public policy makers ought to develop a systematic program to test for the HIV virus and to provide accurate information that can be used to plan prevention strategies, develop treatment options, and determine appropriate use of resources. There are difficult issues here, including whether testing should be mandatory, as well issues of confidentiality that each state ought to work out. Testing remains a crucial part of any broad approach to the fight against HIV/AIDS.[104] Mandatory testing of pregnant women is done in many countries now. Concerns about the violation of privacy are legitimate, but one must also realize that detecting the seropositivity status of the mother has given health-care workers the means to work with the mother to prevent mother-to-child transmission.

I do not think that even if one tests positive his or her name should be put in some national register because that would pose a danger for many people living with HIV/AIDS who already face discrimination. In South Africa, members of her own community beat Mrs. Gugu Dlamini to death after she informed others that she was infected with the virus and became an AIDS educator and activist.[105] The dialogue on HIV/AIDS has been started in Africa largely by activists; it is important that the decision to go public about one's status in a world where discrimination prevails should be that of the individual.

Sixth, public policy makers must take all measures within the law to stop sexual violence against women and girls, which continues to increase the already high rate of prevalence of HIV/AIDS among women. The 2004 joint report of UNAIDS, UNFPA, and UNIFEM indicated that nearly half of the people living with HIV/AIDS worldwide are women, with 17 million of them between the ages of 15 and 49.[106] By the end of 2003, the Global Coalition on Women and AIDS (GCWA) estimated that about 58 percent of all people living with HIV/AIDS in Africa were women. A recent survey by the Department of Health in South Africa of 16,643 women attending antenatal clinics revealed that about 27.9 percent of pregnant women tested positive for the HIV/AIDS virus in 2003. The number had grown from 26.5 percent in 2002, an indication that the spread of the disease among women has not slowed down; instead this survey indicates the increase has been dramatic, because only about 0.7 percent of women at antenatal clinics tested positive in 1990.[107] Many women are infected as a direct result of violence.

Here are some of the things we know about the pandemic among women. The HIV/AIDS pandemic has hit women and girls in Africa in apocalyptic proportions. Over half of the people living with HIV/AIDS in Africa today are women and girls. That number will grow if leaders do nothing to curb gender imbalance and violence in Africa. P. Piot of UNAIDS, describes the impact of HIV/AIDS on women as "a particularly insidious aspect of the AIDS epidemic."[108] To say that the magnitude of the devastation of HIV/AIDS on African women is a tragedy is an understatement. Reflecting on statistics indicating that by the year 2020 HIV/AIDS will have caused more deaths than the World Wars of the twentieth century, Stephen Lewis, the United Nations secretary general's special envoy on HIV/AIDS in Africa has stated:

> The toll on women and girls is beyond human imagining; it presents Africa and the world with a practical and moral challenge which places gender at the center of the human condition. The practice of ignoring a gender analysis has turned out to be lethal. . . . For the African continent, it means economic and social survival. For the women and girls of Africa, it's a matter of life or death.[109]

Concrete steps to stop the devastating effects of HIV/AIDS on women should be part of a comprehensive gender analysis which highlights the following realities.

(1) Young women are three times more likely to be infected with the HIV virus than young men. Since many girls now have their first sexual experience at an early age (11 years), many of them are infected before they reach their thirteenth birthday. (2) Women at all levels have little bargaining

power in sexual relationships and cannot negotiate whether to have sex or abstain. In many cultures they are expected to have sex with their husbands even if they know that their husbands have had unprotected sexual relations with other women. The Global Coalition on Women and AIDS reports that in Zambia 11 percent of the women who were interviewed believed that a woman has no right to demand that her husband use a condom. Despite the great strides made by feminism around the world, women still do not control their own bodies. Since women biologically are more likely to get the HIV/AIDS virus, HIV/AIDS transmission is twice as likely from male to female as from female to male.

(3) Most HIV/AIDS transmission among women in Africa is directly connected to violence against women that has reached epidemic proportions. In one year, about 54, 310 sexual crimes were reported in South Africa alone.[110] Structural inequity has left many women poor and exposed them to sex work and the growing exploitation of "transactional and intergenerational sex," facilitated by the sugar daddy phenomenon.[111] Although transactional sex involves the exchange of sex for money or service, researchers draw a distinction between transactional sex and sex work because transactional sex takes place in the context of unbalanced power relations between the male and female. Transactional sex tends to take place between older men and young women, many of them students at all levels, ranging from secondary school to university students.

Violence against women should be seen in a broad context because it involves a range of abuses: rape, including marital rape; a social praxis such as domestic violence that forces women into dependence; divorce laws that discriminate against women; unfair inheritance laws; sexual exploitation of women and girls in employment and school recruitment; and limited access to education and health services, including reproductive health service. "The plight of girls affected by AIDS in Africa, as of all AIDS orphans, constitutes a human rights emergency."[112] It is tragic that African cultures that take pride in children cannot protect their young girls from violence. If public policy makers are going to stem the tide of HIV/AIDS, some direct action must be taken to stop these abuses. African leaders have an obligation to implement all international agreements which they signed, and which provide for the protection of women's rights as human rights.[113] The Zimbabwean government has passed a sexual assault act, which criminalizes sexual assault in general and in cases where the one who perpetrates this crime infects the victim with the HIV virus. The act also requires that any individual convicted of rape must undergo mandatory AIDS testing.[114] Although some observers argue that measures like these treat HIV as an exception, I am convinced that the high rate of the epidemic of violence against women justifies such measures for now. In addition to passing such legislation, African governments ought to start a systematic education campaign denouncing violence against women, paying special attention to the sexual behavior of men, and seeking to promote the message of the 2000 World AIDS Campaign. Men were the focus of this campaign because UNAIDS rightly called attention to men's health, to risky and unsafe sex practices that endanger the lives of women, and the fact that AIDS has a devastating effect on the family.[115]

A number of sensitization campaigns against violence called "men working to stop the spread of HIV/AIDS" have been organized by men in collaboration with women's groups in Kenya. Conferences were held in Ethiopia, Kenya, Zambia, and Malawi on World AIDS Day 2003, in which men led discussions on ways to change the attitudes toward women, as a way of ending violence. The New York-based non-governmental organization called EngenderHealth, started Men as Partners (MaP) to give voice to gender issues and train peer leaders to discuss gender roles in the community. Women Against Rape (WAR) was started in Botswana to provide support for women and girls who suffered violence and rape, and to provide assistance in dealing with all forms of abuse and discrimination against women. They organized a march in 2003 that many people attended, including secondary school girls.[116] These activities indicate that some small steps are being taken.

The community has to restructure its power base and help men realize that acting to protect the lives of women serves their own self-interests as well as being a moral imperative. Society has to come to grips with issues of femininity and masculinity and work with men to reorder their perspectives on masculinity.[117] Public education should address perceptions of masculine identity and the responsibility that comes with manhood. Communities must contextualize what it means to be a man in relational terms: a man is a son, brother, boyfriend, husband, father, uncle, alongside and in equal partnership with daughters, sisters, girlfriend, wife, mother, aunts. These social relations involve other responsibilities beyond sexual privileges. Sex is not a male prerogative and certainly not a license for violence against women and girls.[118] Masculinity should be reconceived to empower women as equal partners in the journey of life.

Seventh, public policy makers should pay special attention to children and youths who are disproportionately affected by the pandemic. Children who are infected with HIV/AIDS through mother-to-child transmission often die early. Most of them die within the first years of their lives. Infant

mortality has risen in all countries in sub-Saharan Africa. With youths however, we have a tragic story that continues to baffle all concerned with
HIV/AIDS. Statistics from several countries indicate that youths have sexual
experience as young as 11 years of age. While it is true that by the time a
young person reaches 15 or 16 they yearn for sex, social conditions such as
unemployment and poverty increase the drive to find sexual fulfillment at all
cost. What is alarming about teenage sex in many contexts is that it often
involves violence and an inappropriate exercise of power by the male over the
female. At an early age, young men think already that they own their girlfriends and can treat them as their property. In the Eastern Cape of South
Africa some boys told researchers that they reserve the right to monitor their
girlfriends and control their conversation partners and to beat them if they
stray from these restraints.[119] Furthermore, the pattern taking root among
young men is their belief that they have a right to consume alcohol when
they have sex. This is a proof of manhood.

Eighth, public policy makers in Africa should standardize HIV/AIDS
education throughout their countries. Education ought to begin at an early
age in schools. Given the age at which a young person has his or her first sexual experience, sex education in the context of a comprehensive health and
wellness education is not too early in the fifth, sixth, or seventh grades of ele-
mentary schools. At the secondary school level, mandatory classes on sex
education should be part of the curriculum. To ensure that this obligation is
taken seriously, the materials used for sex education should be part of the
general certificate of education syllabus, or whatever constitutes the exit certificate examination. This requires close collaboration between the education, health, and social and cultural departments of state governments. Such
education should acknowledge sexual realities, but stress the responsibility
that human sexuality places on everybody. It should provide specific information about sexuality, sexual abuse, and the dangers posed by current cir-
cumvention of sociocultural norms in order to achieve pleasure for pleasure
sake. Caution is called for because some young men working as peer educators with knowledge of contraceptives have used the classroom to exploit
young women for sex.[120] Peer educators ought to be trustworthy individuals
who will not betray the trust they have been given.

Finally, policy leaders ought to address as a matter of urgency the issue
of food security posed by the HIV/AIDS pandemic. Men and women who
cultivate farms and grow food for family consumption and the market now
spend time in a hospital bed, or are often so weak that they cannot do farm
work. As more people become ill, less food is produced. The threat of hunger

looms large in many countries. Not only can people not work their own farms, but with so many infected people unable to earn money to buy food, many families will certainly go hungry. Department of agricultures in Africa need to plan ahead and deal with this situation, by not only providing food subsidies to affected areas, but also coming up with ways of ensuring that the food supply of the country will not be depleted.

Chapter 2

The *Imago Dei* and its Implications for HIV/AIDS

Is there no balm in Gilead?
Is there no physician there?
Why then has the health of my
poor people not been restored?
—Jeremiah 8:22

Preliminary Questions about Theological Imagery

In this chapter, I propose the *imago dei* as a basis for grounding and for scaling up the church's practical obligations in dealing with the HIV/AIDS pandemic. I argue that the *imago dei* calls for an ethic of love and compassion.[1] The HIV/AIDS pandemic calls for a critical and humble reading of the Bible. The passage from the Hebrew Bible quoted above bespeaks a yearning for answers that is found among many Christians in Africa as they confront the mysterious disease, HIV/AIDS. The *imago dei* does not speak directly to illness, but offers a perspective on the human body battered by HIV/AIDS, inviting us in the midst of the pandemic to honor each human being that bears the *imago dei*.

While I am committed to the view that the *imago dei* compels a loving and compassionate response to HIV/AIDS, my reflections do not exhaust the possible implications of the image of God for the divine human

41

relationship. The *imago dei* offers one window into the divine economy of the relationship between divinity and humanity, especially evident in the prophetic traditions of the Hebrew Bible and the teachings of the New Testament, by which to highlight the Christian community's obligation to love and care for those whose bodies are battered by HIV/AIDS. My working assumption for this chapter, and the theme of this book, is that the idea that humanity is created in the image of God is a summons for Christian communities in Africa to mobilize their people to work locally and with the international community to establish a broad-based, multisectoral fight against HIV/AIDS and to renew their commitment to one another. The magnitude and complexity of HIV/AIDS demands an ethical position grounded on the idea of the image of God that defies a particular ethical theory—whether one thinks of deontological theories or utilitarian theories. The *imago dei* is a theological motif that offers a different way of thinking about and cultivating relationships with human beings who live in and with extreme pain and sorrow because they have been subjected to an invasive and destructive virus.

Having said that, I should also state that the *imago dei* does not provide a "foundation," if by foundation one understands some Archimedean point for a theology of HIV/AIDS. I am even hesitant to call *imago dei* a leitmotif because there are other motifs that could also provide a way for addressing the human condition in a world complicated by the crisis of HIV/AIDS.[2] However, in taking the *imago dei* as scriptural motivation for Christian communities to scale up their fight against the HIV pandemic, I echo the declaration of the World Council of Churches (WCC): "The Church's response to the challenge of HIV/AIDS comes from its deepest theological convictions about the nature of creation, the unshakable fidelity of God's love, the nature of the body of Christ and the reality of Christian hope."[3] The creation narrative, which affirms that humanity is created in the image of God, links human beings to the love of God, which is modeled in the incarnation of Jesus.

My reflections in this chapter follow the tradition of theological ethics that derives perspectives from the historical, textual, liturgical, and philosophical influences that have shaped the Christian worldview. I use the *imago dei* in conversation with the theological and philosophical tradition merely as an anchoring motif for members of various Christian communities as they seek to address illnesses like HIV/AIDS themselves and as they dialogue with other communities of discourse and practice.[4] Some Christian ethicists have argued that Christians have their own perspective and ought to address world issues from that perspective. For example, Stanley Hauerwas has argued:

> The Church does have a social, ethical responsibility toward wider society, but it is a task that she must fulfill on her own terms. The first task is to be a community that keeps alive the language of the faith through the liturgical, preaching and teaching offices of the community. In other words, the church serves society best by striving to be a community of truthfulness and care.[5]

I do not pursue the debate whether this position is "sectarian," because others have expressed those concerns and Hauerwas has responded to them. My own view is that with HIV/AIDS, the Christian community would respond in an informed manner if theologians maintain a robust conversation with the scientific community, medical experts, healers, public policy makers and other groups that seek to forge a new meaning of health and well-being in a situation of great stress and gloom.

The *imago dei* is a springboard to invite a multisectoral acceleration of the fight against HIV/AIDS. Martha Nussbaum, who has articulated the notion of human flourishing in a world where limitations abound but human excellences can cultivated to realize the good, dismisses ethical perspectives motivated by transcendence. Nussbaum prefers instead: "a delicate and always flexible balancing act between the claims of excellence, which lead us to push outward, and the necessity of the human context, which pushes us back in."[6] While I share some of Nussbaum's concerns (I do not think we need any theological foundationalist approach or claim that ethics and morality must be grounded on religion), I do however think that theological claims have a legitimate place in the formulation of ethical perspectives on contemporary issues if one uses his or her theological perspective as one view among other competing views. Responding to HIV/AIDS in Africa calls for a new pluralism because each community is party to a vast array of responders. HIV/AIDS has taxed the resources of the Christian community to its maximum. The church should work with other religious (and secular) communities that have a strong presence in Africa.[7] There is no doubt that in the early days of the HIV/AIDS crisis certain people in the church took sectarian positions and proclaimed an apocalypse, seeing HIV/AIDS as a divine visitation on a world that had ignored God. It is now painfully clear that this approach was mistaken and the church must reach out, take its place in the social world, and share the responsibility for protecting human well-being. In order to do that, it is necessary for the church to come up with new ways of being part of the healing process.

The *Imago Dei* and its Implications for HIV/AIDS

The book of Genesis states several times that God created human beings in God's image. In Genesis 1:26 we read: "Let us make human-kind in our image, according to our likeness; and let them have dominion over the fish of the sea, and over the birds of the air, and over the cattle, and over all the wild animals of the earth, and over every creeping thing that creeps upon the earth." Later the narrator reports God saying to the first humans: "Be fruitful and multiply, and fill the earth and subdue it; and have dominion . . . over every living thing that moves upon the earth." Similar language is found in Genesis 5:3 with reference to human procreation: "When Adam had lived one hundred thirty years, he became the father of a son in his likeness, according to his image, and named him Seth." Then, in Genesis 9:6 we read that God told Noah: "Whoever sheds the blood of a human, by a human shall that person's blood be shed; for in his own image God made humankind."

Scholars of the Hebrew Bible and theologians have wrestled with these passages, although some consider these texts insignificant to the overall account of creation.[8] Anders Nygren takes the position that these passages come from the priestly writer and are alien to the biblical thought of the ancient Semitic world.[9] I am convinced that this priestly addition constitutes an important part of the creation narrative and contributes significantly to a deeper understanding not only of the creation story but of the divine/human connection.[10] The words of Genesis 1:26-27, from a priestly author who wrote during the exile, displacement, and sociopolitical dislocation under a foreign imperial order, attempt to provide theological reassurance that God has not forsaken the Jews. The author comforts the people by proclaiming a close relationship or an ontological proximity between God and human beings. By contrast, the Yahwist author of Genesis chapter 2, who wrote his own account of creation first, perhaps during the high point of the monarchy of Solomon, does not articulate such a close connection between Yahweh and humanity, but instead establishes a hierarchy and distinction in the divine-human relationship.

In the New Testament the notion of the *imago dei* is used with special reference to the divine-human relationship in its christological dimensions because Christ "is" the image of God. The apostles Paul and James also use the idea to reflect the spiritual life of the believer. Paul indicates that humans are "predestined to be conformed to the image" (Rom 8:29) or "transformed into the same image" (2 Cor 3:18) or "renewed according to the image" (Col 3:10) or "made in the likeness" of God (Jas 3:9).[11] I must follow Cairns and underscore some distinctions here. First, I do not think that the terms image and likeness refer to different things. Scholarly consensus after Eichrodt sees the two terms as an example of Hebrew parallelism, with the term likeness explaining the term image.[12] Since image and likeness mean the same thing, I will not address the issues raised by Genesis 5:3, where we read that Adam fathered his son Seth in his own likeness, and after his own image—the image of Adam. This particular text forces us to think about the corporeality of God. Can we say that humans are like God in the sense that Seth the son of Adam was like Adam? If we take the view that God's image and likeness is physical or bodily correspondence what are the implications when we transfer that image to contemporary discussions of difference? Frederick McLeod has argued that Antiochene theologians, some influenced by Origen, thought that the body was part of the notion of the image of God. Adam carried the *imago dei* "in the sense that he serves in creation as a concrete, living, and visible symbol that points to the existence of God."[13] A more useful perspective is to read the image of God as a complex reality encompassing the totality of the human being: body, soul, spirit, etc. The *imago dei* reflects all of what human beings are as people created by God.

The Christian tradition sees the body as a part of the economy of creation. Human beings belong to God and live under the sovereignty of God. They come from God and go back to God; therefore, one must see life and death in the light of God's economy of existence. Whether people live or die, they are God's. The Apostle Paul, in his letter to the Romans, said: "We do not live to ourselves, and we do not die to ourselves. If we live, we live to the Lord, and if we die, we die to the Lord; so then, whether we live or whether we die, we are the Lord's. For to this end Christ died and lived again, so that he might be Lord of both the dead and the living" (Rom 14:7-9). HIV/AIDS touches human bodies with a force that has been and will likely be fatal for many. It forces the body to waste away and finally succumb to death, but the *imago dei* in that body survives because humanity belongs to God. This perspective serves as a reminder that one should not discriminate against people living with HIV/AIDS because they have the *imago dei*. Christians are not entitled to demonize anyone who is HIV-positive because, even in that state, that individual has the *imago dei*.

The image of God in humanity does not imply that human beings are more valuable than other things God has created. Instead, one must see it as a relational category that is rich and pregnant with profound possibilities for human and divine interaction. This relationship lies behind the acts of God in the Hebrew Bible and the covenantal relationship that God established with Israel. One can appropriate the *imago dei* motif without limiting oneself to the view that the *imago dei* refers to spiritual superiority, rationality, self-consciousness, and self-determination.[14]

As one who speaks the *Limbum* language of the Wimbum people in the Northwest Province of Cameroon, I have wrestled with how one could talk about the idea that humanity is created in the image of God or the view that the image and likeness of God refer to one thing. In Limbum, the word image could be translated *rlingshi*, a term that means "shadow" or even "photograph." The second Limbum word, *bfissi*, means "resemblance" and comes close to the word likeness which is used in the text. To say in Limbum that humans have the *rlingshi* (shadow or picture) of God may not quite communicate fully what one understands by the image of God. However, to say that human beings *bfissi* God conveys the idea that they bear a resemblance to God. Thus, to convey the notion of *imago dei* among the Wimbum people one would have to come up with a phrase such as *nyu am boo nnwe iba ambo yi nyu yu* (God created humanity to be like God). One could also maintain the expression that people "*bfissi* God," refers to the fact that human beings resemble God and then work out what such resemblance implies. For instance, one could explain then that a human being is like God because a human being has a body and mind, hence thinks, desires, acts, loves, chooses, and exists in freedom.

What then are the implications of the idea that humanity is created in the image of God? First, the *imago dei* is a relational term that spells out God's relationship to humanity. The image of God is not restricted to the Godhead but extends to humanity. Human beings are related to each other and to God. The image of God therefore establishes a vertical and horizontal communion. It is a communion of outreach; a project that begins with God when God reaches out to establish an identity with humanity. The establishment of such an identity is also an invitation to humanity to participate in the image of God and extend that sense of communion to others. The image of God brings God and people into a communion that is inclusive in all ways.

The image of God also establishes a bond that cannot be destroyed, even if it is distorted by sin. According to Christian teaching, individuals enter into a special relationship with God through their commitment to Jesus Christ, but being committed to Jesus Christ is not the basis for being made in the image of God. Rather, a *koinonia* already exists between God and humanity. Moreover, it is clear that this *koinonia* extends to individuals, not simply to humanity collectively. Each person who carries the *imago dei* is special and all people ought to follow God's example and treat others with special dignity because they too bear the image of God. God's presence points to ways in which the human being resembles God and reflects the divine nature.[15] Community life structured in recognition of the *imago dei* is therefore central to the good of all persons in a given context.

Furthermore, the image of God is expressed concretely as female and male. The priestly passage in Genesis claims explicitly that God created both female and male in the image of God. This view establishes ontological equality between the sexes. Therefore human existence and destiny are linked to the proposition that male and female share one thing in common—the *imago dei*. In the struggle against HIV/AIDS such a position is important because it invites the Christian community to rethink and combat violence against women: such violence which compromises the security of many women and makes them vulnerable to the HIV virus also violates the *imago dei*.

The idea that all people, women and men, are created in the image of God demands deeper reflection. African women experience various forms discrimination based on class, race, ethnicity, and religion. Many of them share one thing in common: they also experience gender-based discrimination. Many people in Africa argue that they do not practice gender discrimination. Others simply argue that the very idea of gender discrimination has been introduced by feminism, which is a Western construct. Studies consistently demonstrate, however, that in many areas of social and family life, men have a stronger position and play a dominant role, often at the expense of women.

God made no distinctions about the quality or quantity of the divine image deposited in male and female. This distinction made at creation between a man and a woman was not a mechanism of subordination, but the establishment of difference in the economy of relations; it was intended to strengthen the human family. The image of God is present in all its fullness in male and female, and the one is not subordinate to other at the ontological level. All cultural concessions that have led to the diminution of the female have effectively sacrificed the image of God in its female expression in the same way that the marginalization of other races has compromised the *imago dei* in its cultural expression.

I am convinced that the central issue in the creation narrative is not what God created Eve to do or be for Adam. Such distinctions are elaborations of roles in the economy of existence that is already grounded ontologically in the *imago dei*. It is wrong to use the emphasis on complementary roles to justify the domination of females by males, even if such chauvinism is ostensibly grounded in the interpretations of creation narratives offered by Saint Paul. I am convinced that the central idea remains the proclamation that God created female and male in the image of God. This claim should be the basis for the church to work for the elimination of discrimination in its own community and in society. This task is easier said than done because cultural and social norms around the world still give preference to men and women remain second-class citizens. The Christian community can contribute to a new dialogue by teaching and living the reality of what it means to claim that all people are created in the image of God.

Men and women are related to God on equal terms because they both have the image of God. This is the revolutionary idea that feminist scholars have articulated since the last half of the twentieth century. Patriarchy had reinterpreted human relations by placing the male on top. What we need is a balance that will restore respect to the image of God in the female member of the human race. The female body, made in the image of God, has become a field of conquest and domination. The female body in some cases has also become a space of cultural bargaining, where practices that no longer serve the spiritual or economic needs of women such as female genital cutting, polygamy, levirate marriages, and widowhood cleansing continue to receive justification in the name of culture. Ignoring the image of God in women has created a culture where poverty, the demand for sex workers, rape, and preferential treatment for male offspring have long compromised the position of women in society. Such compromises have hindered many women from making decisions about their own safety in the context of HIV/AIDS.

Members of the Concerned Circle of African Women theologians have identified gender discrimination and the violent abuse of women among the main causes of the HIV/AIDS crisis in Africa.[16] Their work reflects the Genesis narrative which establishes a community of equals where a man and woman are companions for each other because both have the image of God. Jürgen Moltman argues: "It is not against his or her fellow human beings nor apart from them but only in human fellowship with them and for them that the individual can correspond to his or her destiny as created in the image of God."[17] The idea of community implies a new mode of being in relationship across and beyond all boundaries.

Restoring respect for the image of God in women is an obligation that the church cannot ignore. The standard of what it means to be human is not the male, but God. The mold and measuring rod is God, and God's qualities and character. The question is not who was created first, as Saint Paul argues in the New Testament. The question is what does it mean to be human and bear the image of God! The priestly author of the Genesis narrative did not distinguish between men and women in exile and captivity.

Instead in light of their common situation, the priestly author pointed to a common standard shared by male and female—the image and likeness of God. The teaching programs of the church could help individuals in the fight against HIV/AIDS if leaders emphasize that male and female possess all the possibilities and capacities that reflect God because God has given those qualities in equal measure to men and women.

Like many institutions of society, the church is afflicted with sexism. Sexism is inconsistent with the *imago dei*, but it is part of an old order. Margaret Farley has argued that Christian theology has supported this old order for a long time "by refusing to ascribe to women the fullness of the *imago dei*, and by defining women as derivative from and wholly complementary to men."[18] It is time for this old order to go away so that a new order and new day might be established not only as part of the church's theological obligation during a pandemic crisis but as a quest for justice and recognition of the *imago dei* in men and women.

In order to restore respect for the image of God in the female, Christian communities have to come to terms with the female body. The female body is not merely a receptacle for male seed, a view that in some cultures means that the woman has value only when she gives birth to children. Besides being a limited view of the body of women, this idea is especially dangerous in a time of HIV/AIDS, because women are expected to submit to sexual procreation—even when their partners are HIV-positive. Moreover, some women who are HIV-positive conceal their status in order to continue sexual activity and procreation. But Farley argues women have begun to object to the idea that "anatomy is destiny," and that a woman's essential role is receptivity or submission. The "flight from receptivity in modern theologies of Christian love parallels a general fear of receptivity in a modern age when for Sartrean man, 'to receive is incompatible with being free . . . such fears are the result of an experience and an interpretation of receptivity which is oppressive, deceiving in its illusory offer of meaning and happiness, destructive in its enforced passivity.' "[19] The belief that all women must procreate sexually needs rethinking at a time when the life of the woman could be placed at risk. The woman's body is made in the image of God and that image is not defined primarily by its procreative capabilities.

The *imago dei* spells human dignity. The image of God places on each person a special and immeasurable worth. In simple terms, each person is dignified just by being human. Individuals have that dignity not because they are rational or spiritual beings but because they are created in the image of God. Therefore, one could claim that the *imago dei* makes all persons sacred in the general sense that they are set apart, even if they are not particularly religious.

From this perspective, since the person is sacred, the human body is also sacred. Saint Paul even calls the body the dwelling place of the spirit of God, making his claims about the sacredness of the human body in the context of a discussion of human sexuality. When considered within the context of a pandemic, Paul's claim could mean that one must not allow any activity to harm or destroy the body. Under Paul's economy, one has to flee fornication or sexual relations outside the bonds of marriage. Today, while some people may not share that view, the human body remains sacred and it is prudent to protect one's body in every sexual act because of that sacred quality. Christians have an obligation to work with other communities of discourse on protecting the body. I do not imply that the church should become a social police force, but instead offer counsel for situations where people engage in activities that might sacrifice the sacredness of the body and compromise human dignity.

In a culture where so many already carry the HIV virus, the idea that the body is sacred and bears the *imago dei* also implies that the virus cannot take away one's sense of self and dignity. Since every person has special value, church life should be structured in such a way that all the members of the community have ample opportunity to protect, care for, and sustain human dignity when it is assaulted by disease. Those who suffer do not have to do anything to earn this respect from the church community because they already have a God-given dignity that calls for respect. Human dignity has been bestowed on each person. Each person has within him or her what Martin Heidegger has called "the idea of transcendence." Heidegger refers to what lies beyond the individual and his or her intellect.[20] This sense of transcendence can be understood in several ways as it relates to human dignity. Human beings are connected to something outside and above their humanity. They are also linked to something that transcends present limitations, which our being-in-the-world cannot compromise.

Fourth, the *imago dei* also includes human sexuality. Humans are sexual beings and sexuality cannot be removed from any configuration of the human. We understand sexuality in a profound sense when we see it as part of who we are in God's image. Vincent Wilkin has argued: "God created men and women. Sex was entirely his idea."[21] Although we are all created as sexual beings, sexuality has a very personal and intimate dimension. For many people, sexual bonds are an ultimate expression of love and desire. Expressing that love and desire calls for a level of caring that takes the body seriously enough to protect it. One guards his or her body and sexuality by giving the very best of himself or herself to another person with whom he or she shares the divine image. The question then is not whether human beings will have sex or not, but how people can express their sexuality with a dignity consistent with the *imago dei*! Christians ought to join others in thinking of creative ways to employ cultural and spiritual resources to manage sexuality in a dignified manner.

One useful cultural example, which one must deconstruct because it reflects a traditional male bias, comes from the Wimbum people. Wimbum elders employ a euphemism to refer to the male sexual organ, *rkong nshep*, a term that literally means, "medicine spear." Some men boast that they possess a powerful instrument and can now plant their *rkong nshep* everywhere and procreate at will. Some of their actions distort the rich symbolism of this venerable, though admittedly gender-biased expression. Wimbum elders say that although all men have a *rkong nshep*, not everyone is qualified to carry *rkong nshep*, and that those who do qualify to carry it should not place it everywhere. It should only be placed in its proper place. One could read this to mean that one should only place *rkong nshep* in a proper and committed relationship. The moral values involved in this perspective, once divested of their male bias, could be used to make a point to young people today. Wimbum area churches, for example, ought to remind young men that there is something sacred about sexuality, that merely recreational sex, without responsibility, violates cultural as well as spiritual norms.

My argument is that members of the community have a responsibility to scrutinize the values of their culture, remove gender discrimination, and open a new space for the celebration of human sexuality. Progressive and liberating cultural values could help individuals bring respect to the *imago dei*, celebrating sexuality as a gift of love which they have received from God. Speaking about this sexual connection, Linda Hogan argues: "If the body is the way we mediate our connectedness, then we must have reverence for the body. We must nourish and care for the body with as much attention as we would nourish the spirit. Respect and care for the body and one's sexuality is not an optional extra, but is one of the ways in which the value of each person is affirmed."[22]

The image of God also invites the church to defend human flourishing. Christians do not have a monopoly on what it means to flourish. People search for basic needs, food, clothing, clean water, good health, a secure political climate, and absence of violence; all these are conditions for individuals and members of a community to flourish. Meeting these needs requires careful public and private sector planning in most countries and it is a matter of debate often dominated by politicians and policy makers. It seems as though Christian leaders and theologians have lost their critical voice on the allocation of resources. Lisa Cahill argues that theologians must not neglect their contribution to the debate on bioethics issues because of the dominance of science, technology, and policy experts. A new dialogue needs to take into account historical and contextual moral knowledge, the dynamics of social sin, and the effects of globalization, scientific advances, and capital that offer new opportunities for transformative action.[23] In an earlier essay, Cahill argued that people employ new criteria in allocating resources. Theologians should not remove themselves from conversations intended to establish such criteria because "a distinctive contribution of theology, especially but not exclusively Christian biblical theology, can be to challenge exclusionary systems of access under the aegis of love of neighbor, self-sacrifice, or the preferential treatment for the poor."[24] These theological perspectives are also informed by other interpretations of human thriving. I have focused on the *imago dei* because it invests the human being with value and serves as a starting point for Christians to support the search for the common good not only for members of their own community, but for all human beings who share with them the *imago dei*.

Christian service under this perspective is a shared responsibility; all are called to serve others and seek to make their life meaningful. One cannot claim to serve God if he or she refuses to serve other human beings. It is only when people serve others that they fulfill the divine purpose for which they were created in the image of God. In serving others and helping them experience the good, humans engage in a mimetic activity. The paradigm for this activity is God, who provided humanity with all the good things of life (Psalm 103). God is a God of action, and God's activity in the world protects and provides at times of great crisis. God carries on this activity through human agency. Christian service today calls for specific actions and advocacy on behalf of all people living with HIV/AIDS. Such service has eschatological implications, because Jesus told the disciples that the basis on which people would be condemned on the day of judgment would be what they have done or refused to do the for the least in society. Acting and speaking on behalf of the poor, the sick, the orphans, widows, and those neglected by the political and economic systems of the world is consistent with carrying the image of God.

The *imago dei* affirms the divine-human relationship as a model for personal and communal relationships. The *imago dei* unites individuals with God and creates a community. It is a community where the love of God reigns and where a principle critique of human culture is offered when the human community falls short of standards of human decency. The church community is structured on the message and mission of Jesus and must reflect on its praxis to ensure that it is building and restoring the broken image of

God. The church's reflection on its thoughts and values took a revolutionary turn following World War I and World War II with the emergence of political theologies, liberation/regional theologies, feminist/womanist theologies, and process theologies. Starting with Walter Rauschenbusch, theologians have criticized social injustice in national, regional, and global contexts. In doing so, they have restored the prophetic tradition of the Christian religion which has always taken sides with people who suffer. In Africa, the prophetic voice has articulated contextual theologies of cultural retrieval and liberation to underscore the fact that human beings matter to God. Feminist theology continues to highlight injustice and gender disparity in the church and society on similar grounds: humanity is one and shares the image of God.

The decline of the postneocolonial state demonstrates that earlier cultural theologies did not go far enough in defending the search for a common good, human rights, and justice. The end of apartheid testifies to the fact that faithfulness to the prophetic message and collaboration with progressive forces around the world can change social realities. African theologies of adaptation have revitalized and restored African culture that was distorted in the encounter between Africa and modernity. What is needed in the current crisis is a creative theology of suspicion directed toward cultural and political forces that perpetuate marginalization, poverty, and an environment conducive to the spread of HIV/AIDS. Such a theology becomes effective if thinkers unmask and target for reform those aspects of culture that impede the quest for human thriving and flourishing. The growing inequalities and marginalization aggravated by the HIV/AIDS pandemic remind us that the prophetic task of the church is not over. This prophetic task includes listening and collaborating with other communities of discourse to defend and sustain the *imago dei* in a world of suffering. The church could use its prophetic voice to articulate two messages.

First, the African church should join the medical community in defining HIV/AIDS as a medical crisis and, in doing so, reject a facile or simplistic view that it is a punishment for sexual sin. Churches owe this obligation to people living with HIV/AIDS. Second, the church should speak the word of God's love and care to the power brokers at this time of crisis, conveying the fact that God condemns all stigmatization, discrimination, reckless behavior, and political and economic injustice that keep people in poverty and create a climate for risky behavior. The church needs to stand shoulder to shoulder and walk hand in hand with the public in isolating and ameliorating social inequities that promote the spread of HIV/AIDS. In doing this, the church derives from the prophetic tradition not only a confrontational style but also a substantive message that invites critique, dialogue, collaboration, and engagement in the struggle both to defend and provide help and hope for people living with HIV/AIDS and to prevent the spread of the HIV virus. Justice can only be meaningful if Christian practice, in light of the *imago dei*, prioritizes the personal in communal activities.

This calls for a critical theology of HIV/AIDS that begins with a self-probing inquiry as it seeks to address local and socioeconomic inequalities. Such a theology should offer a critique of negative cultural practices that have outlived their usefulness. It should also condemn political practices that have marginalized people. A progressive theology in a world of HIV/AIDS should also offer a critique of the kind of biblical interpretation that absolutizes spiritual perspectives alone at the expense of social and scientific analysis of the human condition. In the light of challenging issues like the AIDS pandemic, theologians have an urgent task to examine critically all practices that weaken the *imago dei*.[25]

One example of a cultural practice which many people fear place women at risk is female genital cutting (FGC). The fight against FGC has taken place in many places in Africa and over many decades. Opposition to this practice dates back to the early 1900s in Kenya. Nyambura Njeroge points out that most people know about the conflicts surrounding the Scottish Presbyterian Church in Kenya and the missionary doctor, John Arthur, who opposed FGC. However, many people do not know that Kenyan Christian women formed Kaima kia Ngo, to protect their daughters from FGC.[26] During the colonial struggle, Kenyan nationalist leader Jomo Kenyatta celebrated Kikuyu rituals in his work *Facing Mount Kenya*, giving some people the impression that all Kikuyu people celebrated the practice, when there were other voices that favored moderation of the practice. The international outcry against FGC and the provisions of the African Human Rights Charter strengthen the case for alternative rituals that would recognize the coming of age in young women. The likelihood that the HIV virus might be transmitted through such traditions compels church leaders to carry out a dialogue with indigenous religious leaders in areas where FGC persists. Such a dialogue needs to explore alternative rituals that would celebrate individuality and community.

I recognize that others might see the involvement of the church in rituals that do not draw on Christian symbols as further interference in matters that do not affect the Christian church. These people would likely charge that the church continues its colonial policies of destroying traditions of which it does not approve. Such complaints have historical foundation and cannot be ruled out; some African churches have a history of disregarding local values in the same manner that the Scottish Presbyterian mission did in colonial Kenya. However, if churches initiate a constructive dialogue with indigenous religious leaders, which demonstrates the risks involved in FGC, alternative rituals could perhaps be found to replace FGC. If people have learned anything from the past, it is the fact that such traditions do not go away easily. The church will need to prepare its members for a tough and patient dialogue on this issue in order to protect the *imago dei*.

Other cultural practices that the church could address in its prophetic proclamation are rites associated with the widow and levirate marriages. Some have argued that widowhood rites such as widow cleansing and levirate marriage contribute to risk of infection for the widow, the person who performs the cleansing ritual, and the person who remarries the widow. The church needs to revisit this issue and think carefully about it because even in the absence of HIV/AIDS, widowhood rites have been unjust to women. Many people are becoming aware of the possibility of contracting or passing on the HIV virus in situations where the partner of the widow or widower died of complications from AIDS. In rural areas where some have never taken the HIV test, it is possible that a person infected with the virus will pass it to his or her spouse. Inheriting the wife of a departed relative who might have died of AIDS-related complications exposes the inheritor to the risk of transmission.

The tragedy here is that were the virus to be transmitted, the woman would be blamed for bringing the disease and bad luck into the family, and for infecting both the first husband and the one who has inherited her. No one would even bother to consider the fact that her first husband might have infected her. A woman infected in the first marriage and now blamed for the situation in the second marriage in the same family is likely to be treated as an outcast and deprived of care and support. One could argue that the new husband ought to assume the responsibility of taking care of her, but this never happens. Bolstered by a theology that demonstrates that a widow continues to exist in the image of God and should not be subjected to negative rituals to restore her dignity, church leaders have an obligation to work with local leaders to help write a new chapter in the lives of African women. Church leaders could undertake these discussions as part of a prophetic response to the reality of the *imago dei*.

Finally, with respect to HIV/AIDS, the *imago dei* calls for a critical appropriation of the theological tradition. Early theological interpretations privileged the rational capacity of human beings, and interpreters argued that rationality per se defines the *imago dei* in humanity.[27] Augustine restricted the image of God to our rational capacity which motivates the human quest for God. "For not in the body but in the mind was man made in the image of God. In his own similitude let us seek God; in his image recognize the creator."[28] Augustine thought that the human soul bears the image of God because God gave that image to enable the individual to understand and behold God.[29] Augustine's reflections were centered on his attempt to understand the Trinity, but he explored other images such as mind, memory, understanding, will, and self-transcendence, and his reflections have informed what later theologians have said about the *imago dei*.[30] Augustine presented a complex way of understanding the Trinity as a system of relations, which can be extended by analogy to divine-human relations.

For his part, Saint Thomas argued that God's image in humanity was identified with humanity's intellectual nature.[31]

> In one way, according as [man] has a natural aptitude for understanding and loving God, and this aptitude consists in the vary nature of the mind, which is common to all [men] in another way, according as [man] by act of habit knows God and loves Him, but imperfectly, and this is the image by conformity to grace. And in a third way according as [man] is the image according to the likeness of glory.[32]

Thomas highlighted the human capacity to understand and love God, although such human love is imperfect. The image of God in an individual includes the capacity to respond to the grace of God. Both Saint Augustine and Saint Thomas intellectualized and spiritualized the *imago dei* to a point where it lost some of the meaning that we find in the narratives of the priestly writer in Genesis. They focused completely on God and one gets the impression that the *imago dei* was only there to drive and direct human strivings to love and be like God. One could argue that this is what humanity is supposed to do in fellowship and community with God, but such a position ultimately diminishes the dignity implied by the priestly writer in the claim that God made male and female in the image of God.

Protestant reformers perceived the *imago dei* in Christocentric terms and linked the idea to the moral and spiritual orientation of the creature towards the Creator (a move made by Saint Augustine when he postulated the eternal longing of the soul for God). Protestant reformers also argued that although the fall of humanity damaged the image of God, the grace of God restored that image. Martin Luther asserted that the image of God referred to original righteousness that was lost with the fall of Adam but restored in Christ. John Calvin believed that the image of God set humanity above all else in the created order. God created humanity in God's image so that God's truth would shine through humanity. Humanity was created in the image of

God to reflect the glory of God.[33] In his commentary on Genesis 9:5-7 Calvin pointed out that despite the fact that humanity is fallen, God still respects humanity, loves humanity, and is violated if one commits an offense against another human being. In this passage, despite his remark about the image being damaged by the fall, Calvin restored the *imago dei* to the position of respect that could reflect the account of the priestly author. For Calvin and other reformers, the image of God that was damaged at the fall was also restored through the Word of God and the Holy Spirit.

During the twentieth century, Emil Brunner and Karl Barth introduced Martin Buber's categories of I-Thou into the discussion, arguing that persons are commanded to love one another because such human relationship expresses the divine human relationship. Emile Brunner argued: "the term *imago dei* is always used to describe [man] as he now is, and never a mode of being [that was] lost through the Fall."[34] While acknowledging that the "material" image was lost in the fall, Brunner argued that human relation and human responsibility before God was not destroyed and therefore, the "formal" image was not destroyed by sin.[35] However, the material part of the image was damaged because humanity sinned. The act of faith in Christ, which restores this image, is always a renewal of *imago dei* in humanity.

Barth, in opposition to Brunner, maintained that the divine image was lost in the fall, thus destroying the point of contact, and could only be restored through a divine miracle. Barth later would clarify his position when he argued that God created humanity as male and female. He equated the relationship that exists between male and female with the one that exists in the Trinity.[36] Barth argued that the image is restored as humanity hears and responds to the Word of God, and serves God. Regarding the relationship of man to the woman and other people, Barth argued that such a relationship consisted in a bond of helpfulness, which is natural and does not depend on grace. Barth shaped contemporary interpretations of the image of God, arguing that it involved four points. "Firstly, that I should see my neighbor as a real [man]; secondly that I should speak to him, and receive his answer as a real answer. Thirdly that I should help him; [and] fourthly, that I should do these three things gladly."[37] Speaking about a man's relationship to a woman, Barth stated that they stand before God in relationship to one another. While we cannot baptize Barth into a feminist, his critics ought to recognize that Barth articulated an important perspective when he insisted that male and female relate to each other as they relate to God.

Cairns rejects Barth's "attempt to give moral content to the universal humanity" because all people cannot meet its conditions.[38] Since Barth rejected general revelation, Cairns believes that Barth's positions then are untenable. Indeed, Barth's position would seem to be limiting because on his terms only Christians could meet the criteria of a restored *imago dei*, when they submit to the Word of God, Jesus Christ. Cairns prefers Brunner's distinctions between the formal and material aspects of the *imago dei*. While human dignity depends on God's self-giving love, all created human beings have dignity, sinners and saints alike. "Having given this dignity of personal being to [man], God values it. . . . And this dignity of [man], universal, whether [man] be sinner or saint, is also something that we must call good and which we must value."[39]

Having said that it is puzzling that Cairns introduces what he calls a comparative worth to human dignity because God may value some people more than others. By endorsing Brunner's notion of the formal aspect of the *imago dei*, Cairns subscribes to the view that the image of God invests in human beings dignity whether they establish any other relationship with God through Christ or not. But the idea of a comparative worth, which implies that God might relate to some people in a better way, privileges the Christocentric agenda of the reformers and sets up a scale of value which individuals have to meet in order to retain human dignity already implied in the notion of the *imago dei*. Therefore, Cairn's own position returns us to a God who plays favorites, rather than the God who created all humankind in his divine image and likeness.

This is not to deny New Testament passages where the writers claim that people who have placed their trust in Jesus have a special relationship with God. This is the position Paul takes in Colossians 3:9-10: "Do not lie to one another, seeing you have stripped off the old self with its practices and have clothed yourselves with the new self, which is being renewed in knowledge according to the image of its creator." The text further states that in this new relationship with Christ there are no ethnic distinctions. However, texts like this do not warrant the views of Protestant reformers that the image of God in humanity was destroyed by original sin. One could use specific language to describe the fact that some people are out of fellowship with the Creator and need to establish that fellowship through a conversion experience. However, there are no sufficient grounds to suggest that the divine image was obliterated by the fall. Such a position would imply that the fall wiped away the human capacity to relate to God, other human beings, and the rest of creation. But the innate qualities with which the Creator endowed human beings remain and serve as the basis for human rationality, emotions, freedom, capacity to relate and interact with one another, act, and carry out responsibilities, and even make a conscious decision to approach God in a direct way through Christ. The image of God in humanity was not destroyed in the fall, even if one concedes that it was weakened to the extent that one could affirm (with the Reformed tradition) that any move individuals make towards God depends on God's initiative. Leroy Howe has argued: "But nothing that we can ever do and nothing that we ever leave undone can destroy the divine image in us, and nothing can compromise finally our God-given power to conform ourselves to that image."[40]

While I do not think these issues can be resolved easily, it is important to come to terms with Barth's famous claim in *Dogmatics* III, 2 that as human beings we stand at the crossroads and are invited to recognize the sacredness and dignity of humanity.[41] It is useful to paraphrase Barth's position today in light of the HIV/AIDS pandemic. The question is: Will the Christian church today affirm humanity or ignore it and let it perish? Will the Christian community do something about the human condition in light of the fact that human beings bear the *imago dei*? At a time when HIV/AIDS inhabits and destroys the immune system and eventually the body, will the church stand shoulder to shoulder with people living with HIV/AIDS, their families, and the rest of the world, in facing the threat, and working to eliminate that threat and the devastation it is causing? Barth wrote his theology in reaction to the devastation that led to two world wars. The HIV/AIDS pandemic is likely to kill more people than both world wars. The church today is therefore invited to reconsider what it means to claim that humanity has the *imago dei*.

The *Imago Dei* Invites an Ethical Approach to HIV/AIDS

The perspective that human beings are created in the image of God calls for an ethic of love and compassion. The Christian story emphasizes that God is love and has established a relationship to humanity based on love. The Christian tradition interprets the acts of God in creation, the fall, and restoration as a manifestation of divine love. New Testament accounts claim that Jesus incarnates God's love and the Christian community has its *raison d'etre* in the faith that Jesus of Nazareth embodied the love of God to a fallen humanity. Regardless of where each faith community stands on the question of who Jesus is, they all take the life and teachings of Jesus as a manifestation of the love of God. Therefore, the Christian tradition also takes the exhortation of Jesus seriously: "I give you a new commandment, that you love one another. Just as I have loved you, you also should love one another. By this everyone will know that you are my disciples, if you have love one to another" (John 13:34-35).

I have maintained the "commandment" language of the New Testament to emphasize its prescriptive tone for those who follow the ethic of Jesus. There is no reason to read the commandment given by Jesus as an internal ethic intended merely for the disciples and the church. The command in the passage reaches all domains of the community. The Christian church has proclaimed that Jesus, the incarnation of God's love, served, healed, and laid down his life on the cross to redeem all people and give them his vision of a human community. Therefore, the commandment to love is a mandate for churches to love and care for all people, including people living with HIV/AIDS, and their families. Some of those afflicted with AIDS have been despised and neglected by their families on grounds that they have brought shame to the community by contracting the HIV virus. Others have been terminated from work because of their condition, still others told to leave government hospitals because some in those hospitals have unfounded fears that one can be infected with the virus from casual contact. People living with HIV/AIDS face all kinds of hurdles and find it difficult to live where the love of God is preached but discrimination reigns.

The church is commanded to love all people, especially the most vulnerable in our midst. Such love at the time of HIV/AIDS cannot be cheap love, but a generous and sacrificial love that reaches out and touches those who are created in the image of God yet are infected and affected by HIV/AIDS. Love for others transcends economic considerations. Such loving care would bring light into the darkness that has not only obscured the image of God, but also snuffed out love in some communities. It is possible for the Christian church to act in such a way that the darkness of discrimination and neglect are banished, replaced by a new light made possible by the love of God which shines in all communities. The work of Christians then includes engaging in activities that would usher in a new day in each human encounter. A Jewish rabbi reportedly told his students: "It's dawn when you can look into the face of another human being and recognize him or her as your brother and sister. Then you know the night is over."[42]

The type of love members of the Christian community are invited to share with one another, especially people living with HIV/AIDS, is unconditional love. It requires that members of the community reach out, embrace, and celebrate the humanity of people living with HIV/AIDS because they are part of the human family. The Christian community is a place where people need to do everything to make all feel at home, knowing that they are welcomed because they are made in the image of God. Although their physical bodies may waste away, the *imago dei* is not destroyed. Christians ought to learn to relate to those suffering from

HIV/AIDS as Saint Francis of Assisi did when God responded to his prayer by saying that he ought not run away from lepers. Jerome Miller has described this vividly: "Only when he [Francis of Assisi] embraced that leper, only when he kissed the very ulcers and stumps he had always found abhorrent, did he experience for the first time that joy which does not come from this world and which he would later identity with the joy of the crucifixion itself."[43] This is an example of unconditional love.

Grounding praxis on love would encourage Individuals to question certain beliefs before they subscribe to those beliefs. For example, some people have passed on the view that a seropositive individual can get rid of the virus by having sexual intercourse with a virgin. The church must reject and condemn this fraudulent claim as unscientific, selfish, self-serving, evil, and deadly.[44] Such an assault on children and young women is carried out in the vain hope of benefiting the HIV-positive individual alone. It not only exposes them to unwanted sexual advances but threatens them with exposure to the HIV virus. There is no doubt that perpetuating the belief that sex with a virgin cures HIV is a declaration of war on young virgins. The church must stand against it.

At the same time, the church must stand with those suffering from HIV/AIDS, regardless of the circumstances of their infection. The ethic of Jesus prioritized the personal. Most of the public ministry of Jesus was dedicated to individuals who were ignored or rejected by society. One of the narratives of the New Testament deals with a woman caught in the act of adultery. The individuals who brought this woman to Jesus wanted him to condemn her to death. When Jesus spoke to the woman's accusers, he said that anyone among them who was not guilty of any sin should cast the first stone. No one did. Jesus told the woman to go and sin no more. My point is that mistreatment of people because they might have done something wrong to bring about their HIV-positive status is not consistent with the ethic of Jesus.

Members of the church could also explore the teachings of Saint Paul as they seek to practice love in the day of HIV/AIDS. Paul's controversial teachings on subjection have been rightly criticized on grounds that he made too many concessions to prevailing views of women in the society of his time. However, Paul also prioritizes the personal through several propositions that spell out intersubjective relations in society. Paul, like Christ, calls on members of the church to love one another. He tells Christians in the church at Rome: "love one another with mutual affection" (Rom 12:10). In Ephesians 4:2 he tells his readers "with all humility and gentleness, with patience, [bear] with one another in love." Paul tells the Philippians, "And this is my prayer, that your love may overflow more and more" (Phil 1:9). Paul calls on the Colossians to be united in love (Col 2:2). Paul prayed that God should increase the love of the Thessalonians (1 Thess 3:12).

Reaching out to others in love calls for a new *diakonia*. The New Testament invites members of the church to serve one another. Saint Paul exhorts the Galatians to serve one another (Gal 5:13). The words used for service in the New Testament often refer to the Christian responsibility to minister to one another. The word deacon is derived from this concept. Christians share the world with others whom they are to serve in love. Christians are invited to serve the weak among them and are reminded that such ministry will be rewarded in the eschaton.

The *Imago Dei* Invites Compassion and Care

The conviction that human beings are made in the image of God serves as a motivation for members of the Christian community to show compassion and to care for all who suffer. "Compassion" means experiencing sorrow at the sufferings and pain of another person and doing something to relieve that suffering. In other words, compassion is "hands on"; it involves acting to ameliorate and bring relief to the pain and suffering of another person. Several biblical terms connected to compassion include sympathy, empathy, and pity.[45] In Christian tradition and in the philosophical literature, the term pity was equivalent to compassion, but, as Martha Nussbaum points out, since the Victorian era this term has been corrupted and taken on meanings of condescension.[46] Other terms associated with compassion include benevolence, care, and love. Most discussions of compassion distinguish it from care, but feminist scholars have challenged this view and employ compassion and care as related emotions and activities.[47] I discuss compassion and care together because to be moved to suffer on behalf of someone should not mean a detached sympathy but a desire to act to remedy that situation as a moral responsibility of care. One could argue that it is necessary to separate compassion and care because an individual may be moved to compassion but, for a variety reasons, have no means of providing care to the one that is suffering—lack of resources, distance, or legal restrictions.[48] While such a scenario is possible, in the Christian tradition to feel or suffer with someone also implies doing something to relieve that suffering and pain.

Compassion is an affective and cognitive activity that involves what Lawrence Blum has called "imaginative dwelling on the condition of the other person, an active regard for his good, a view of him as a fellow human being, and emotional responses of a certain degree of intensity."[49] However, we do this as distinct individuals who may be connected to the sufferer or because we are a part of the community of faith to which the sufferer belongs. Compassion is also a moral disposition that involves an active engagement with all who suffer. While such a virtue is based on what an individual has observed in a person who is suffering, compassion arises from the observer who then makes a decision to act on his or her feelings of empathy for the suffering of the other person. Compassion as a moral virtue binds one individual to another and has the potential of bringing people together to build stronger community bonds. In endorsing the ethical dimensions of compassion, it is not necessary to go as far as Schopenhauer to argue that compassion is the basis of ethics.[50]

Other interpretations of compassion suggest that in being compassionate, one is actually "infected" with the suffering.[51] Max Scheler, Friedrich Nietzsche, and Immanuel Kant all discuss the notion of infection. Nietzsche thinks one is infected with the suffering of the other through pity, but Scheler thinks pity can actually take care of the infection. Kant on the other hand distinguishes between the capacity to share in the feelings of other people, and the susceptibility of feeling sadness with other people. Kant thinks that one could freely share the feelings of other people, but he also thinks that susceptibility is communicable and spreads naturally among people who live close by. While this might indeed happen, it is not the active sharing and involvement in the suffering of the other person that compassion involves.[52] What we are dealing with in compassion then involves observation of suffering, feelings of genuine sorrow, and the development of empathy that moves one to do something about it.

In her recent book *Upheavals of Thought*, Martha Nussbaum has amended the account of compassion offered by Aristotle which defined compassion as a human emotion extended to another individual's suffering or misfortune.[53] Nussbaum distinguishes three cognitive elements in Aristotle's argument. First, there should be the belief that other person's suffering is genuine. Second, there should be a belief that the person who is suffering does not deserve it. Third, there should be a belief that the one who observes the sufferer could be in similar circumstances. Nussbaum does not think that Aristotle's third belief is necessary. Instead, Nussbaum substitutes the third with the view that the person who is suffering is an important part of my goals and agenda and thus his or her good should be promoted.

Later on, Nussbaum argues: "If one believes that the misfortunes of others are serious, and that they have not brought misfortune on themselves, and in addition, that they are themselves important parts of one's own scheme of ends and goals, then the conjunction of these beliefs is very likely to lead to action addressing the suffering."[54] With this amendment of Aristotle's position, Nussbaum lays new ground rules for compassion. The new criterion would seem to suggest that one cannot show compassion to someone who is suffering from self-inflicted pain. This sets a controversial standard for compassion, namely that compassion can only be shown for innocent suffering. The third criterion shows compassion to be self-interested: the person who is suffering is an important part of one's ends and goals. There is a vested interest in the act of caring. I find these formulations inadequate because if followed, they leave very little room for altruism; one could find a lot of reasons to refrain from responding in compassion to some people living with HIV/AIDS.

If we take Nussbaum's first criterion and apply it in the context of HIV/AIDS, one would have to find out if the seropositivity status of an individual will eventually lead to great suffering before one was prompted by compassion to do something about it. In most cases, perceiving this is easy because the infected person might be experiencing health problems or suffering from clinical AIDS and living in constant pain. Applying her second criterion is problematic, because I have to know if the infected person is innocent. The question here would be what counts for innocence in the case of HIV/AIDS? If a person acquired the virus through risky sexual behavior, then is this person innocent or not? If one were to claim that this individual is not innocent then one would have to know that the individual had the opportunity to avoid this risky situation but chose not to take precautions. Take the case of a woman who has not had any sexual contact outside marriage who becomes infected because her husband was infected from a casual sexual encounter; is this woman innocent? There are a number of scenarios that one can analyze here and if one were to conclude that all infections resulting from sexual contact outside marriage means that the person is not innocent, then according to the criteria articulated by Nussbaum, one cannot show compassion to this person. It would be a tragic position to take in a world where people are dying and need assistance. The literature on compassion also suggests, and Nussbaum concurs, that the feeling of sorrow and determination to do something about it might also reflect the fact that I see in the other person's condition my own potential suffering. This prompts compassionate action because it is possible that I might be in a similar situation in the near future. While this reasoning is logical and one could argue that people actually think and operate this way, it rules out altruism as an ethical activity.

Responding to the suffering of the other person because I could be in a similar situation in the future is related to but somewhat different from what Noddings describes as "engrossment" with the suffering person, so that one feels "impelled to act as though in my own behalf, but in behalf of the other."[55] Noddings' position means that if a person is HIV-positive, I am to respond to that person as if I were acting on my own behalf. The point here is that to be moved to help the other person, I should think of myself going through that situation and then act on behalf of that person. If I see a woman suffering from HIV/AIDS, I could imagine how she feels, and how long it might take her to develop opportunistic infections. I could imagine and share her fears that the infection could end her life. If she develops clinical AIDS, I could imagine her emotional sufferings, frequent illness, frequent trips to the hospital where she may not even get any medicines. I could also imagine the pain she bears in her body. I could also worry about the fact that she lies on her bed helpless. She coughs frequently, suffers from diarrhea, and has painful bouts with malaria. I could also imagine the confusing emotions, the shame brought about by stigmatization that is very prevalent in society, or the shame this person feels because the one mistake she made in life turned out to be fatal. I could also imagine the pain this individual has because she cannot communicate these feelings with her loved ones for fear that they will further ostracize her. Such an engrossment should lead to feelings and to acts of compassion. When a woman named Rachel knew she was facing her last days in the hospital in the Northwest Province of Cameroon, she told her sister that she regretted what she had done that led to this condition. She told the sister that she had made peace with God. She committed her children to the care of her siblings and told the sister to tell her children not to be deceived into taking her path.[56] Rachel was fortunate that her siblings loved her and cared for her. They extended empathy to her and did not need to imagine themselves in her situation to show her compassion.

One could also imagine a person living with HIV/AIDS worrying about money. If he had enough money, he might be able to see a doctor who could help him. If he had enough money, he could have gone to a reputable herbalist for treatment. If he had money, he could make the pilgrimage to the churches in Nigeria where miracles are being performed and ministers claim that they can cure HIV/AIDS. Such a person might actually come to terms with death, and wish to die, but the sickness will tarry for a while and his body will continue to deteriorate and he will feel the pain every minute that he is alive. I could imagine him worrying about his spouse, children, and the old parents he used to support! He needs no longer worry about himself because he has lost the battle, but what about his loved ones! What will happen to them when death takes him?

These imaginations and sensations that I experience could be merely my own imaginations and nothing more. They could also be full of presumptions about the feelings of the other person. Feelings for the other person must be factually based. One has to guard against appropriating the suffering of the other person, and focusing one's imagination in a way that may not at all reflect the actual condition of the other person.[57] The one who wants to show compassion needs to recognize that he or she cannot replace the other person's suffering. One may imagine what it would be like for him to be in the situation in which the other person is, and often do because that is part of the process of developing the emotion of compassion and care. But as caregivers, individuals have an obligation not to pretend that they can take over the emotions of the other person or make themselves equal with the person that is suffering.

If one takes these limitations seriously, then compassion would not be a false emotion. One may imagine the suffering of an individual this way, and as members of the church, one could also imagine what individual members of the community who live with HIV go through. If one individual could develop a spirit of compassion, the community could do the same. It might take some education and coaching to have members of the community think that way, but helping people develop the emotion of compassion is necessary in light of the pain and suffering which HIV/AIDS causes.

HIV/AIDS is a catastrophe that brings about severe suffering. It is a condition, which should evoke compassion and care from us. The Christian community in Africa and around the world has an obligation to share the pain and suffering of people living with HIV/AIDS, even if the people are not "innocent." Compassion and responsibility are what we owe people whom we encounter in face-to-face relations. In such encounters, where there is suffering, the proper response is compassion.

A compassionate response according to Emmanuel Levinas would include desiring or welcoming the other person, an act that places us at the disposal of the other person and inviting him or her to be part of our lives.[58] Levinas describes welcome and desire as that which overflows and escapes our attempt to contain. However, welcoming and desiring the person also indicates that we identify with the person who is suffering. Caregivers in this context can always show compassion in acts that alleviate suffering.

The goals and aims of compassion are to make a positive difference in the lives of people living with HIV/AIDS. First, compassion and caring would help one promote the well-being of such people.[59] The person who has been infected with the HIV virus would like to get rid of that virus and be free from its future scourge. The person who is developing symptoms of full-blown AIDS would like to live a normal active life and not lose his or her freedom to the disease. The person who has developed clinical AIDS desires treatment and recovery of health and the chance to avoid death. If death overtakes this individual, as it has for more than 20 million worldwide, he or she dies desiring that loved ones will be taken care of and not subjected to stigma and discrimination. Compassion implies that we share the sorrow of people living with HIV/AIDS and desire these things with the same passion that they do.[60]

If one suffers with others, one restrains his or her suffering from eclipsing the suffering of the one who is the object of one's compassion. One must maintain what Emmanuel Levinas calls a radical difference "between suffering in the Other, which for me is unpardonable and solicits me and calls me, and suffering in me, my own adventure of suffering, whose constitutional or congenital uselessness can take on a meaning, the only meaning to which suffering is susceptible, in becoming a suffering for the suffering . . . of someone else."[61] Our desire ought to be to hear the people infected with HIV virus speak to us about their suffering, and teach us even when we least expect such instruction. Even in the large world of non-governmental organizations and faith-based organizations dedicated to the cause of HIV/AIDS, we cannot allow the voices of the caregivers to suffocate the voices of those who suffer. We have an obligation to hear their call and respond to that call. We cannot identify, in the sense that we cannot get ourselves infected with the virus, but we can teach ourselves to be sensitive to their pain and suffering.

Once caregivers know the desire of those infected with HIV/AIDS, they need to work with others to meet those desires with concrete actions. Those who are sick but desire to work ought to keep their jobs. Members of the community should organize and cultivate farms and raise crops for those who are suffering so that there will be enough food for the family during the year. Where there are young children in the house, the community could set up a roster for people to cook meals for the family. The task of caregivers is to enable the infected to live a responsible life so that the infection will not spread. Members of the Christian community have an obligation to join those who are suffering in advocating for their right to access to treatments. Sometimes little things go a long way in enhancing the quality of life for a person living with HIV/AIDS: one can go with them to the hospital, encourage their children to stay in school or perhaps provide financial assistance for those children to stay in school.

The situation I describe here works in contexts where we love the people, have a personal connection, and can see ourselves in the situation. In the case of HIV, it works for a village setting where most people know each other and people actually settle according to large extended families. What about people who live in other villages? In other words, what about strangers, people to whom we have no connection? Noddings suggests that caring should be premised on "the existence of or potential for present relation, and the dynamic potential for growth in relation, including the potential for increased reciprocity and, perhaps, mutuality."[62] In order words, individuals can show compassion to strangers only when there is a potential for a relationship to exist, where there is a potential for reciprocity, and where the act is completed in a visible way. Nodding's position limits compassion to proximity.

Compassion in light of what Noddings suggests can only take place if there is the possibility of establishing a relation and seeing the compassionate act completed. While one could argue that if we demonstrate compassion in our own community, and others demonstrate compassion in their own community, the act of caring would go round, such an approach would restrict our understanding of the biblical idea of a neighbor. In the gospel narrative, when thieves attack a traveler and leave him for dead, two "local" individuals come by and walk away; it is an outsider, a Samaritan, who provides care to the person in need. The Bible argues that my neighbor is anyone in need, or anyone who provides for anyone in need. Diana Cates rejects Noddings criteria for caring for strangers and argues: "Being compassionate and just within our modern global context requires recognizing that every human being is a neighbor who has some claim on us to be received and responded to with attention, affection, beneficence, respect, and fairness."[63] Cates further explores the subject of compassion to strangers based on the work of McNeill, Morrison, and Nouwen who argue that people ought to love and befriend strangers because of our friendship with God.[64]

When we respond in compassion we follow the example of Jesus. In the Gospel of Mark we read that a man who had leprosy came to Jesus and kneeled before him and asked Jesus to make him clean (Mark 1:40-42). Jesus was filled with compassion and reached his hand out, touched this man, and said "be clean" and the man was cured of leprosy. Leprosy was a dreaded disease, and lepers were often isolated from the community. Yet Jesus reached out and touched someone who had this frightful condition and healed him. Christians ought to copy the example of Jesus and show compassion to people who have been despised by the community. Touching people living with HIV/AIDS today involves more than giving them the occasional hug, embrace, handshake, or a wink of affirmation and support. We may not have the miracle touch of Jesus, but our touch ought to communicate love and not merely sympathy. An effective touch is one which includes verbal support with an active involvement to make life better for people living with

HIV/AIDS. Even where physical touch is not involved, effective action that improves the social conditions for people living with HIV/AIDS would go a long way in making their lives better. We are invited to give a sustaining touch because the dignity of others is at stake. Our touch must reach across all types of barriers. Christians are all related to God and are part of one human family. Their locations and cultures may be different, but they have one common heritage because all people come from God. The image of God is not limited to our particular community of faith or discourse. It is not limited to our circle of friends. We all share in the image of God and have an obligation to respond with compassion to uphold the dignity of all persons.

Christians proclaim that human beings are created in the image of God. This image involves the totality of everything human beings are, including their relationship to God and other people. The idea that all people are created in the image of God rules out discrimination. I have argued that since all people have the image of God, members of the Christian community ought to join other communities of discourse and show love and compassion to those who have been affected by the HIV/AIDS pandemic. In the next chapter I will discuss virtue ethics in the light of HIV/AIDS.

Chapter 3

HIV/AIDS and Human Virtues

Theoretical Considerations

In this chapter, I explore virtues of hope, fidelity, care, justice, and prudence in light of HIV/AIDS because the pandemic threatens *eudaimonia*.[1] Virtue theory has enjoyed a revival in ethical discourse during the last two decades, since Alasdair MacIntyre, a leading proponent of virtue theory, decried the loss of virtue in the modern world.[2] In *Whose Justice? Which Rationality?* MacIntyre, discussed four moral traditions: the Aristotelian tradition; the Thomistic synthesis of Augustinian and Aristotelian traditions; the seventeenth- and eighteenth-century Scottish tradition; and liberalism. As in *After Virtue*, MacIntyre rejected the view that the liberal society could provide a coherent account of moral virtues and facilitate the practice of justice in the post-Enlightenment era.[3] MacIntyre preferred the notions of justice reflected in the Thomistic synthesis of the Augustinian and Aristotelian traditions.[4] In the African context, some ethicists, especially in South Africa, have called for the appropriation of *ubuntu* values that promote togetherness in the pursuit of the common good. The employment of *ubuntu* as an ethical priority has special prominence in South Africa, where it has been part of the discussion on life after apartheid.[5]

Feminist scholars, since the publication of Carol Gilligan's book *In a Different Voice*, have contributed significantly to the discussion of virtues, especially on crucial questions like care and justice.[6] Kathryn Tanner argues that feminist scholars have shifted their focus from the "dualism of moral orientation in public and private spheres . . . by a process of mutual critique, so that, for example, the family becomes a place of justice and public life an arena dedicated to nurture."[7] Feminist scholars have addressed issues related to women's experience and reformulated ethics, arguing that these issues cannot be defined in abstraction from contemporary experience.[8] In theology, some scholars have argued that the Christian tradition and its narratives provide a guide to the community.[9] Others have taken a broad approach, using the Christian tradition and its texts in dialogue with critical perspectives in other disciplines to discuss virtues and moral issues in society.[10] A theological dialogue on virtues in Africa must be pluralistic because HIV/AIDS has raised moral issues that involve religious, scientific, medical, cultural, economic, and political perspectives.

I consider human virtues as character traits and dispositions necessary for the good and for humans well-being and flourishing. These traits and dispositions remain valid for every community.[11] I do not propose a new set of rules (deontology) or call for a return to some natural ideal (natural law), or argue that one way of doing things would benefit the greatest number of people living with HIV/AIDS (utilitarianism). Rather, I call attention to selected virtues that could energize dialogue and praxis in personal and public life. Virtues are public values which a community should promote in an open dialogue to enable its inhabitants to acquire those dispositions that would help them achieve the good. I take a minimal and contextual normative approach because in the context of HIV/AIDS some people, especially African women and children, do negotiate their marginal existence in ways that might appear to an onlooker as if they lack virtue or acquiesce to forces that dominate them. Their actions, which seem to violate norms of virtuous action, might also be taken to affirm life and therefore be praiseworthy.[12] Contextual nuances differ, but in the main, people around the world share the virtues of a good life, even though the technical language and descriptions which scholars employ emerge in different contexts.

I do not share the view that moral agents must always act as autonomous and reasonable individuals. In a context of HIV/AIDS, where the politics of neglect, discrimination, marginalization, and stigmatization have created risk situations for many, rationality is often compromised. For example, a woman, let's call her A, whose husband takes a second wife, widow B, without knowing that B's husband died of HIV complications, is in a difficult position. In many cultures, A cannot prevent the marriage, and cannot refuse to have conjugal relations with her husband because she does not have the autonomy to ask questions about the health of B, the new wife. Therefore A is not in a position to make rational decisions about her sexuality in what has become a risky situation. Two philosophers, Julia Driver and Normy Arpaly have argued persuasively that people do not always act with autonomy and rationality.[13] Their perspectives offer a necessary corrective to the intellectualism of Plato, Aristotle, and Saint Thomas, whose works provide the background to discussions on virtue ethics today. There are indeed individuals living with HIV/AIDS because they exercised poor judgment, lived risky lifestyles, rejected the warnings about the virus, or denied that HIV/AIDS is real. But many people who live with HIV/AIDS, especially women and children, had no choice. They are not sinners or immoral people.

I return to the virtues because given the right context and adequate support from the political community, individuals could be encouraged to deploy character traits that would lead to flourishing. Aristotle articulated his ethics in a context where the state served as an educator and authority to enable some of its members to achieve the good and moral virtue. In both the *Nicomachean Ethics* and *Politics*, Aristotle stressed the role of a structured political community with its legal instruments—calling it authoritative, and a voice of reason—as necessary to instruct members to attain virtue.[14] The good in Aristotle referred to a life lived by people who took morality seriously and who were prudent, were raised in a noble manner, and lived and acted justly, employing moral virtue as their disposition. In the political community, virtues enabled members to actualize the good by living in the mean between excess and deficiency of what is *deon* (proper). Achieving this mean was also a rational activity. The view that the virtues concerned the political community is important because the failure to act and redress social problems, which has exacerbated HIV/AIDS in the postneocolonial state, has compromised the life of virtue for many people in Africa. Therefore, the priorities of the state should be changed if it is to enable its constituents to experience well-being and pursue the good, and in the process thrive and flourish. In the context of HIV/AIDS, the question then is how a state can act as educator and guardian of the common good—in this case, good health.

HIV/AIDS may be here for a long time. Individuals and communities need moral perspectives that will strengthen them in the struggle to protect themselves, prevent the spread of the virus, and work together to provide comprehensive care to people living with HIV/AIDS, and also provide support for their families and friends who have been affected in different ways. Such an ethic cannot be written down as a series of rules and handed down to people in African communities; nor can one simply adumbrate some belief in natural law. An ethic in the time of HIV/AIDS must emerge from dialogue in each moral community; participants in such a dialogue should think of new priorities that would encourage and enable people to live a life of virtue. Cultivating virtues could foster an atmosphere where people make rational and good judgments that would promote an enabling and ennobling debate about distribution of resources crucial to the well-being of those who have been made vulnerable by the HIV virus.[15]

It is important to emphasize the role the state could play because they have failed to energize the population. There are ethical perspectives that must be adopted and the state ought to play its role as educator. Some demographic studies have suggested that African societies do not have any moral foundation on which to ground family life or if they do, the logic of such a moral foundation does not encourage the kind of traits implied in virtue theories. Such a perspective was articulated several years ago by Caldwell, Caldwell, and Quiggin in their thesis on African sexuality.[16] While I strongly dispute these findings, I would contend that the leaders of the postneocolonial state have not played the role of educator but have perpetuated a view that the only thing that matters is making money, taking care of one's family, and pushing other members of the community to the bottom of the heap.

I do not think that virtue ethics could further strengthen the stigma people living with HIV/AIDS already face. The political community has an obligation to promote well-being and work with people living with HIV/AIDS and to help them flourish; all people in a political community, including those who have been affected by HIV/AIDS, ought to experience *eudaimonia*. Admittedly, experiencing *eudaimonia* in such a context poses a number of challenges and calls into question the contemplative happiness proposed by Aristotle or divinely ordered theological virtues articulated by Saint Thomas. However, individuals and communities owe each other the search for life-enhancing virtues under all circumstances. Put differently, I can talk about virtues in full agreement with Rosalind Hursthouse, who says that "in evil times, life for most people is, or threatens to be, nasty, brutish, and short and *eudaimonia* is something that will be impossible until better times."[17] Hursthouse also argues that during such times parents should raise their children to be prudent, less gullible; in other words, more careful as they live in society. Ultimately she argues, and I agree with her, that those who possess virtues will reap the benefits of a virtuous life. I now turn to the specific virtues of hope, fidelity, caring, justice, and prudence.

Hope When There Is No Reason to Hope

Hope is the virtue which deals with expectation. To hope is to expect that something will go well, a circumstance will change, a difficult situation will be resolved. Some people bring religious dimensions to hope: for them hope means an expectation that God will do something about their situation or the human condition. Hope could be an act of faith or might be based on some concrete facts. If someone has hope that he or she is going to make some money, this person must take the initiative to start a business and invest time and money into that business. The person must work hard to ensure that his business performs well. Someone who already has an established business might base hopes on certain facts: for example, the fact that the economy is doing well, that there is demand for the product this individual makes, or that another business that employs many people has moved into the area and given the local economy a big boost.

To take another example, a person may hope that longstanding conflicts in the family or in the community will be resolved. He may base his hope on the fact that he has made some contacts with different parties in the dispute. This hope may also be based on the past history of this family, especially if the members of the family have always acted in love to protect the family from disintegrating. However, a person may hope that things will go well and not have any concrete data to back up that expectation. This type of hope, based more on faith or fate, might pertain to someone who is undertaking a mission of mediation but has never met the parties in a dispute. Such a person may expect that mission to go well, but he really has nothing to ground this expectation on. His hope is an act of faith.

Both individuals and communities can have hope. In both cases, those involved have the expectation that things may change for the good. When individuals and communities have hope, they may also do something to bring about the situation that they hope for. Therefore, hope is active because people are engaged in doing the things that could fulfill their expectations. When a community hopes that it can avert disaster, say a famine, its members are going to plan, strategize, and do everything to ensure that they are able to get the supplies they need for their community. If they have only the anticipation and do nothing about it, their expectations may not be fulfilled.

There are times when it is difficult to have hope, yet hope persists. There are more than 27 million people in Africa living with HIV/AIDS. Some of these people have been aware of their condition for a long time. Miss Ana Asa has known now for many years that she has HIV/AIDS. She became aware of her situation many years ago when her doctor told her that her husband had died of HIV/AIDS. At that time, she did not fully understand the disease. But she followed the doctor's advice and goes to the hospital every time she has a fever or illness. She says that every time she goes to the hospital she takes tests. She is hospitalized several times a year, but she continues to follow the doctor's advice and takes her medicine. She also says she watches what she eats, and makes sure that she eats well. She has recently started taking antiretroviral drugs through a program administered by the Cameroon Baptist Convention Health Board. She has hope that things might get better. For now, she does not know if she will be able to afford all the medications, but she hopes that with the support of her family, she will have the money to pay for the medications. Miss Ana Asa continues to thrive because she is in good spirits and has the support of her family. Other people who live with HIV/AIDS are not as fortunate as Miss Ana Asa because they are not taking any antiretroviral medications. Every time they are ill, they try different remedies from traditional healers and people who sell drugs in the market on the weekly market days. They hope that all these medications will make them feel better.

I have talked to many people in Cameroon who know that there is no cure for HIV/AIDS, but hope that the government will reform and revitalize the public care system so that they can receive treatment for opportunistic infections. Many express concern about stigmatization, and hope that even if the society despises them, their families will provide support for them during this difficult time. Many hope that medical experts and scientists will discover a cure or vaccine for HIV/AIDS. Researchers themselves share this hope that they can discover new treatments or a vaccine that will bring remedy to the millions of people infected with the virus. Professor Victor Anomah Ngu from Cameroon has named his clinic Clinique d'Espoir (Hope Clinic). Here Professor Ngu has carried out his research and has discovered, he claims, a vaccine for the HIV/AIDS virus. He has given this vaccine to some of his patients. Few seem to have been worried about the debate raging regarding the integrity of that vaccine. They need help and they have taken the vaccine in the hope that it might change their lives.

Hope as a virtue can only be meaningful if individuals and community leaders could come up with a vision of combating HIV/AIDS, articulate it to all people, and take steps to see that vision come to fruition. For example, those who hope that the rate of infection will decline should join the campaign against HIV/AIDS and educate people to recognize and avoid risk situations and behavior. Those who hope that orphans will not live a miserable life should do something to help them stay in school or enroll in vocational training to acquire useful skills and become self-sufficient. Politicians who hope that violence against women will cease ought to propose and pass enforceable legislation to provide maximum support and protection for women. Hope must be accompanied by a drive to promote the well-being of the members of the community.

Fidelity to One Another

Fidelity encompasses the second aspect of the ABC campaign, "Abstain, Be faithful, and use a Condom." Fidelity describes faithfulness and loyalty to the people with whom one has established connections. This is a more neutral term than faithfulness, but shares meanings with faithfulness. Fidelity calls for commitment in relationships within the family, with friends, colleagues, partners, or other associates and acquaintances. Fidelity is a deliberate commitment a person makes out of his or her own free will. Margaret Farley has described fidelity as "[yielding] to the other a claim over one's free choices."[18] It also implies that a person is willing to place his or her life at the disposal of another person without fear that he or she will diminish who they are. Although maintaining fidelity is a deliberate choice, the decision to enter into a relationship already puts one under obligation such that we can say that fidelity becomes a mandate of that relationship. Fidelity does not dissolve the self and does not diminish the stature of either partner in a relationship. Instead, fidelity establishes mutuality grounded in the good will of each party.

As a moral virtue, fidelity is also a commitment to a friendship and a nurturing relationship to one's friends. This nurturing calls for a spirit that is willing to make sacrifices on behalf of one's friends, to take action to preserve and protect their well-being, and to honor the friendship by avoiding competing relationships that could jeopardize the health of the other friend. We could learn some lessons about friendships in philosophical literature. Aristotle devoted books 8 and 9 of the *Ethics* to a discussion of friendship.[19] He used the word friendship in various ways to include family, business, civic, and political associations.[20] *Philia* referred to reciprocal well wishing and well doing. Aristotle identified three types of friendships. The first is friendship for utility, which Aristotle calls incomplete, and dissolves when it ceases to be useful.[21] Pleasure friendship is based on feelings and emotions and often shifts as pleasure and emotions shift. Virtue friendship exists among good people. This is unconditional and enduring friendship. Such friendships are rare. They take time and the parties involved must be lovable and willing to be friends.[22]

In the context of HIV/AIDS what would count for what Aristotle calls virtue friendship? It is friendship between people of character who have chosen to be one's friends not for the mere utility of such friendships, but out of a dependable character. Such a friend will be there in times of difficulty and provide support even when the other party has been told that he or she has the HIV virus. It is such good character or virtue, that makes friendships endure. People who have good character take the priorities of their friends seriously; they are friends for the sake of the other person.[23] In the context of HIV/AIDS, these friends will spend time with those who have been infected, or affected. What is deemed worthy in this context is the very dignity of the person who is suffering. While the person who is suffering may not be able to reciprocate fully in this context, friends of good character will stand with him or her and provide all the support they can. Aristotle thought that older people do not have this kind of friendship because they do not have enjoyment. I do not see any reason why older people should be excluded from good and lasting friendships. In the African context, particularly where the elderly stay with family members, it is important that their friends stand with them, especially when they go through the agony of seeing their children and grandchildren come down with a disease that continues to baffle everybody. One could agree with Aristotle that good friends are limited because good friendship is like a passion (erotic) that one can direct only to a few individuals. But the important point is that such passionate commitment, even if it is limited to a few individuals, demands that one stand with his or her friends, especially through the agony of HIV/AIDS.[24]

Aristotle's account of friendship was not perfect. For example, for Aristotle's use of *philia* to refer to what might be termed a voluntary association, business, or political partnership seems to exclude those who were outside such circles. While the Wimbum people do not use the same categories as Aristotle, friendships, *bkar* (singular *nkar*), are important relationships. People recognize good friendships and talk of *nkar bongbong*. This is a friend who will stand with you through difficult times, often called in Wimbum society *nfi nge* (literally, "time of suffering"). Such a friend will be there for you at all times, when you are ill, have an illness in your family, experience some misfortune, or need long-term care. In Wimbum society, these friends are often called *nkaro wob mntii* ("a friend of your heart," an expression that might be described as a close friend). Sometimes people use the expression *nkaro shi mini* (literally, "a true friend"). People often count on their friends in times of difficulty to give them support and encouragement. Eleanor Humes Haney has argued that friendship is central to feminist ethics and is the basis for a relationship that takes the "other" seriously on his or her own terms as a genuine "other"—not as an extension of myself. "Friendship is a relation of mutuality, respect, fidelity, confidence, and affection. It is impossible in, and therefore a rejection of, most competitive patterns, adversarial patterns, exploitive patterns, authoritarian patterns, and paternalistic patterns of relating. To begin to make friendship a reality is to begin acting as a friend. That is to demonstrate in one's speech and behavior that one is not superior or inferior and that one will no longer countenance being related to in those ways."[25]

Maria Cimperman who has written about HIV/AIDS in the African context has argued that fidelity involves three aspects: "honest communication, embodied expressions and consistency."[26] Fidelity requires that friends—and especially sexually intimate partners—listen to and communicate with one another. Communication should include a open discussion of sexuality and sexual histories if such a history is relevant to the present circumstances. Partners should be willing to talk about this without fear that there could be reprisals from the other partner. If a partner has been unfaithful, it is important that the issue be discussed openly and steps taken to ensure that the other partner is not at risk. Fidelity also involves sharing and honoring each other's body. Finally, Cimperman has argued that fidelity involves consistency over a long time. "Consistency is about seeing the other as the main partner through which community with others grows. Consistency is also a faithful response in the midst of a society constantly seeking new stimulation and quick answers. In the midst of frenzied activity, fidelity calls us to attentiveness on a regular basis."[27] Fidelity, or faithfulness, is no longer something that reflects what some considered old conservative values. It is about life and the life of one's loved one.[28] In circumstances where fidelity has been compromised and the well-being of one's partner has been compromised, it is important that both partners have open communication and seek supportive ways of resolving the problems.

HIV/AIDS, Caring, and Self-Care

There are two important aspects of care: caring for one's self and caring for others. Recent feminist work, in response to Carol Gilligan, has called attention to the practice of care and to caregivers, and also focused on an inclusive view of justice because it relates to caring. For example, Susan Okin has argued that the support and caring roles women typically have in the home have been part of a power imbalance that has been dictated for them. The justice component comes in because in a relationship of equality, men and women should share the caring.[29] Configuring caring as a moral responsibility that involves both men and women is an important check on power relations between men and women. It could also offer insights on paternalistic relations between caregivers and receivers. Kathryn Tanner has argued that "the danger of patronizing paternalism . . . has to be offset by a more democratic structure comparable to that found in the public sphere on a larger, more impersonal scale."[30] Care giving should be a mutual relationship where the concerns of the receiver are taken in consideration. This works best when the person receiving care is alert and makes the most of his or her own decisions. When people are very sick and lack the ability to make their own decisions, the caregiver ought to make every effort to ensure that the rights and wishes of the person who receives the care are not violated.

In the many years since HIV/AIDS has hit African communities, women have carried the burden of care more than men. Many a mother has cared and nurtured her sick children, grieving why such an illness has afflicted her sons and daughters. In some contexts, the same mother has cared for several of her own grandchildren and watched them slowly die from HIV/AIDS complications. Women have also provided care to their husbands and nurtured them until their death. Since their husbands often infect them with the virus, many of these same women who have cared for their husbands do not receive the same quality of care they have provided. The division of labor that makes women caregivers is not a responsible way of dealing with such a great disaster. Caring in the day of HIV/AIDS should be a family affair that involves both men and women. It is not enough for the men to argue that they provide the money for treatment. They should also share in the responsibilities of the home.

Michael Slote has argued that caring is an admirable virtue that provides the basis for ethical judgment. I think that caring is an important trait, but I do not think that it should be elevated as Slote does. What further complicates his position is the view that caring must be balanced; by that he means that one has to attend to his or her intimates before others, or even if one could have done more good for humanity. He justifies this perspective by resorting to intuition, and one wonders what following that could lead to? For instance, in the case of HIV/AIDS, the question could arise about the allocation of critical drugs. Following Slote's argument, one could choose to make drugs available only to his or her relatives and loved ones and allow many others to go without them.[31]

The virtue of care requires that communities and leaders think carefully and establish a rational basis for caring for people living with HIV/AIDS, rather than assuming that one ought to care exclusively for his or her immediate loved ones and allow others to suffer. Perhaps what Slote intends can be summarized with clichés like "charity begins at home" or compared to the instructions one is given on the airplane: in case of an emergency, put on your own oxygen mask before trying to help other people traveling with you. Slote argues that the "help those closest" principle could be generally applied. A virtuous approach, however, calls for careful planning and coordination of health services to ensure that everyone is treated fairly. How one establishes such a criteria cannot be spelled out completely because it is going to depend on the needs of patients, available resources, the seriousness of each case, and the overall impact the chosen approach could have on saving lives.

An important aspect of caring involves self-care. Aristotle considers self-love a source of friendship because friends do for the other what they wish for themselves. Friendship involves goodwill, concord, active and unselfish benevolence, and proper self-love.[32] The things that a friend does for the other—pursuing his good, spending time with him, making the same choices, and sharing the joys and distress—the virtuous also wishes for himself.[33] In the *Ethics* Aristotle says, "The decent person, then, has each of these features in relation to himself, and is related to his friend as he is to himself, since the friend is another himself."[34] Friendship is, in a curious way, the loving of oneself.

HIV/AIDS has called our attention to self-love and self-care as an important virtue not only because it is part of the structure of care, but more importantly because it is a necessary and crucial dimension of prevention. There is no doubt that if one wants to avoid being infected with the HIV virus, self-love and self-care are indispensable. For example, a woman has to love her own self so that in socially unencumbered situations she will think of the dangers of unprotected sexual relations regardless of how committed she might be to her partner. It is clear that many of the women who are infected do not have those opportunities, but on the whole a large number of young women attending university in Africa today could love themselves at that level. If a woman were to take self-love and self-care seriously and decide to protect herself by abstaining from unprotected sexual relations even in a committed relationship, she would have acted in a virtuous manner.

Such a decision reflects a virtue that fosters an overall healthy state of mind and state of being. It is a state of mind that recognizes that to protect others from the HIV virus one must be prepared to make the right decision about his or her own health. One cannot save the world if one lacks the strength and emotional resources to do the right thing in a personal relationship. It is a character trait that requires an individual to assume the responsibility to take care of himself/herself, as Keenan suggests, "affectively, mentally, physically, and spiritually."[35] Self-care is an important activity that would help an individual avoid being infected and in that way stop the spread of HIV/AIDS, but it requires individuals to make deliberate and conscious decisions to think, act, and live responsibly.

The opposite of self-care is self-absorption, which could lead to neglect of the self. One cannot take this lightly in the context of HIV/AIDS in Africa where many women and children are vulnerable to HIV/AIDS. Many vulnerable women are so busy caring for others that they cannot do anything to help themselves. Their "mission" to care for all others except themselves can lead to excessive self-sacrifice. A failure of self-care can lead women to sacrifice themselves as caregivers.[36]

Exercising the virtue of self-care involves three things: knowledge, a determination to thrive, and a constant self-affirmation. First, one should have adequate up-to-date knowledge about HIV/AIDS, including modes of transmission and the implications of living with the virus. Information is available in urban centers, but leaders of the community must pass that information on in the rural areas where some people may not be able to read. The Christian community has a responsibility of educating its members on a regular basis and should provide individuals with information on prevent-ing HIV/AIDS and the risk situations that facilitate the spread of HIV/AIDS. People should be given information about safe sex practices. Women should also be given information on reproductive health.

Self-care also involves making a conscious decision to thrive and flourish. This may entail setting up peer groups where people can provide support for each other. To thrive and flourish physically, emotionally, and spiritually, one needs to take care of his or her body. If an individual becomes infected, then he or she should seek medical help and learn how to live "positively." This calls for more than a spiritual state of mind. Persons who have the infection need medications, adequate food supply, access to a physician/healer, and so forth. For women, the ability to live positively and to thrive will depend to a large extent on the kinds of decisions they make about their commitments to others. This is where the whole question of self-sacrifice needs to be taken into consideration again. A person cannot thrive with a debilitating disease like clinical AIDS if she does not place limits on what she does.

Family members should support people living with HIV/AIDS to help them flourish even as they cope with this infection. The community also has an obligation to provide support to people living with HIV/AIDS so that they can live as full and rich a life as possible. Community leaders and reli-gious leaders should reach out regularly both to those with the virus and to their relatives who, though physically well, are affected greatly by the condi-tion of a family member. Churches should arrange logistical support and help people living with HIV/AIDS deal with legal issues concerning illness and death. Ciperman has argued: "persons on the margins of society and at risk for HIV infection may not easily find supportive relationships or community support. Self-care requires supportive relationships because there are times when we all need to lean heavily and depend on others. . . . Self-care is about how we take care of ourselves, and this includes allowing others to care for us. . . . Supportive relationships assist us in growth and healing."[37]

Self-care requires constant self-affirmation. I cannot pretend to understand what it is like for someone living with HIV/AIDS who knows that if there is not accelerated treatment he or she is likely going to lose the battle against the disease. Mustering the courage to affirm one's self under these conditions must be difficult. Many people who are diagnosed HIV-positive think the diagnosis is already a prescription of death. Because of misinformation about the disease, an HIV-positive diagnosis not only places one on a death list but also brands him or her as a promiscuous individual. In the case of a woman, she is often shunned as a prostitute who has infected her husband and brought suffering to the children. Even after an HIV-positive individual has gone through denial and finally accepted the condition, he or she will still struggle with the impressions people have that this individual lived in an irresponsible manner and is now facing the consequences. In such a situation, I can imagine how it would be difficult for someone to engage in self-affirmation.

For persons living with HIV/AIDS to affirm themselves and practice self-care, they need to cultivate courage to believe some truths. They have to accept what experts in the medical community say: as deadly as the virus is, a positive diagnosis is not the end of life. The HIV virus does not take away what constitutes personhood, humanity, or in the case of those who subscribe to the Christian perspective, an affirmation that they still exist in the image of God. As the viral load increases and the person's immune system succumbs to attacks, the individual is going to have difficulties and may have to deal in a realistic manner with impending mortality. However, before one gets to such a stage, intervention from the community can provide the individual a reason to hope and to live positively, knowing that he or she has so much to look forward to in the context of family and community. It is such an awareness that should motivate the individual to affirm his or her self. Such self-affirmation is an antidote to fatalism. People develop a fatalistic attitude when they are disappointed and bitter.

Some people have become bitter about their condition and embarked on a life of revenge, seeking to infect innocent people. Recently, Cameroonian discussion groups in the United States passed on the names of certain Cameroonians who are allegedly infecting others because these individuals are angry that someone gave them the HIV virus. A similar message was also posted in an online chat room that a young Kenyan woman had vowed to infect several men. People pass on these messages on the pretext that they want to protect the public, but I am not sure that public safety is enhanced if people compromise the privacy of others.

A person living with HIV/AIDS cannot successfully practice the virtue of self-care alone. We belong to communities and our ability to thrive and practice self-care will depend on the support we get from that society. As humans, we need the love and good will of others in order to thrive. The question this raises is, why should someone care for the person or people who have been affected by HIV/AIDS? The virtue of justice provides some answers.

HIV/AIDS Calls for the Virtue of Justice

Justice is an important virtue because it has both individual and political dimensions. Aristotle described justice at the individual level as that characteristic which disposes an individual "to do just things, act justly, and wish just things."[38] He classified justice under two parts, the general and the particular, to reflect lawfulness and fairness. General justice is lawfulness and is the sum of all virtues directed toward the good of another person. Particular justice is the right disposition towards good things such as security, money, and honor in a political community.[39] Aristotle further defined particular justice as equality or fairness with respect to the common good in the political community. He called general justice complete because it is based on laws, directed toward another person, and claimed: "justice alone of the virtues is thought to be for the good of another."[40] He also expanded the concept of particular justice by differentiating between distributive and commutative, or corrective, justice. Distributive justice deals with the equal distribution of the common goods such as honor, money, and the good things of life. Distributive justice involves proportional distribution, or fairness and equilibrium in society. Commutative justice involves contracts and other legal transactions.

Saint Thomas described justice as the virtue that provides the mechanism for distributing the common good.[41] At the particular or individual level, justice deals with restitution, recompense, or what is called compensatory justice. In the community, justice involves the fair distribution of the resources of the state. At both levels, every member of the society expects the good and has a right to that good. The question for us is what people can do as individuals and as a society to ensure that justice is ongoing, since the quest for the good is itself an ongoing project of individuals and the state. This is where the idea of justice involves politics and political life. Aristotle and Saint Thomas provide similar answers, except that Thomas provides theological grounding for his discussion of social justice.[42]

Aristotle assigns to the state an important role in helping its citizens live virtuous lives for the sake of the good. Justice means acting fairly to promote the good of others in the political community. This is an important perspective in Africa, where the postneocolonial state has failed to promote justice and, as a result, inequality has reigned. Without making further distinctions, I discuss justice in this section as the virtue that addresses the needs of others.

Recent discussions of justice have wrestled with the groundbreaking work of John Rawls, *A Theory of Justice*, in which he argues: "justice is the basic structure of society . . . the way in which the major social institutions distribute fundamental rights and duties and determine the division of advantages from social cooperation."[43] Central to the Rawlsian idea is the notion that justice involves public reasoning, deliberation, and debate to arrive at "agreement in judgment among reasonable agents."[44] A community should work to reach a consensus on seven primary goods desired by individuals and distributed by the "political constitution and the principal economic and social arrangements." These primary goods are: rights, liberties, self-respect, power, opportunities, income, and wealth. These form what Rawls calls a "thin theory of the good" which he considers crucial for the well-being of individuals and society. He argues that the principles for allocating these goods are general and can be intuitively recognized. They are also universal, public, should offer preferences to conflicting claims, and must be final. Rawls states that the choice of these principles ought to be made in the "original position," a hypothetical situation that could be compared to some prior position before human sociality. At such a hypothetical position, members of the political community are expected to be free agents, equal, rational, self-interested, and ignorant of their position, or their preferences and religious beliefs. This should not be taken to mean zero knowledge about the society; members should have general information about the human society. However, in the process, conflicting aims could not be used to advance an individual's claims at the expense of other claims to ensure impartiality in the choice of principles of distributing primary goods. Rawls offered an overlapping consensus to address competing interests in a liberal society where members shared common values such as democracy and similar visions of the political economy. Such a broad consensus would ensure that "all social values—liberty and opportunity, income and wealth and the bases of self-respect—are to be distributed equally unless an unequal distribution of any, or all, of these values is to everyone's advantage."[45]

Reaction to Rawls has varied but in general reflects the view that Rawls proposition assumes western democratic liberalism, as capitalism, and does not adequately address human rights. Some argue that his theory does not give adequate consideraton to gender and other social inequalities. Rawls's view that there is a hypothetical situation devoid of preconceptions where the principles of justice could be determined seems unrealistic.[46] Feminist scholars contest the view that justice can be a dispassionate construction. Seyla Benhabib has argued contra Rawls that an ethic of justice must consider not only the concrete history of people, but also the "identity and affective-emotional constitution" of others in the community.[47]

This is a crucial dimension of justice, because one cannot talk of justice and ignore effective communication with other people or segments of the political community. In order for such a communication to be effective, it must take into account the viewpoint, social location, and needs of others, as well as the resources available to the state. Justice that is conceived as autonomy and rationality is meaningful if it is inclusive. Justice conceived as rights in each context means positive rights that contribute to the well-being of all in the political community. As Tanner has pointed out, "A just society is not simply a society that allows people to go their own way, a just society is one that actively cares for its members by providing the 'institutional conditions that enable people to meet their needs and express their desires.'"[48]

Amartya Sen has argued that Rawls's view that justice as fairness articulates a transcendental perspective that focuses on the nature of a just society in contrast to a comparative approach which considers alternative arrangements and asks whether some approaches are more or less just than others.[49] Sen prefers the comparative approach because it gives a community an opportunity to advance justice by including social policies that might eliminate hunger and illiteracy—even though its implementation might violate the transcendental requirements of justice that include "equal liberties and distributional equity."[50] Sen also argues that the transcendental approach cannot offer more than it proposes. The transcendental approach ignores "comparative distances" such as different starting points, different dimensions of transgressions, and different ways of measuring infractions, and cannot offer an adequate way of ranking justice. Furthermore, even if one conceded that there is an inviolable best alternative in justice, it does not prevent one from considering the relative merits of alternative approaches.[51]

Sen acknowledges that his comparative approach may be incomplete, but it offers a compelling argument about injustice at a time of prosperity and the ongoing subjugation of women. According to Sen, despite durable ambiguity, we may still be able to agree readily that there is a clear social failure involved in the persistence of endemic hunger or exclusion from medical access, which calls for remedying for the advancement of justice, even after taking note of the costs involved. Similarly, we may acknowledge the possibility that liberties of different persons may, to some extent, conflict with each other (so that any fine-tuning of the demands of equal liberty may be hard to work out), and yet strongly agree that arbitrary incarceration of accused people, without access to court procedures, would be a just violation of liberty that calls for urgent rectification.[52]

Sen emphasizes that even where people have a specific nation of justice, shared beliefs could provide partial ranking, making "evaluative incompleteness" relative to a theory of justice.[53] Finally, Sen argues that the institutional requirements of the Rawlsian approach would be difficult to meet in the context of global justice, even with Rawls's new starting point that includes negotiation with different peoples and giving reasonable help to decent societies that may not be just.[54] Sen argues that what emerges from Rawls's transcendent perspective is a silence that inhibits public reasoning about justice. Rawls's idea of a common starting point ignores the possibility of impartial arbitration, shared beliefs and prejudices that might offer an opportunity to examine the issues from the perspective of people who do not belong to the same society.[55]

Theologian L. Gregory Jones also takes issue with Rawls, arguing that the notion of an overlapping consensus as suggested by Rawls is misguided because the contemporary society is morally bankrupt. "It may be that it is not that religious beliefs and competing conceptions of the good have precluded rational agreement about the good, but rather that our institutions . . . have so corrupted our shared social practices that we no longer have the character by which we could reach some level of agreement about, as well as to embody, principles of justice."[56] Jones is more pessimistic about the idea of pluralism which Rawls and other proponents of social justice assume.

While aspects of Rawls's thesis are problematic, his central claim that justice calls for deliberation on the common goods remains appealing because it is not structured on the notion of desert but on the idea of fairness. Rawls's focus on distributive justice ignores deontological concerns, but one could argue that the notion of deliberation allows the community to debate the legal mechanism that is best suited for distributing the goods of the community. The assumption that in a free society individuals can engage in meaningful dialogue on equal footing may not always work, because even in free societies members do not have what MacIntyre calls a common story through which they can seek or appeal to the common good.[57] This poses a real problem for many postneocolonial states which are not "free societies" and do not have a common story or narrative. In addition, dictatorial regimes have held freedoms hostage by preaching equality but institutionalized inequality and keeping the masses on the margins. Politicians have restricted public discourse on the nature of a political economy and its common goods that ought to be used to enhance the quality of life for all members of the political community. Therefore, in light of growing inequities, Rawls's notion of equality deserves further reflection in every context.

Despite these problems, justice as a virtue is also social justice and calls for a radical rethinking of the idea of fairness in the context of HIV/AIDS. To begin with, a new dialogue ought to start in the postneocolonial state about the idea and parameters of justice. A deliberative process in that context could use the notion of a minimum consensus with all perspectives in play to forge a hopeful path forward. Such an approach could work well for the church in its fight against HIV/AIDS; members of the Christian community cannot impose their view that response to HIV/AIDS must be grounded on the *imago dei*. An uncritical commitment to one's perspective, especially the theological position on social justice, is problematic because it might demand compliance from communities that do not share that moral ethos. In this context, what might emerge as a minimum consensus on social justice that could embrace theological proposals on the *imago dei* and its implication for a life of love and compassion ought to be cultivated in tandem and tension with other positions.[58] Theologians and religious ethicists have mechanisms to make necessary compromises to achieve a minimum consensus because the claims of justice in the Christian tradition prioritize the person and his or her needs, rather than deserts or reciprocity. The poor and needy of the community deserve justice, and those infected with the HIV virus deserve justice simply because they are human beings.

I do not suggest that Christians should abandon their texts and tradition. The Christian tradition that has drawn from the heritage of the Hebrew prophets and the teachings of the New Testament as well as the vast literature on the social teachings of the church brings a perspective that employs transcendental language, divine mandates, and moral obligations. The message of the Hebrew prophets generates a provocative dialogue on justice which theologians should use to establish dialogue with other communities of discourse to champion the common good. Rather than talk about the demands of God, or the uniqueness of the Christian perspective in the fight against HIV/AIDS, theologians and Christian community ought to place their ideas on the table for free and open dialogue with other communities. People share a common humanity, as well as basic desires and needs, and can meet those needs more effectively if they collaborate. If Christians maintain a privatized discourse on justice, their voices will not be heard on this crucial debate about justice in a world of HIV/AIDS.

When theologians approach the idea of justice in tandem with others, what constitutes justice? The face of someone living with HIV/AIDS defines or provides a context to redefine justice. Karen Lebacqz has written broadly about justice and argued that justice and acts of justice center on carrying out the obligations of human relationships.[59] As members of the human community, we are engaged in various relationships. We are related to others because they belong to the same family. We have relationships with friends, occupational colleagues, and members of a religious or social community, in addition to all kinds of proximal relationships. Finally, we have relationships with others because of political configurations called constitutions and institutions, and the nation state.[60] Therefore, at a minimum, justice calls for a reasonable recognition of the rights of others. These include the right to equality as a human being who desires liberties, self-respect, good health, power, opportunities, income, and wealth. Each member of the community is invited to participate in the creation of these goods, to participate in making decisions about how those goods will be distributed, and, where necessary, to seek actively to redress the wrongs that have deprived others from participating fully in the goods and opportunities that exist in the political community. Justice also refers to those practices that ought to be cultivated, because failure to engage in acts of justice will not only diminish others in society, but also deprive them of experiencing the good. In the case of HIV/AIDS, the practice of justice might involve two broad agendas, a civic praxis and a theological praxis that would concretize the pursuit of justice to promote the common good. I will discuss the civic praxis here and discuss the theological praxis in the next chapter.

In order to maximize justice, each community needs to establish a civic praxis that is rooted in human values. I have already argued that the state has new priorities in light of HIV/AIDS. Building a civic praxis requires some basic information. First, every member of the political community should have a clear understanding of the HIV virus and the ways in which it is spread. The leaders should pass on this information to its citizens on a regular basis. They need this information to think correctly about HIV/AIDS and make reasonable decisions about risk situations. Second, every member of the community ought to participate in creating a safe environment. I am not referring to the absence of guns or spears, but to a social atmosphere that is free from domination and abuse. Such an atmosphere would empower

women, children, and other members of the community, such as those who
are engaged in commercial sex, to exercise their freedoms and demand equal
rights to engage in activities that would minimize their risk of infection.

Third, those who govern ought to provide health care and devote the
resources of the state to the fight against HIV/AIDS, not simply waiting for
the resources to come from non-governmental organizations and other relief
agencies. The number of resources each political community devotes to
fighting a pandemic that is claiming so many indicates the value that political leaders place on the lives of their citizens. A political community cannot
be committed to the survival of its members if it merely pays lip service to a
deadly disease such as HIV/AIDS.

Finally, assuming civic obligations to promote justice might involve taking a stand and playing an advocacy role for those who have been affected
by the disease. Such advocacy might involve forming pressure groups to
demand that government leaders take their responsibility to people living
with HIV/AIDS seriously. For a long time, many people in Africa have
assumed that their countries are poor and that they cannot therefore expect
their governments to do anything for them. It is time for people to begin to
raise more questions about the role of government in situations where political and economic marginalization exists. So much has happened to change
public perception about HIV/AIDS in Nigeria and South Africa because of
a few individuals who played an active role in calling on politicians to fulfill
their obligations to the people. I will discuss access to medicines in chapter
5, but for now I only emphasize that if members of the political community
take their role as activists seriously, it could lead to a new accountability on
the part of political leaders who will be forced to act or face civil strife. Such
activism ought to emphasize the fact that health care can no longer be the
privilege of the few who can afford to buy it.

The second broad agenda that members of the community as individuals and groups could undertake is narrower because it is a theological praxis,
which may not be shared by all people in the political community. Christian
communities have a worldview that is structured in the belief that all
humanity is created in the image of God. These communities also proclaim
that the God who has created humanity loves everybody, and has set an
example of love for humanity to follow. One way to demonstrate that love is
to speak and act as a community on behalf of the many who are on the margins of society, especially people living with HIV/AIDS. With values that
differ from one community of discourse to another, theologians would have
to recognize that their communication will be heard in a significantly different manner if they themselves listen to other voices that do not come from

within their community. I am not suggesting that religious communities should ignore their core values, but am calling instead for what Stephen Hart has described as "recovering the capacity to express moral outrage, universal claims of justice, and visions of a better society [which] is essential if progressive political initiatives are to prosper—or deserve to prosper."[61]

Such a critical voice against injustice must be raised in a society where a few members of even the elite class have access to health care and the masses have none at all. In many African countries, members of the governing class travel overseas for medical care, often at taxpayers' expense, while most of their citizens do not even have access to good health-care facilities, let alone medicines. In societies where this is the norm, theologians ought to raise critical voices and join other communities of discourse to debate social practices that could contribute to the well-being of all. Thomas Ogletree has argued: "When some fare well and attain much, it is almost always at the expense of others, indeed, not infrequently by virtue of the domination and exploitation of those others. Excellence achieved at such a price is morally dubious at best. It takes on a morally negative cast insofar as it is a function of structural forms of social injustice."[62] As I have argued already, theological commitments do not have to be abandoned completely because they could provide the basis from which to engage in a critical prophetic project that moves the political leaders to practice justice. A further articulation of justice through a theological praxis requires elaborate efforts in Christian communities to educate people and combat HIV/AIDS. I discuss some of these efforts in the next chapter.

HIV/AIDS and the Life of Prudence

I have left the idea of prudence until last because I think that social justice should exist to facilitate acts of prudence as people search for the common good. Prudence is the human disposition to use good reasoning and judgment in actions that one pursues. One could also argue that to act out of prudence is to act out of one's own interests. I would like to link the idea of prudence to what the ancient philosophers called *phronesis*, to refer to judgment, or practical wisdom which one employs to make decisions about life.

What is important at this point is not whether one can argue that a person can always do what he or she ought to do. The idea of prudence suggests that an individual will deliberate about the kinds of things they ought to do in every situation, taking time to think about what is the good and wise course of action. If the person is reasonable, he or she will decide not to do certain things because she knows they would not be good for her. In a world of HIV/AIDS, given all the information about transmission of the virus, a rational person would be prudent about his actions and not engage in behavior that would place him at risk. In making that argument, one assumes several things. First, the person is rational and has taken time to reflect on his or her choices. Second, this person has the freedom and capacity to make choices. But this is not always possible. The wife whose husband has had an extramarital relationship may not have that information and may not know that she is at risk. Even if she knows that her husband has had an extramarital relationship, she may not know with certainty if she is at risk because she has no information on the health of the other partner in this relationship. The husband may also lie to his wife about the extramarital affair, claiming that he used a condom when in fact he did not. The prudent thing for the wife in this circumstance would be to insist on using condoms or insist that her husband take a test to be sure she is not at risk.

Other factors may further complicate this. One of the partners may know that he or she is HIV-positive, but still decide to have unprotected sexual relations because he or she wants to have a baby. In some cases, the partner who acts this way may not disclose his or her intentions to the other partner. Yet this person is acting to promote what she considers a very important cultural value, having children. This is not a hypothetical situation. In my conversation with one of my informants in Cameroon, she told me that a friend of hers who is HIV-positive met someone working in Cameroon from the West. She did not disclose her status to the man because she wanted to get pregnant and have a child by him. The prudent thing would have been to discuss this situation with the man and ask his opinion. Both parties deserve to know this crucial information, because they could have a child who is HIV-positive, and because the man could become infected with the virus and return to the West and infect his own wife.

The woman in this situation might argue that she has considered the risks to the child, and plans to take medications available to prevent mother-to-child transmission. It is still clear that the woman is not acting with prudence because if she is not taking any antiretroviral drugs, she may develop clinical AIDS and die, leaving her child as an orphan. She might then argue that even if this were to happen her lover could take her child back to the West where the baby would be raised under better circumstances, her assumption being that the man would take responsibility for the baby and that the man would not become infected and would therefore be around to take care of the baby. In the worst-case scenario, the woman might think that even if she dies and the man deserts her, she has a family that will raise her baby. The ultimate goal for this woman is to have a baby, and she considers that a virtue. Having a child may indeed be a worthy goal, but getting pregnant through sexual intercourse when one is already HIV-positive is not prudent because it poses a lot of risks to both parties and to the child born of such an encounter.

On the other hand, the man who has left a family in the West and gone to Cameroon on assignment may or may not know the plans that his temporary partner has. From his perspective, all he wants is recreational sex. His partner looks good, shows no signs of illness, and there is no reason for him to be suspicious. However, it is possible to raise questions about his judgment. He has not taken time to find out the health of his potential partner. He is at great risk and does not know it. When my informant told me this story, she did not know if her friend had infected the male partner. My informant wondered several times if the "innocent" man is now infected with the virus and will infect other women too, before he leaves Cameroon. She also wondered what will happen when he returns to the West! If he is infected she worried, he is likely to pass the virus on to his wife and other women in his life. One can say, however, that whether he is infected or not, in this situation, he did not act prudently.

One could make several generalizations about enacting prudence in this situation. First, the Cameroonian woman and her western lover could have talked openly about their sexuality before deciding what to do. In the context where the rate of HIV/AIDS prevalence is so high, both parties should have asked each other questions about their past sexual life. Both parties could have taken their act of prudence to a higher level by making a conscious decision to do voluntary testing and counseling. Both parties could also have chosen to use a condom. If they used a condom, they would of course have jeopardized the woman's goal of getting pregnant. This is a situation where it would have been prudent for the woman to think of alternative ways of having a baby, including adoption.

It is easy in the context to blame the woman because she is the one that was infected and to argue that she did not act in a prudent manner. That in fact is my position, but one should not ignore the cultural or family pressures that might have been placed on her to have a child. Even if there were no outside pressures, and she acted on her own, then one would need to ask if she was sufficiently "educated" to seek alternative ways of fulfilling her dreams of becoming a mother. Furthermore, one would also be assuming that if she took the risk of informing the potential father of her future child, he would have understood the situation and taken steps to protect her privacy. The dilemma here is that the development and response to HIV/AIDS in Cameroon and other African countries has not given us concrete information to sufficiently assign blame in a situation like this.

I also conclude that the man did not act prudently. First, his decision to seek a sexual partner because he is on assignment and away from his family leaves many questions about his own fidelity. Second, there is no indication that he wanted to know anything about the sexual history of his partner. If he did, he did not act with prudence when he had unprotected sex. He could have insisted that both of them do voluntary testing and counseling. It is also possible that he wanted to have a child with this woman. In that case, he too should have talked to a physician and considered alternative ways of having a child. It would seem that regardless of what the woman planned to do, if the man had acted in a prudent manner, he might have minimized the risk situation.

When one thinks of prudence by thinking of concrete situations like this, it reinforces the idea that individuals should employ *phronesis* and not only reason alone to make decisions. People live in contexts where cultures and traditions provide a background on which to draw to make decisions. Sometimes one faces a crisis because those contexts themselves face new challenges and cannot provide a clear-cut answer on what to do. The virtue of prudence and the employment of *phronesis* become all the more important and challenging.

In this chapter I have explored a set of virtues that could be employed by individuals and their communities to prevent the spread of HIV/AIDS. Promoting these virtues is a task that individuals and their political communities must strive to accomplish because living a life of virtue constitutes an important weapon in the fight against HIV/AIDS. In the next chapter I will discuss what religious communities can do at the local level and within ecumenical groups to scale up the battle against HIV/AIDS.

Chapter 4

The *Imago Dei* Invites a Bold Community Praxis

The AIDS epidemic has a profound impact on economic growth, income and poverty. . . . Women and girls are more vulnerable to HIV/AIDS and are disproportionately affected and infected by the epidemic. In both rural and urban areas, the epidemic adds to the already heavy burdens women bear as workers, caregivers, educators, and mothers. I will do my best to persuade this new church in Cameroon to also deal with the HIV/AIDS epidemic.

—Dr. Catherine Akale[1]

In this chapter, I argue that the idea of the *imago dei* invites members of the Christian community to engage in a bold praxis, at the local level and at the national and international levels. I will talk about the local level first and then address the role of national (denominational and ecumenical) organizations. I will conclude by discussing the role of Bible reading in the faith community in the context of HIV/AIDS. I consider these issues as an extension of the questions addressed in previous chapters about honoring the *imago dei* through love and compassion, and creating a social context for people to cultivate a disposition that enables them to pursue the good and flourish. This chapter emphasizes praxis because I am convinced that actualizing love, compassion, and the virtues calls for a combination of thought, devotion, and action that would prevent the spread of HIV/AIDS and strengthen people living with HIV/AIDS to "live positively."

Responding to HIV/AIDS Requires a Reorganized Local Praxis

The first place for the church's action is the local congregation or assembly. This is crucial because the brunt of HIV/AIDS is felt within the local congregation. The majority of people living with HIV/AIDS are no longer in urban centers and cities as was thought at the beginning of the crisis. Even those who live in urban areas often go home to the rural areas in search of herbal treatments or, when they no longer have any options, they return to the rural areas to die. Those who die in urban centers are often transported to the rural areas for burial. The urban centers serve as denominational headquarters where most of the campaigns against HIV/AIDS are organized. Urban churches are likely to have a highly educated pastoral staff that can access and deploy some of the resources available for fighting HIV/AIDS from the state, non-governmental organizations, faith-based organizations, and other international agencies. In addition, these communities also have members who can provide medical services. This is far from true in the smaller rural congregations.

Local congregations, whether rural or urban, can do a number of things to be an effective channel of love and compassion. First, church leaders could talk openly about the reality of HIV/AIDS and place it at the center of its worship and teaching, as well as its *diakonia* (service). Such a conversation need not take place only through lectures and sermons. Important steps have been taken already in using music, drama, poetry, and art to teach people about HIV/AIDS. However, songs, prayers, announcements, fellowship time, teaching, and preaching ought to include direct references to the pandemic because it is part of people's lives in various ways. Regular and direct references could help keep the issue alive in the minds and daily practice of the people. It will remind people that information about HIV/AIDS is not only available when special visitors come into the community nor is it a set of ideas and lesson materials imposed on the local church from denominational headquarters.

Second, churches should develop a systematic education program about illness, especially HIV/AIDS, prevention strategies, and ways of caring for people living with HIV/AIDS. People know about the disease and have local names for it. In the Wimbum area, people sometimes just wonder if a person has *nje yang ha* (that type of disease) or "this illness that is killing us." Sometimes they come out and say that they suspect that the person has *wammi*, the local name for HIV/AIDS. Education programs should address the disease specifically. Many pastors in Cameroon talk about HIV/AIDS in very general and vague terms. Few pastors talk about it openly, but instead do so as a way to highlight the theological dilemma HIV/AIDS has introduced; why has God has allowed such a thing to come to us at this time! Short-term and occasional training programs led by experts and a systematic training program in local churches should replace education by non-governmental organizations.[2] If you drive on the road from Bamenda to Nkambe in Donga Mantung Division, you find sign boards on a house that indicates that the local AIDS Committee meets there. Yet most of the local committees depend on outside resource personnel to do their work. Local churches could supplement the work of local AIDS Committees by providing an organized education and prevention program in the community. In order to provide such education and counseling, local churches need financial resources and support from other organizations and public health officials. Training people would require a financial commitment that may not be feasible in some local churches. However, several denominations could work together to set up training sessions with their churches in a given region. Pastors and other volunteers who attend the training sessions would then take the materials back to their respective churches. This process could be done every six months and repeated for about three to four years until a large section of the local community has been trained in key issues about HIV/AIDS, including prevention, voluntary testing and counseling, assistance for persons who have tested positive, care for the sick and support for someone who is facing death, support for families caring for someone living with HIV/AIDS, and comfort for those who are bereaved. The training program should also teach volunteers basic religious perspectives on illness, healing, and the role of medicine and faith in the healing process. Disease and healing are important aspects of church life in Africa, yet they have typically been left to the denominational leadership. It is now time that churches should make these issues local concerns. Local education programs should draw from the services of medical experts.

Local churches ought to encourage voluntary counseling and testing (VCT) as an overall prevention strategy. Supporters of VCT recorded some success in Kenya because workers promoted it by making door-to-door visits.[3] The Kenyan program involved three steps: (a) pre-test sessions during which the individual learned of the risk factors of HIV transmission and the meaning of the test; (b) collection of the body fluid samples for laboratory; (c) post-test counseling when the counselor informed the individual of his or her result, discussed the meaning of the results, gave support, counseling and made a referral if it was necessary. The epidemiological impact of this method of prevention was determined by behavior changes such as the modification of lifestyle to prevent transmission and the use of pharmaceutical products to prevent the transmission of the virus or slow the progress of clinical AIDS. Denominational health boards should send mobile medical teams to rural areas to train local volunteers to assist in VCT. Church health boards should also provide test kits and make sure that they work properly. Where it is not feasible to have test kits in local churches, they should be made available in local health clinics. Local churches should open up their facilities to be used as makeshift clinics if mobile teams deliver services. Churches and community centers have provided such services in the past. In addition to offering their facilities to be used for VCT, churches can train people to serve as volunteers in such a testing program.

Volunteers should be trained to respect confidential information and individual privacy. Some people do not like to take the HIV test because they fear that other people will learn about their status. If people were assured that no information about their condition would be compromised, they might be more likely to participate in VCT. An individual may choose to let people know if he or she is HIV-positive; people should be encouraged to do that. If the individual chooses to make his or her condition known, the Christian community has an obligation to provide counseling and support, to relate to the individual in a normal way, and to encourage the person to live courageously and wisely. If the individual develops AIDS, members of the local congregations have an extended obligation to provide compassionate care for this individual. Church leaders should organize support groups within the church to handle visitation if families are open to the idea, and a regular supply of food in critical situation when a seriously sick individual needs nutrition. People could take turns to visit, cook, and help the children with housework, as well as performing other necessary tasks such as household cleaning and even farm work. Arrangements should be made with local government authorities about what to do if violations of confidentiality occur.

Outside the VCT setting , pastors remain first responders in most rural areas. Many of them do not have adequate information about HIV/AIDS to be able to counsel effectively. Theological seminaries in Africa are just beginning to include HIV/AIDS into their curriculum. James,[4] who was an active member of his congregation, recalls when he first had his test results back. James told me that since he could not talk to his local pastor, he depended on the counseling that he received from the staff at the Baptist hospital. He was fortunate that his wife was not positive. She accepted him and provided support to him to the extent that James said that his only reasons for living were the love of his wife and the support he received from the counseling staff at the hospital and one of his siblings in whom he confided. He said he depended on his wife alone and this sibling to protect the rest of the family from this horrible news. He could not tell them for fear that they would disown him. He did not tell his local pastor about his condition because he feared that his pastor would criticize him. Most local pastors were not yet trained to handle the AIDS crisis. This incident underscores the importance of training pastoral counselors to respond to the HIV/AIDS crisis with love and compassion. The counseling ministry of the CBC Health Board under the direction of Rev. Tani has been very effective. The Health Board has worked in the past few years to extend its counseling program to local churches in the Northwest Province, and it is now carrying out extensive training in churches in the Southwest Province.

Local churches also need to start a conversation on sexuality. Some scholars have argued that the introduction of Christianity to Africa inhibited dialogue on sexuality because the missionaries imposed a new sexual morality on the converts. In trying to override cultural perspectives on sexuality, missionaries drove discussion of sex underground but did not stop sexual intercourse among members of the church.[5] An open dialogue is needed to refute false generalizations that Africans do not talk about sex. Celebration of human sexuality abounds everywhere in music, literature, and art. Religious and secular rituals celebrate, regulate, and enhance human sexuality and human reproduction. The fact that people are unwilling to talk about sexuality is seen as a kind of ingrained modesty on the part of Africans. On a continent where Christianity continues to spread with its own indigenous forms, turning away from a dialogue on sexuality on grounds that Christians "do not talk about such things" is heretical. Additionally, the refusal to talk about sexuality that masquerades as African modesty could actually be a massive conspiracy of silence. The age at which young people have their first sexual experience continues to drop, making this a truly sexual generation. An informative discourse on sexuality could dispel fears and the stigma attached to HIV/AIDS. Madeleine Boumpoto has stated that to talk about AIDS "is to speak of sexual matters. It is more than that, it is to expose to the light of the day a noxious sexuality, a profligacy; it is to mention the unmentionable. This is the reason why people living with AIDS and their families prefer to remain silent."[6] The dangers posed by HIV/AIDS invites the church and its leaders to break the conspiracy of silence and speak openly and honestly about human sexuality. An honest conversation on sexuality should not be a witch hunt or a time to demonize people for being promiscuous but should be a time for a new dialogue that affirms human sexuality as a gift from God that should be used appropriately in a committed and responsible relationship. Therefore a dialogue on sexuality ought to deal with difficult questions like multiple partners, sex outside committed relationships, and unprotected sexual practices.

A dialogue on sexuality in the African church should also recognize homosexuality and condemn discrimination against gays and lesbians. Many Africans think that homosexuality is a Western lifestyle, although evidence of homosexuality abounds in African communities.[7] Africans who boast that they are tolerant typically deny that same-sex relationships exist in African communities. Many Africans who live in the diaspora and who have come to treat homosexuality as a civil rights issue still argue that homosexuality works for the western society but not African societies. A dialogue on sexuality should help participants recognize that gays and lesbians have the *imago dei* and, like other members of the community, they want to realize the reign of God here on earth.[8] It should also discuss ways in which homosexual relationships (like heterosexual relationships) can be abused and become dangerous. When both heterosexual and homosexual relationships are celebrated and handled with responsibility rather than fear, hatred, and blame, the community will make progress in its campaign to prevent HIV/AIDS. President Robert Mugabe has attacked gays and lesbians in Zimbabwe in order to build support for his failed political agenda. Gays have been dragged to court in Cameroon in a shameful witch hunt that is abusive and deflects attention from the massive problems that the Cameroonian society faces. The recent threat by the Anglican bishop of Nigeria to pull out of the Anglican communion over the ordination of a gay bishop in America creates a crisis where the church ought to respond in love, affirmation, and inclusion.

An open dialogue on sexuality needs to dispel false views about black sexuality. The boldest claim in recent years that black sexuality departs from the human norm is that of John Caldwell et al., who from their studies in Nigeria and a broad sweep of selected anthropological literature map out what they claim is an excessive female sexual freedom, in contrast to Eurasia models.[9] Caldwell and his colleagues decry transactional sex and what to them is a "distinct and internally coherent African system embracing sexuality, marriage and much else."[10] Their selective use of data details frequency of sexual activity, the number of partners, and sexual networks in different regions of Africa. The theme, which they sustain throughout the study, is that chastity has little value in African sexual ethics. This is not the place to refute the Caldwell thesis; others have done so eloquently.[11] Church leaders ought to remind members of their communities that many African communities condemn both premarital and extramarital sex.[12] The so-called virginity tests, which have now been prohibited in South Africa, were an attempt to demonstrate that African societies did not tolerate premarital sex in the manner Caldwell and his colleagues claim.[13] I do not support virginity tests and I do not think that they should have been started, but the idea of such a negative practice likely indicates that African communities expected a bride to be a virgin. Wimbum elders refer to pregnancies out-of-wedlock as *bipsi* (from the verb "to spoil").[14] The dialogue that takes place at the local church must be the type of conversation that is divested of these patriarchal concerns and encourages sexual responsibility. The church ought to be a safe place for open conversations so that members can flourish emotionally and otherwise.

Dialogue about sexuality should restore it to God's plan within the social order. The North African Bishop and theologian Saint Augustine, whose turbulent journey to conversion is well documented in his classic work *The Confessions*, adopted an attitude to spirituality which echoed Saint Paul's strongest critique of sexual sins. Augustine's hermeneutics of sexuality reflected his perceptions of the debilitating effect of his passions and led Augustine to link sex to sin and shame. Augustine's view of sexual sin was also reflected in his interpretation of the collapse of civilization in *The City of God*, where Augustine talked of shame as an aspect of all "sexual intercourse."[15] A new dialogue should depart from this negative portrayal of sexuality and encourage people to celebrate sexuality in a responsible manner.

An honest conversation about sexuality should also address and endorse the use of condoms as safe-sex practice. Since some Christian leaders recognize that condoms can be used as part of a general prophylaxis in order to save life, local churches should emphasize the benefits of condoms as a component of safe sex practices. The claim that distribution of condoms will only promote more sexual intercourse should also be discussed openly and refuted. Parents ought to be presented with the information that their young people engage in sexual activity whether they have condoms or not and then be given the opportunity to think about the outcome of sex with or without condoms.

There is no doubt that condoms could indeed give young people false security and undermine a commitment to abstain from sexual intercourse. However, if they have sex, and we know that many of them do, they should use condoms to be safe. Public health officials have made it clear that condoms are just one method of preventing the spread of HIV/AIDS. The most effective tools remain abstinence and faithfulness to one's partner. Local church leaders should support the distribution of condoms and support local production of condoms in Africa.

In order to have an effective dialogue on sexuality, leaders should develop a relation of trust with the people, especially people living with HIV/AIDS, and make them feel safe to talk about their experience. People with HIV/AIDS, and their families, have a right to know that others will not accuse them and shun them for bringing shame to the community. Church leaders who lead these dialogues ought to receive some basic training on handling sensitive information. The aim of dialogue is to educate people, create awareness, and build a climate of tolerance and acceptance to enable people celebrate their sexuality in the right context. At an ecumenical gathering in Nairobi in 2001, African church leaders confessed that:

> Today, churches are being obliged to acknowledge that we have—however unwittingly—contributed both actively and passively to the spread of the virus. Our difficulty in addressing issues of sex and sexuality has often made it painful for us to engage in any honest and realistic way, with issues of sex education and HIV prevention. Our tendency to exclude others, our interpretation of the scriptures, and our theology of sin have all combined to promote the stigmatization, exclusion, and suffering of people with HIV or AIDS. This has undermined the effectiveness of care, education, and prevention efforts and inflicted additional suffering on those already affected by the HIV.[16]

Fortunately, some models offer clues and ways of talking about sexuality. A study by the United Nations Population Fund (UNFPA) has employed a culture lens in selected cases to contribute to the fight against HIV/AIDS.[17] The project was implemented in Uganda, where UNFPA workers collaborated with church leaders and community elders to develop strategies of talking about the threats early marriages pose to women, the right to safe delivery, adolescent sexual behavior, and HIV prevention. Workers used African music and poetry to reach the right audience with information about reproductive health and HIV prevention.[18] UNFPA did not impose its perspective on local leaders, but instead allowed religious leaders to promote "family values, abstinence and faithfulness in marriage [rather] than promoting condom use. The religious leaders were encouraged to follow their mandate. At the same time, it was agreed that they would not undermine those whose mandate it was to promote condom use."[19]

Project leaders in Uganda sought and received the support of elders, church leaders, and even kings on all the major initiatives. UNFPA formed a partnership with the Sabiny Elders Association to address reproductive health. The initial goal of the project was to eradicate female genital cutting. UNFPA workers and the elders respected cultural values, highlighted problematic issues, and proposed alternative practices. A cross section of people including women and traditional health providers participated in the project. This educational effort demystified female genital cutting and the practice dropped by 36 percent.[20] UNFPA also worked with leaders in the

Kinkizi diocese of the Church of Uganda in 1999–2000 and identified the following as issues: "early adolescent sexual activity; sexually transmitted infections, including HIV/AIDS; teenage pregnancy; school leaving; and early marriage."[21] A program was initiated that focused on consensus building and engaged volunteers to use popular culture, especially music and drama, to communicate messages about sexual health and sexually transmitted diseases (STDs). The project recorded impressive results; all parties agreed to prevent early marriages, retain girls in school, and promote the self-esteem of young girls and women. Many people also decided to participate in voluntary testing for the HIV virus.[22] The case study demonstrates that involving people in new programs that address sexuality and probe problematic practices could be effective.

An effective campaign against HIV/AIDS at the local level must address the vulnerability of women to HIV/AIDS. Women in Africa face discrimination and domination as wives, daughters, and members of the political community. African women who have worked hard to keep African cultural heritage alive have also been victims of some cultural practices that should be discarded or amended to meet the exigencies of today. Structural and ideological imbalances in the postneocolonial state have restricted women's full participation in the economy. A transformation at all levels is needed to guarantee and protect the rights of women and it should start at the local level, where women form the bulk of the membership in churches. Churches have an obligation to discuss cultural and institutional arrangements that make women vulnerable to HIV infections, and to acknowledge that certain religious perspectives on gender roles perpetuate that vulnerability. Margaret Farley has argued: "It would be naïve to think that cultural patterns that make women vulnerable to AIDS infection are not influenced by world religions whose presence is longstanding in their countries. Fundamentalisms take varied forms, but many of them are dangerous to the health of women."[23] Farley has stated that the world cannot make real gains in the fight against HIV/AIDS if gender discrimination that has marginalized women from social, economic, and political power is not addressed.

As an important step in education and prevention, Christian communities could involve older women in mentoring younger women, helping them fight barriers that prevent them from achieving thier full potential as equal partners in society. In the area of sexuality, where women are most vulnerable, Carolyn Baylies has demonstrated that older women in Zambia who have raised families are economically secure and less vulnerable to coercive sex, have also achieved status within the community that allows them to have an impact in the fight against HIV/AIDS by "teaching, cajoling, persuading" and in some cases opposing practices that would put younger women in risk situations.[24] One older woman insisted that her granddaughter and her fiancé get an HIV test and when the fiancé tested positive, the older woman used her influence to call off the engagement and prevented a marriage that might have led to the infection of the young woman.[25] Cameroon Baptist Convention churches in Yaoundé Cameroon now require that young people who show an interest in each other take the HIV test. If one of them tests positive, the pastors have resolved to discourage them from moving on with the engagement. These programs raise privacy questions and the right of an individual to make a decision about whom and when to marry, but church leaders argue that since there is no vaccine or cure for HIV infection, they have a duty to help stop the spread of infections.

In addition to focusing on the threat women face in the area of sexuality, Christian communities should also address inequality. Christian churches have stressed obedience and promoted a culture of subjugation that relegates women to supportive roles. Local churches could work with their denominations, faith-based organizations, and non-governmental organizations to train and empower women to be self-supporting since there is very little employment for them in the villages or even in the urban centers where many have moved in search of jobs. In Bamenda, in the Northwest Province, many young women who have earned university diplomas have no employment. They face obstacles because the corrupt culture requires people to bribe before getting jobs. Some young women claimed that after bribing the recruiters, they were still expected to provide sexual favors. The economic climate in African countries makes it difficult for women to become independent and self-sufficient. They face unscrupulous municipal authorities, and gendarmes who come frequently to harass entrepreneurs and demand bribes. Church leaders should raise a prophetic voice against corruption, and set up advocacy groups that will draw support from legal experts. Elected officials who are members of Christian churches should take up the cause of women in their parliaments. Advocacy groups should work with women who need to secure business permits and press charges against those who harass women who want to establish businesses.

Churches must target men and work with them to combat gender discrimination and violence against women. An overwhelming number of studies on HIV/AIDS and sexuality indicate that women have little or no power to negotiate sexual relations. Men have often used culture to justify their sexual behavior. Churches can no longer stand by while abuse is justified in the name of culture. Aspects of any culture that promote domination of women and place them at risk should be rejected. Aberrations such as the sugar daddy phenomenon, multiple partners, and extramarital relations should not be dignified as "African culture." An honest dialogue must name the sugar daddy phenomenon for what it is: a bizarre culture, which "spoils" young women, as the Wimbum people would say. Sexual partners outside the marriage union are not unique to the African context and Africans ought not to rationalize it as a cultural norm.[26]

Men have a key role in redressing the spread of HIV/AIDS and other STDs. Since some men have multiple sex partners, marriage may no longer reduce a woman's risk of being infected with an STD. Young women are vulnerable to HIV infection if they become sexually involved with older men who have not changed their sexual practices.[27] Men should collaborate with church and community elders to address delicate situations where one of the partners is HIV-positive. In such a case, preventive methods that include regular condom use should be encouraged to prevent the other partner from being infected with the virus. If an individual is infected, he or she needs the support of a strong partner, one who can be there for the children should the infected partner die from complications from the infection.

There are mixed stories here to tell from Africa. A physician in Cameroon tells the story of a husband who knew he was infected with the HIV virus, but practiced safe sex to protect his wife from being infected.[28] Schoepf reports the opposite example of a woman in the Democratic Republic of Congo who suspected that her husband was HIV-positive and suggested that they should use condoms. The husband refused and his family threatened to send the woman away and take her child from her. When the husband died from AIDS-related complications, his relatives accused the wife of infecting him with the HIV virus and abandoned her. The woman also died two years later.[29] Churches ought to educate people on a responsible expression of sexual desires. Men should be responsible for their own health and the health of their partners. In addition, if the wife is seropositive, the husband has a responsibility to protect her privacy and not to abandon her.

Churches should teach men to read the Bible from an egalitarian perspective, especially texts that address male-female relations. For example, men's groups should study passages from the New Testament such as Galatians 3:28, where the Apostle Paul argues that there is neither Jew, nor Greek, slave nor free, male nor female, that all are "one in Christ Jesus." The idea here is that men are not superior to women because both are one in Christ. The second passage is Ephesians 5:22-23 where the apostle tells wives: "be subject to your husbands as you are to the Lord. For the husband is the head of the wife just as Christ is the head of the church, the body of which he is the Savior." Bible teachers might begin reading this passage in a different light by starting with verse 1, where the apostle calls on Christians to imitate God and walk in love. The verses that follow outline ways in which men and women could walk in love. When the apostle turns to inter-personal relations in the domestic and public sphere, he prefaces his com-ments in verse 21 with the command: "be subject to one another in the fear of Christ." He then spells out dimensions of this subjection. It is in this con-text that Paul makes what some consider too many concessions to the pre-vailing culture when he orders women to be subject to their husbands. Christian men ought to have the opportunity to reflect on the command in verse 21 to practice mutual subjection. Such a reflection could help men rethink their attitude and actions towards women. Men should reflect on what it means to imitate God in whose image we are created, and to live in love. This is a fundamental obligation that requires rethinking of all social practices that conflict with the *imago dei*.

If readers ignore Paul's anti-Jewish polemics and his concessions to the prevailing culture of his day, then men could articulate a more egalitarian reading of the text. In keeping with the motif of the *imago dei*, one could read the Ephesians text in a more radical way. As carriers of the *imago dei*, Christians ought to imitate God, and walk in love as Christ has loved them and sacrificed for them. This calls for a reversal of roles. Rather than having women sacrifice and place their bodies at risk, men ought to engage in self-sacrificing behavior that would take away that risk. One important message from the Galatians text is that in Jesus all people have equal status. Thus, any cultural and social praxis that exposes women to danger is not Christlike.

Addressing risks to women calls for a rethinking of both the issue of multiple partners and the longstanding practice of polygamy/polygyny. Prevention campaigns promote monogamous relationships, and often target people who have sexual relations with several women or men at the same time. The sugar daddy phenomenon is a particularly egregious lifestyle because some sugar daddies "keep" several young women for their sexual pleasure. The argument in favor of monogamous relationship is that if part-ners are faithful to each other, their lifestyle would reduce their risk of being infected with the HIV/AIDS virus and other STDs. Sexually active people ought to remain faithful to one partner. When and why people change part-ners is up to them; the idea is to discourage people from hopping between partners. In the incidence of multiple partners, men bear much of the responsibility, and Christian churches need to come up with new ways of communicating the dangers to the men. However, a recent study of female motor park workers in Lagos, Nigeria demonstrates that young women also participate in "sexual networking" that can be very dangerous for all involved.[30] In principle, it is time for churches to work with community leaders to promote a culture of faithfulness in monogamous relationships because this could contribute significantly to the effort to stop the spread of HIV/AIDS.

The case of polygamy/polygyny is a little different because the partners are already married. The only threat to such unions would be for one of the partners to engage in unprotected sexual behavior outside the union. If that happens and the person is infected, this person is likely to put the other members of the union at risk. In the 1980s, social scientists argued that polygamy could actually reduce the risk of infection if the man remained faithful to all his wives. However, studies carried out in the Mbale district in Uganda indicated that women in polygamous homes were at risk because some of their husbands had additional partners outside the home; polygamy did not provide a shield from the risk of infection.[31] When churches address this issue it is important to stress that the problem is not primarily the institution of polygamy as such but extramarital relations which create a risky situation for all in the family. When such an understanding has been created, it is possible then for the church to explore the institution of polygamy itself and the health implications for those involved, and to work to evaluate risk factors and create strategies to minimize those risk situations.

Churches should also work with local elders to address the cultural and structural imbalance that works against young girls. The recommendations of the United Nations Task Force on Women, Girls, and HIV/AIDS in southern Africa could provide a launching pad for this type of intervention. The task force has recommended that communities (1) "collapse the bridge of infection between older men and younger women and girls"; (2) protect female enrollment in schools, because AIDS may be taking many girls away from school; (3) Work to protect women and girls from long-term risks of HIV infection; (4) "Protect the rights of women and girls to own and inherit land"; (5) Introduce a volunteer charter on rights and responsibilities of men and women to take care of people who are sick and orphans; (6) "address gender norms, violence, stigma and discrimination as potential barriers to women's access to care and treatment."[32] These may sound like large projects that are out of reach for the local church, but on close examination, local communities committed to dialogue could address them. Local pastors and community leaders need to think boldly and begin a dialogue to address these issues.

Local churches also have a special obligation to widows and orphans. These two groups are living examples of the devastation of HIV/AIDS on individuals and the community. The widow, for instance has to deal not only with the loss of a spouse, but with possible infection with the virus as well as responsibility for the children, some of whom may also be infected through mother-to-child transmission. In addition, the widow faces cultural rites and expectations that might bring stigma or discrimination, and hinder her ability to cope with her new status as a widow. The orphan faces a different set of circumstances. An orphan deals with the grief of losing one or both parents. Many orphans face stigmatization and discrimination from others who know that their parents died from AIDS complications. Some of the orphans receive support from the relatives of their parents but even in such circumstances, life is not always easy. At a very tender age, many orphans now have to work to support their siblings. This makes them vulnerable to the very disease that might have taken their parents.

Church leaders must establish a dialogue with community elders to address longstanding cultural practices that have marginalized widows. Scholars have recently called attention to many of these rites, arguing that they not only discriminate against women, but also put women at risk of infection with HIV/AIDS.[33] Practices like levirate marriages and widow cleansing should be scrutinized and appropriate action taken to create a safe environment for widows and other members of the community.

Evelynes Agot has addressed different aspects of widowhood in the Luo community in Kenya and called for a more nuanced exploration of the subject. Agot has noted that the term "widow" is inappropriate, because the Luo call her simply the wife of the departed relative. A widow who has been inherited continues to live on her late husband's estate and the new man cannot move in with her because a woman cannot bury two men in the same compound.[34] The widow refers to the new man as the man who takes care of her. She is not inherited like property and is not remarried because she was never divorced. The advantages for the widow include financial support, the chance to bear children if she is childless, and access to sexual rites, performed at the beginning of the planting season.[35]

In the Luo widow cleansing rite the widow has sexual relations with another man before the planting season to fulfill the tradition established by the first wife of Luo's primordial ancestor, Ramogi, who ordered it to ensure that all wives had conjugal rights. The ritual linked sex to food and shelter and represented continuation of the biological and social reproduction of the community. Widows could not be exempted from this rite, and for that reason it was necessary for a widow to have a male partner to fulfill this rite with her so that she would be ready to participate in the agricultural cycle. However, today widow cleansing rites have become "a world of romance, exploitative sex, and lavish food."[36] Professional inheritors now work with several widows and depend on them for the inheritor's livelihood. Some of the new inheritors do not care about HIV. Some women think an outside inheritor is more suitable if it is known that the late husband died of AIDS-related complications. Placing conjugal relations in a broad reproductive cycle that includes the fertility of the land is sacred and noble. However, at a time when HIV/AIDS has become an issue, it is likely to expose either the widow or the one who inherits her to the HIV virus.

Agot's greatest contribution to the debate is her insightful discussion of the different perspectives of vulnerability, which presupposes that, given the right information, a widow will make the right decision. A widow's background, relationship to family members, society, and religious affiliation determines how she understands vulnerability to HIV/AIDS.[37] The level of vulnerability is low for a woman who has grown-up male children who can carry the father's legacy; a widow who is at menopause and less sexually active; one who is economically independent; a widow who is educated and has cosmopolitan and cross-cultural views on inheritance. A widow who falls in one or all of the above categories is less likely to be inherited. The widow's relationship within the family also influences inheritance. She is a sister-in-law, a daughter, daughter-in-law, or co-wife, and what she decides to do influences many people. Finally, her religious affiliation may affect her decision on inheritance.

> It is usually in situations where factors supportive of the practice reinforce each other (and are also counter to her own decisions) that a widow becomes more vulnerable because she may be forced to be inherited against her wishes or else resort to a type of inheritance that would expose her to more risk for HIV, such as being inherited by a serial inheritor.[38]

Since sexual rites are always conducted at planting season, sometimes there is little or no time to do background checks of the inheritors and this heightens the widow's vulnerability.[39]

Given this information, Agot questions interventions based on assumptions that the women who enter such unions dislike inheritance. Widows do not interpret risk in the same manner as researchers. Furthermore, leaders of African Initiated Churches (AIC) support widow inheritance on biblical grounds.[40] Leaders of mainline denominations, on the other hand, oppose the practice because the New Testament has given the widow freedom to marry someone else in the Lord after the death of her husband.[41] But supporters of widow inheritance argue that both the Hebrew Bible and the New Testament endorse such practices.[42] These supporters encourage a more open, and probably safer and less risky behavior, than those who oppose it. But on the other hand, it is also possible that being assured of support from one's church, it becomes easier for the widow to decline to be inherited because the church would 'bail her out' in events where she would otherwise be expected to observe the sexual rite.[43]

The risk and vulnerability must be seen in relation to the social location and spiritual context of the widow.[44]

The Christian community could work with some of the perspectives that Agot has articulated to initiate dialogue on widowhood rites in contexts where the practice of cleansing exists. Since the rites are tied to the productive cycle of the community, it is necessary that local church leaders work with elders to redefine vulnerability in a manner that could encompass the risks the widow faces. Such a definition needs to be formulated in light of the long-term goals and well-being of the widow, her children, and the rest of the community. Such a definition of vulnerability should take into consideration the feelings of the widow and all others who may be part of the sexual relations established by the remarriage or inheritance of the widow. Sexuality as a rite should be explored and discussed. Members of this community face a situation now where in trying to fulfill the will of the ancestors, individuals could be exposed to danger. The long-term goal of the rite requires that people weigh vulnerability to infection with HIV/AIDS against the immediate need to fulfill the demands of this rite. This is an issue for the community to work out with the elders.

Mandating that only married couples practice the Luo sexual rite during planting season might be one way of modifying this tradition. The rite would survive, but women and men who are not married or are widowed would not have an obligation to practice it. Such a revision of the rite would free widows from the need to hire a professional inheritor to fulfill those rites. The precedent for this is a practice whereby a relative inherits an older widow but does not consummate the sexual rite. In areas where the widow is not able to determine on her own terms if she would like to marry and is vulnerable because of the high level of seroprevalence in the area, the Christian community could use its persuasive voice to discourage rites of inheritance. This is a delicate negotiation to carry out: if the deceased died of clinical AIDS, the question is, do you tell his family that he died of AIDS complications and might have infected his wife? In cases where the wife knows the cause of death, she is often not at liberty to disclose that information because her late husband's family could accuse her of defamation and take steps to ostracize her. In some cases, the family might accuse her of infecting their dead relative. If the risk and level of vulnerability have been assessed and all in a given community agree that the level of seroprevalence is high, the Christian community has a moral obligation to negotiate the abandonment of widowhood inheritance and cleansing.

For a long time the church has ignored its obligation to care for widows. HIV/AIDS has reminded the African church that it is the responsibility of the local church and their community to care for widows. In James 1:27, the Apostle James wrote, "religion that is pure and undefiled before God, the Father, is this: to care for orphans and widows in their distress, and to keep oneself unstained by the world." The church in Africa cannot abandon its mission of providing for widows and orphans. Widows and orphans face new and more disturbing violence in the wake of the HIV/AIDS pandemic. International organizations and local non-governmental organizations can provide assistance, resources, counseling, and other support, but the local church where the women fellowship ought to serve as the primary response group.

In the Northwest Province of Cameroon, Mrs. Mirabelle Jato Karawa started a Hope for the Widow ministry in 2000 because "the loss of a husband, the head of the family . . . causes the widow great pain and sorrow. She suffers from insecurity, sexual harassment, poverty/hunger, judicial discrimination, [and] cultural barriers. . . She therefore needs all forms of assistance for herself and the dependent children." The organization Karawa started serves as a voice for the widows and offers them love, acceptance, guidance, encouragement and hope.[45]

HIV/AIDS has created a major orphan crisis all over Africa. UNAIDS defines an orphan as "a child under 18 who has had at least one parent die."[46] Most African communities face an orphan problem that calls for concerted action now in order to avoid further catastrophe in the future. Continent-wide, the age of orphans ranges from a few days to 18 years.[47] The orphan crisis is most severe in sub-Saharan Africa where more than 12 million children have lost at least one parent to the disease. If current trends continue, by 2010 there will be more than 18 million orphans in the region. Children who have lost one or both parents to HIV/AIDS face numerous problems at different levels. They experience the grief of losing one or both parents, financial difficulties, limited access to food, few resources to pursue an education, anxieties that result from new living arrangements that separate them from other siblings, low self-esteem, and problems in foster homes. Outside the home environment, they face discrimination, and exploitation from unscrupulous employers, child labor, and sexual abuse. Therefore, many of them are at risk of being infected with the HIV virus.

In the Wimbum area of the Northwest Province, studies by Save the Orphans Foundation indicate that there were some 554 orphans in Ndu Subdivision alone.[48] The studies do not specifically indicate that these children lost their parents to HIV/AIDS, but given the high rate of prevalence in the area, one can assume many have been orphaned by the disease. Among these were 301 males and 253 females. Save the Orphans Foundation was started bu Dr. Njingti Nfor and launched in 2003 to provide for the needs of these children. In the Ndu area, 443 orphans were between one and fourteen years of age, with 343 of them in primary school. An additional forty-eight had completed primary school, four had the General Certificate of Education at the ordinary level, four at the advanced level, and one had a university degree. Many had dropped out of school and were apprentices in a variety of workshops at Ndu.

The foundation is now established at Mbacourt quarter in Ndu Town and offers services to children that include education, health care, accommodation, employment, computer training, and assistance to those who are not well off in society. The leaders of the foundation spent a substantial amount of money to carry out the surveys and at the time of launching. This was an investment on the part of the founders, because it took some time before they received funding from the government under the Heavily Indebted Poor Countries (HIPC) initiative or any other donations. Organizations like Save the Orphans have very little local funding and continue to depend on and collaborate with international non-governmental organizations, faith-based organizations like World Vision International, Catholic Relief, private volunteer organizations, and the United States Ambassador to Cameroon.

Some agencies prefer not to use the term *orphan* because of the stigma attached to it. The Cameroon Baptist Convention Health Board calls orphans "chosen children." The Health Board started the Chosen Children Program in July of 2001 because leaders and health-care workers of the Health Board realized that they could not do an effective HIV/AIDS ministry without doing something about the "alarming increase in the number of children whose parents died of HIV/AIDS."[49] The initial goal of the program was to provide "timely and quality assistance to HIV/AIDS orphans through family caregivers in their homes . . . [and] practical guides which help lighten the physical burden of caring for these children."[50] The program started with sixty-five children and thirty-five family caregivers who were drawn mainly from Bui Division, where Banso Baptist Hospital, the flagship hospital of the Health Board, is located. The program has expanded to different areas where the Health Board has AIDS ministries.

Health Board guidelines give information about HIV/AIDS, list false beliefs about HIV/AIDS, define it, detail stages in the development of the infection and how HIV is spread, and also provide information on false views about HIV transmission. The manual includes lessons on preventing the spread of HIV/AIDS. Other lessons prepare families to talk to children about HIV/AIDS. The Health Board recommends that information about HIV/AIDS be given to children incrementally, at ages five to seven, eight to ten, and eleven to fourteen years of age. For example, parents and caregivers are encouraged to talk to a five- to seven-year-old child in this manner: "AIDS is a disease caused by a specific germ called a virus. The virus is carried in some people's blood. You can't get AIDS from touching someone or being around a person with AIDS the way you can catch a cold from a friend. You can't get AIDS from being in the same school with someone who has AIDS. You can't get it from pets, flowers, mosquitoes, toilet seats, water glasses or hugs."[51] Such an explanation informs children about HIV/AIDS and how it is transmitted, as well as providing information that could generate a conversation about discrimination and stigmatization. By telling them that if someone in the same school is infected, the school is still safe because the virus is not transmitted casually, parents can dispel fears and reduce the temptations to discriminate against children living with HIV/AIDS.

The manual also has a biblical perspective on orphans, and here the leaders of the Health Board have listed several passages that point out that God cares for them, considers maltreatment of orphans an offense, defends them, helps them, punishes those who oppress orphans, protects them, and provides their needs and sustains them.[52] Believers are encouraged to care for orphans, resist oppression of orphans, give generously to them, involve them in their community activities, and treat them justly. The rest of the lessons discuss nutrition, sanitation, making a will, and the property rights of orphans. The information follows Cameroon civil code in which, depending on whether a person dies as a testator or intestate, when all the issues are resolved, the surviving spouse is to receive 50 percent and the rest of the property divided equally among the children.[53] This is important because in some Cameroon communities the family of the deceased still claims rights over the property and leaves the widow and her children with few resources. Churches should work with their communities to condemn these practices as unbiblical and a violation of the Cameroon penal code.

HIV/AIDS Calls for Bold Leadership at Denominational Level

In the previous section, I have argued that local churches ought to undertake the bulk of the work being done on HIV/AIDS prevention because local churches in Africa now carry a greater burden of the crisis. In this section I discuss praxis that should take place at the denominational level.

First, leaders of Christian denominations should prioritize programs to combat HIV/AIDS by providing spiritual, medical, technical, and logistical support to member churches. Medical services should continue to provide palliative care and work to introduce antiretroviral treatment into their over-all treatment and prevention program. Theological institutions and the educational institutions of every denomination should include HIV/AIDS in their curriculum.[54] Additionally, seminary and Bible college students should take mandatory courses in medical anthropology. These courses, as part of a comprehensive study of HIV/AIDS and other infectious diseases, should be an important aspect of pastoral training, discussing religious perspectives on disease, healing, and different approaches to healing. Each denomination could adopt its own theological rational for such a comprehensive program. In this book I have argued that the concept of the *imago dei* provides justification for an all-inclusive program to combat HIV/AIDS.

For an example of denominational leadership, I highlight the efforts of the Cameroon Baptist Convention in the struggle against HIV/AIDS. Convention leaders have supported the campaigns to promote abstinence. Dr. Dieter Lemke initiated the CBC Health Board AIDS Control and Prevention Program (CBCHB-ACP), which is now based in Mutengene, in 1999. The Health Board sent educators into the communities to sensitize the people on the issue of HIV/AIDS from 1999 to 2002, and trained new educators from 2002. Dr. Julie Stone, Dr. Thomas Welty, and Dr. Edith Welty are cochairs of the CBCHB HIV/AIDS management board. Professor Pius Tih continues to provide overall leadership and Mr. Joseph Fonyuy Nkfusai is the supervisor of the project in Mutengene. The AIDS Control and Prevention Program has eight components which include a community AIDS education program, prevention of mother-to-child transmission of HIV, tuberculosis control, orphan care (Chosen Children), support groups for people living with HIV/AIDS, MTCT Plus Program, Youth Network for Abstinence, and a program that encourages people to adopt a health-care worker.[55] The Health Board of the convention has carried out an extensive AIDS Control and Prevention Program (ACP) in the Northwest Province and is now carrying out a similar program in the Southwest Province at its health complex in Mutengene.

Community AIDS education targets youths, offers prevention information, advocates changes in behavior, trains workers, and provides sensitization through lectures, role-play, and videos. The PMCTC, which started in February 2000 with the support of the Elizabeth Glaser Pediatric AIDS Foundation, provides counseling and support to pregnant women who test positive. The Health Board also provides them medicines, supports them in their decision to raise children, and networks with other agencies working on similar issues. It plans to expand the program to six of the ten provinces in Cameroon and reach 100,000 pregnant women by 2007.[56] The TB program maintains confidential records to facilitate follow-up and treatment, with medications offered by the national TB program. The Chosen Children's program registers orphans, provides support, trains foster parents, and encourages the community to support orphans. The support groups empower those who are infected with HIV/AIDS to live positively, offer nutrition training, encourage members to engage in business activities, train them in handicrafts, work with them on health promotion, prevention of disease, and medical follow up, and provide members with strategies for political activism on HIV/AIDS issues. The mother-to-child transmission plus program monitors the health of infected women, schedules their CD4 count and other tests, and uses highly active antiretroviral treatment to treat infected women. It is a family-centered program, but is limited to only 750 people at Banso Baptist Hospital, Mbingo Baptist Hospital, and at the health center at Nkwen. The Youth Network for Abstinence encourages youths to practice abstinence before marriage and provides HIV/AIDS education. Finally, Adopt a Healthcare Worker provides AIDS medications to health care workers who need them and encourages them to join support groups.

Perhaps the most successful program implemented by the Cameroon Baptist Convention Health Board, which also involves treatment, is the Prevention of Mother-to-Child Transmission project organized as a community-based initiative (bottom-up approach) in delivery of babies. This multi-strategy program includes the training of senior counselor trainers whose responsibility it is to train health-care workers at different sites and voluntary counseling and testing of pregnant women at antenatal clinics, which provide same-day results, care for mothers, antenatal care, follow-up treatment and counseling for HIV-positive women, treatment with antiretrovirals and nevirapine to reduce the risk of transmission to the newborn baby, and training for mothers on the importance and specifics of infant feeding. As part of its strategy, the program also involves training of male partners and involves the local communities by using the services of trained birth attendants.[57]

The Health Board reports that in five years the program has been expanded from two facilities to 124 sites in six of the ten provinces of Cameroon. During that five-year period 492 counselors were trained, 79,307 women received counseling, and 91.5 percent (72,513) agreed to be tested. Of these, 8.6 percent were positive (6,255) and about 40 percent were treated with nevirapine. HIV-positive women were also encouraged to join support groups. There are now twenty-four groups with 800 mothers who receive and participate in different services. The Health Board attributes the rate of success of this program to "the bottom-up approach [which] ensures the full involvement of the community as a key component for the ownership of a PMTCT program: Opt out approach in VCT with same day rapid test results is crucial to increasing acceptability of HIV testing in ANC."[58] The activity of the Cameroon Baptist Convention Health Board is one exemplary program in Cameroon alongside the PMTCT program of the Ministry of Public Health that has 272 facilities in the country. The state has integrated its own PMTCT programs with its work on reproductive health care.[59]

Overall, the Health Board's HIV educational materials have offered basic information on the HIV virus and modes of transmission. The Health Board has also dismissed some of the false views about HIV/AIDS: that HIV is a curse from God, an American way of discouraging sex, a white man's disease; that HIV is caused by witchcraft or is a strategy to reduce population growth in Africa; that condoms are already infected; that AIDS is curable if an infected person has sex with a virgin; that it can be treated by a traditional doctor; that it is a form of Douala fever, Foumbot fever, slow poison, Musong, or typhoid.[60] What is significant here is that the evangelical Baptist convention boldly dismisses speculation that HIV/AIDS is a punishment from God. Health Board authorities stress that HIV is spread in several ways but sexual transmission is the most common. They also dismiss false views that it is spread by mosquitoes, witchcraft, and close proximity or sharing of utensils.

Cameroon Baptist Convention Health Board has distinguished between primary and secondary means of prevention. Under primary, the Health Board argues that abstinence is 100 percent effective, followed by faithfulness to one's partner, premarital testing, knowledge about HIV/AIDS, counseling and testing, and limiting sexual partners. Condom use comes a distant seventh and the guidelines encourage people to use condoms correctly and consistently for all sexual encounters. "Remember that condoms are NOT 100% effective in reducing the transmission of HIV from one person to another."[61] The list here also includes information on breastfeeding and treatment of sexually transmitted diseases, and warns people not to use mind-altering substances such as alcohol or to inherit a widow or widower. The list is progressive, and placement of condoms in the seventh position reflects the uneasiness that the church has about promotion of condoms. The secondary prevention guidelines offered by the Health Board include "living positively with the HIV virus, thus delaying the development of AIDS." [62] This section warns against reinfection through unsafe sex, advises women to avoid future pregnancies and counsels infected individuals to come to terms with their condition, join a support group, avoid intake of substances that could alter their minds, strengthen their relationship with God, and live in the hope that a vaccine or cure could come soon. People living with HIV/AIDS are encouraged to take their medication as prescribed by the physician.

The Health Board of the Cameroon Baptist Convention is not the only religious institution working to combat HIV/AIDS in Cameroon. Other religious groups are engaged in the same fight. I have highlighted the work of the Health Board because, under the leadership of Professor Pius Tih, it has demonstrated love and compassion; the leaders continue to take the message to their member churches, the public in Cameroon, and the international community. Recently, the Health Board was able to persuade the United States Agency for International Development (USAID), which had left Cameroon, to return and work with the Health Board to combat HIV/AIDS. The projects that will receive funding from USAID include prevention campaigns in seventeen other African countries, a testimony to the effectiveness of the initiatives that have been carried out by the Cameroon Baptist Convention.

The Presbyterian Church in Cameroon also has an HIV/AIDS ministry, as is evident in the publications and teaching ministry of the church. A 2004 Presbyterian youth manual carried a message from the moderator, The Right Reverend Dr. Nyansako-ni-Nku, for the church's forty-fifth Church Day Celebration. In the opening paragraph, Rev. Nku states candidly:

> In Cameroon we have the terrifying statistics that 600 people are infected every day and 25 people every hour. Officially, about 12% of our populations, i.e., about 1,800,000 people are sick of this illness. The most frightening thing about it is that this illness has no cure yet. That means that once infected whether young or old, you are certainly going to die. And many are indeed dying every day.[63]

As part of its fight against HIV/AIDS, the Presbyterian Church in Cameroon has appointed a professional health practitioner to be the AIDS coordinator for the church and recommended that all pregnant women who are seropositive be given free treatment to prevent mother-to-child transmission. The church encourages youths planning marriage to take the HIV test. Those who test positive are advised to take medications, which the Cameroon government has made available at reasonable cost.[64] Prevention committees have been organized in all the constituencies of the PCC and the church has joined the government as an active partner in the fight against HIV/AIDS. The Presbyterian Theological Seminary in Kumba offers a compulsory course on HIV/AIDS (3 credit hours) to all its students.

Rev. Nku goes on to say: "In our opinion HIV/AIDS has come to serve as a searchlight exposing certain dangerous habits and awful conditions which had become convenient for us to ignore. Now is the time to face these conditions and face them squarely in love."[65] While one cannot disagree with the perspective that HIV/AIDS requires drastic changes in lifestyle, the view that HIV/AIDS might be a wak-eup call could play into the hands of those who see the disease mainly as a punishment for sin. However, all should support Rev. Nku's call for change in beliefs and lifestyles. He argues: ". . . isn't it time we re-examine such obnoxious cultural practices of wife-inheritance? And shouldn't we think twice before we step into a polygamous marriage? In many of these situations, the carelessness of one could mean death for all."[66] Rev. Nku has called on Presbyterians to avoid discrimination and stigmatization of people living with HIV/AIDS because such prejudicial actions are sins.

He has criticized the culture of denial and silence: "We must admit that AIDS exists as a result of our recklessness and indiscipline and so we can only stop it by cleaning up our behaviour." He has reminded members of his church that HIV/AIDS has touched humanity in the area of sexuality, where they are most vulnerable. This situation invites responsibility in private morality and people ought to take care of the body, which is God's temple. With a realism that acknowledges the limitation of the church in this area, Rev. Nku argues that the church cannot cure HIV/AIDS, but members of the church can help prevent the spread by doing two things: people and especially young people should abstain from sex before marriage; married people should practice monogamy. He notes that condoms are not 100 percent safe; therefore, the church emphasizes abstinence and fidelity. Rev. Nku challenges members of the Presbyterian Church to practice pastoral care, bear one another's burden, and live in the hope of the resurrection, believing that "the bones shall rise again."

The volume in which Rev. Nku's address appears also has poems by youths warning young people about HIV/AIDS. Setah Lydia Ajeitoh has written a piece in which the narrator is AIDS, who claims that he can kill without discrimination and has made many orphans, widows, and widowers. He claims that he has chosen certain segments of society in order to bring people into his kingdom. These people are youths, teachers, drivers, musicians, uniformed officers, prostitutes, and unfaithful partners.[67] Other Presbyterian youth manuals provide information on how one can contract the HIV virus, dispel myths about how the virus is spread, detail protective measures one can take, and suggest how one relates to an infected person.

In its early response in its 2001 *Message of Hope*, The Catholic Bishops of Southern Africa appealed to people to abstain from premarital sex, and practice fidelity or monogamous relationships. The bishops added: "This is the answer, which Christ gives us. With his help we will overcome AIDS and build up a new, happy and healthy South Africa, Botswana and Swaziland."[68] The bishops stressed abstinence and fidelity; they rejected condoms because, they argued, condoms promote immorality and selfish love, and do not give complete protection from infection. They concluded that condoms would be acceptable in a marriage relation where one of the partners is already infected with the HIV virus. I wonder if the bishops' claim that the message of the gospel is all that is needed is realistic. I further wonder why a church that saw apartheid come down because of a combination of forces in collaboration with non-Christian organizations and economic institutions wants to return to a sectarian view of a global crisis! South African Catholic historian Philippe Denis has argued: "too much emphasis on abstinence and fidelity strikes one as being simplistic and narrow-minded. These campaigns take no account of the factors which lead people into behavior patterns that put them at risk, whether physiological, cultural, social, or economic."[69] Churches have an obligation to preach fidelity and hope, but denominational leaders are already aware that HIV/AIDS will have to be tackled from a variety of perspectives and direct action that goes beyond prayer and the message of the gospel.

Denominational leaders need to work with other agencies. This calls for networking with groups where the guiding principles are not doctrinal orthodoxy, but love. The church's message that Jesus saves and heals has been confronted for the first time with a serious challenge because HIV/AIDS is a world where miracles have not yet landed. Unfortunately, that world is part of our world and the domain HIV/AIDS occupies is the human body created by God. In order to heal and save that body from the ravages of HIV/AIDS, the Christian church has to supplement its interventions with programs and projects from other human institutions working on the same issues. A good example of this collaboration is the ABC (Abstinence, Be Faithful, use Condoms) prevention strategy in Uganda that was developed by religious organizations, government, and civic leaders.[70]

Ugandan Churches worked with a variety of partners including Islamic organizations, traditional religious groups, United States Agency for International Development (USAID), the World Bank, as well as the government of Uganda to mount this massive campaign. In carrying out that campaign, about 4,500 agents were trained by the churches to work in the prevention campaign by 1998. Christian denominations acceded to the distribution of condoms and this collaboration made a significant impact on the fight against HIV/AIDS; the infection rates dropped from 30 percent in 1990 to 6.1 percent in 2002. The dramatic story of Uganda's success indicates that churches and Christian organizations could accomplish much more than they do now if they work together with public and international organizations.[71] This broad-based collaboration is what denominational and ecumenical leaders who have access to information and have a national profile should initiate. It calls for humility on the part of religious leaders who encourage praying and fasting, but who must take a more realistic approach, realizing that Kevin DeCock of the Center for Disease Control (CDC), speaking of the U.S. context, was correct in saying: "You are not going to solve the AIDS crisis in a convent in Montana."[72] For Africa, denominational leaders need to take a multisectoral approach grounded in love and compassion rather than doctrinal posturing.

Third, denominational leaders should maintain a critical relationship with the state in the fight against HIV/AIDS. There are broader social and structural issues, in addition to sexual behavior, that denominational leaders should discuss with state leaders. In such a discussion, religious leaders could adopt a prophetic position about structural inequalities that force people to resort to improper relations to deal with deprivation, marginalization, and poverty. A critical engagement with state officials and non-governmental organizations that have expertise, legal resources, and the capacity to address gender imbalance and sexual violence which affects a large number of women, would be a giant step forward.

In addition to sponsoring weekly Bible study, prayer, revival meetings, and summer holiday camps, churches need to study social realities in order to address the issues of the world in which young people live their lives. Brendan Carmody conducted a study on "religious heritage and premarital sex in Zambia" and reported that a great number of young people are aware that premarital sex is wrong. Yet they also indicated in their responses that premarital sex is acceptable if partners use a condom or intend to marry each other.[73] The study revealed, further, that youths admire those who have premarital sex, although they believe that boys and girls should remain virgins before marriage. Boys had their first intercourse between thirteen and nineteen years of age, and in some cases the age was as low as five to fifteen for girls. The survey provides insights into the prevalence of premarital sex among youths who already know that it is not acceptable in their religious community. Youths engage in premarital sex for many reasons: they desire a new experience, are overwhelmed with peer pressure, have a lack of guidance, wish to prove they are adults, or because both cannot control their desires.[74] Therefore, "where churches encourage their members to use condoms, clearly their moral imperative to avoid premarital sex is undermined."[75] This conclusion reflects the data that was gathered, but remains problematic because it does not address the fact that premarital sex is a big issue regardless of whether one uses a condom or not. One could argue that one of the questions included in the survey predetermined the answer and hence the conclusions Carmody has made. For example, the youths in the survey were asked: "If a person is careful (uses condoms) is it alright to have premarital sex?" It should not surprise anyone that youths would answer in the affirmative.

However, Carmody's study shows why denominational leaders and ecumenical groups need to work with the state to address situations that contribute to premarital sex, such as economic pressures and weak support from parents and schools. Carmody suggests that churches need to exert influence on the media to cut down advertising of condoms, provide peer education, and peer support. In order to address the economic problems, churches might have to increase their services and come up with a "a program to combat severe economic hardship forcing young girls into prostitution."[76] Carmody's conclusions that young people will still have premarital sex ought to be a signal for the church that proclaiming that Jesus Christ is the only solution to HIV/AIDS is not working. Rather than ask media to limit the advertising of condoms, denominational leaders should take action on the side of life and advocate the use of condoms as part of an overall safe sex for life campaign.

The time has come for denominational leaders also to work with social services and legal experts on a program that would address the problem of child sexual abuse. In a context where children have sex at age eleven, denominational leaders *must* work with legal experts and legislators to develop new legislation that would declare the age of consent at eighteen and effectively criminalize sex with all children below the age of eighteen. This calls for a massive grassroots campaign and delicate and firm negotiations with chiefs and traditional rulers to solicit their blessing and support for the drafting and passing of such a law and related acts to protect the rights of children, especially girls. If laws are passed that set the legal age of consensual sex at eighteen, religious communities might go a long way in creating a climate where responsible negotiations can take place between sexual partners. Such a legal tool could bolster the efforts aimed at helping youths postpone their first sexual experience.

Opponents of such legislation might see it as a new way of policing sexual desire. Others might argue that in advocating such legislation, churches are infringing on the rights of people to choose their sex partners freely. Still others could argue that such a ban would only delay marriage or sexual activity and, eventually, exposure to the risks of HIV. But if such legislation were in force, the statistics would be reporting that young females from age eighteen to twenty-four have the highest level of infection rather than fourteen- and fifteen-year-olds, as is the case in many countries. At age 18, and with further education, a woman might be empowered to negotiate safe sex more easily than at age eleven.

However, in light of growing violence against girls and the risks of being infected with the HIV virus, which young people face on a daily basis, the church and the rest of the community have high stakes in such legislation. No legislation, though, will provide a magic bullet that transforms the fight against HIV/AIDS. Instead, such action should be part of a comprehensive program that uses all structures of society to prevent new infections. Christian denominations have the resources to mount a national and regional campaign that individual congregations do not have.

Christian denominations should fight stigmatization and discrimination against people living with HIV/AIDS. Discrimination diminishes a person's dignity, ignores, and disrespects the *imago dei*. It creates boundaries on grounds that are unscientific and irrational. Stigmatization and discrimination destroy proximity to the other, an important relational component of intersubjective relations. Such boundaries may give individuals a false sense of security but they circumscribe rather than expand the horizon of the other and severely undercut one's ability to thrive in his or her immediate environment. An exclusionary subjectivity eradicates the benefits that could accrue from community and destroys a central component of being. Finally, discrimination against people affected by the HIV/AIDS pandemic is a form of judgment against them. In light of the discrimination many people living with HIV/AIDS face, one could rightly say that denominational leaders have often joined the broad conspiracy of silence.

Religious leaders who take a prophetic stand should remind African political leaders that they have constitutions that guarantee the human rights of all citizens. Nearly all African governments have established Commissions on Human Rights and Freedoms and have signed the African Charter of

Rights and Freedoms as well as the United Nations Declaration of Human Rights. Yet they have failed to put in place mechanisms to enforce the prohibition against discrimination against people living with HIV/AIDS. Religious leaders and their communities have a moral obligation to work with the state to eradicate discrimination against people living with HIV/AIDS. At the World Council of Churches consultation in Nairobi in 2001, African Church leaders acknowledged that discrimination is a major problem and declared: "the most powerful contribution we can make to combating HIV transmission is the eradication of stigma and discrimination; a key that will, we believe, open the door for all those who dream of a viable and achievable way of living with HIV/AIDS and preventing the spread of the virus."[77] Denominational leaders could translate these lofty desires into reality by teaching through their example: working with families, visiting, interacting, and openly embracing those who are living with HIV/AIDS.

Christian denominations could work with elected officials to pass non-discrimination legislation, monitor compliance with such legislation by government agencies and the public. Churches and affiliated organizations may not have any enforcement authority, but they can work to ensure that justice is done where antidiscriminatory legislation is violated. One objection to this proposition might be that the churches would be in the business of legislating morality, or forcing people into a situation where some feel, justifiably or not, that they might be exposed to the risk of infection with a deadly disease. Were there any medical evidence that casual contact could transmit the HIV virus to a person who was not previously infected, then one would be concerned that mingling freely could pose a threat to the uninfected people. There is no indication that anyone has ever contracted the HIV virus through causal contact. Therefore denominational leaders should address the discrimination against people living with HIV/AIDS that is rampant in many countries in Africa.

Leaders should also work with their constituencies to restructure their educational and social services to address the HIV/AIDS pandemic. Churches in Africa have contributed significantly to education in two ways. First, churches provide education within the church that is often called "Christian education." In Christian education, the church seeks to educate its members about the rudiments of its faith, its practices, and procedures, questions that deal with the daily experience of the members of the congregation. This pastoral and prophetic ministry provides spiritual resources to Christian communities. But churches also provide education to the public through primary, secondary, and sometimes university level classes.

Churches run schools that meet state standards because they follow a curriculum that is suggested by the ministry of education. In the Northwest and Southwest Provinces of Cameroon, churches operate primary schools, secondary schools, and high schools. Such church schools as Cameroon Protestant College in Bali; Sasse College; Saker Baptist College in Limbe; Sacred Heart Mankon; Presbyterian Secondary School and play a major role in the educational system of the country. These schools, along with state schools, should be spaces for innovative and honest education on the HIV/AIDS crisis that goes beyond the rituals of morning devotions, pep talks, or special projects by members of a gospel or medical team.

Students in these institutions have heard of HIV/AIDS. In a recent study in the Bamenda urban area, the students I surveyed all told me that they know someone who has died of the disease. Most of their information about the disease comes from occasional lectures and visits by health-care officials or religious crusades during which the ministers preach to them about abstinence. These measures are all good, but it is necessary to integrate teaching about HIV/AIDS into the curriculum of church schools at all levels. Such a curriculum should include sex education, and courses on human sexuality. Those classes should address the mystery, beauty, and responsibility of human sexuality. Courses should present medically and scientifically sound information as well as interreligious perspectives on sexuality. A broad educational curriculum should also include courses on reproductive health for women and girls.[78] The dangers of STDs should be communicated clearly and a special effort should be made to provide updated information on HIV/AIDS on a regular basis—not only when the school chaplain speaks, or when a gospel team visits the school. Education should deal honestly with the advantages of condom use. Young women should not only be taught how to resist advances from sugar daddies but also be given skills to fight sexual aggression of all kinds. Making HIV/AIDS education a central component of the educational life of the schools would continue to remind young people of the dangers of the disease.

Education in church schools should promote tolerance. School administrators should work hard to prevent discrimination against children whose families have been affected by HIV/AIDS. This should be part of a broad culture of respect for the dignity of all people that students learn on a regular basis. In addition to religious creeds and pledges of allegiance, schools could write new codes of mutual respect which all students and parents would find appealing. Such statements would not have to be long: they could be recited each morning and afternoon to make sure that pledges to respect all people become part of the thought process of every student. In order to avoid any possibility of this slipping into indoctrination, a team of experts should study pledges carefully to make sure that they are devoid of doctrinal content and address only human dignity, regardless of the religious orientation of each student. Schools could also develop a zero tolerance policy and put in place severe sanctions for all who violate this policy. Instructors and administrators should also be taught to handle sexual violence appropriately.[79]

Finally, children infected with the virus should be supported to stay in school without calling any attention to them or exposing them to stigmatization. Financial assistance should be provided to students who have lost one or both parents to HIV/AIDS. Education authorities and denominational leaders should organize special fundraising activities dedicated to this cause.

Nourishing the *Imago Dei*: Bible Reading in Light of HIV/AIDS

In addition to asking what can be done within the local church and at the denominational level, one has to consider what role the Bible plays in the midst of an HIV/AIDS pandemic. Bible reading provides inspiration to many people living with HIV/AIDS in Africa and around the world. There is a new longing for the Bible in Africa in the wake of massive economic difficulties. New Bible churches are springing up everywhere and Bible studies organized by these new churches challenge the attitudes of the older established churches. The new churches hold two or more services during the week where the leaders teach and preach the Bible. Everywhere I travel when I am in Cameroon, I hear people refering to the Bible and quoting Bible passages. Pentecostal religious traditions have not only revitalized interests in Bible reading but popularized the Bible through contemporary religious music with mostly biblical lyrics.

Biblical scholar Musa Dube has argued that the church should read the Bible in light of HIV/AIDS because the disease attacks life and the very idea that God created human life.[80] HIV/AIDS has created fear and a great sense of vulnerability because there is no cure and also has affected social relations at all dimensions.[81] Dube also has included HIV/AIDS in the curriculum at the University of Botswana as she teaches the synoptic gospels and their narrative of the healing miracles of Jesus.[82] Dube advocates an African hermeneutics of enculturation, liberation, and feminist reading of the Bible. She also suggests a thematic approach to Bible study where participants study themes such as "life, sickness, compassion, healing, fear, hope, sin and forgiveness, widows, orphans, advocacy/prophets and human sexuality."[83]

The Bible should not be used by Christian leaders only to scold people. Rather, members of faith communities should appropriate biblical narratives that shape and inform human experience in time of difficulties. I do not imply that where the narrative calls for a critique of improper use of human sexuality that the Christian church should not use it that way. If one takes a broader perspective, however, the texts of the Hebrew Bible and the New Testament affirm life and provide guidance for life. Unfortunately, the church has tended to use the Bible to admonish, scold, and show people how far they have fallen from the will of God. This is an approach that does not build up people.

A remarkable alternative has been developed in South Africa. Gerald West describes a solidarity project at the Institute for the Study of the Bible and Worker Ministry Project (ISB&WM) located in the school of theology at the University of Natal in Piertermaritzburg. This project invites people living with HIV/AIDS to meet together to build a sustainable community where they will offer mutual support, give each other hope, and reach out to other communities.[84] Such initiatives, along with the work of Dube and other scholars, are encouraging the church to appropriate the Bible thoughtfully and deal with the HIV/AIDS crisis faithfully: I believe that they strike the right chord.

The question still remains: What can one say about HIV/AIDS in biblical terms when the linguistic subtlety of the text and the cultural context of the narratives in the Bible do not apply easily to what we know about HIV/AIDS? Johanna Stiebert addresses this problem by exploring the meanings of illness and healing in the Bible.[85] According to Stiebert, the Hebrew Bible claims that Yahweh is in control and sometimes inflicts and takes away illnesses. Such passages have been misinterpreted to argue that HIV/AIDS is a punishment from God.[86] Siebert highlights two texts that remain pivotal in the formulation of a Christian understanding of illness: the story of Job and a question which the disciples asked Jesus in John 9:2. In the first instance, Satan proposed to test Job to show that Job's faithfulness would falter if he lost his wealth and his health. When Job became ill, his friends came to him and suggested that he was suffering because he had sinned and that he needed to repent in order to experience healing. Job maintained his innocence and in the end he was healed and proclaimed his confidence in God as his redeemer. In the second passage, from John 9:2, the disciples brought to Jesus someone who was blind from birth and asked who committed the sin that led to the tragedy that this individual was born blind. This question indicated the disciples' assumption that the blindness was a punishment for sin. This is the view that many Christians expressed when they thought that

HIV/AIDS was limited to people who practiced a certain lifestyle. In both cases, the narratives suggest that the illness did not result from any sin, but came to manifest the glory of God.

Still, these texts do not give us any clue to dealing with HIV/AIDS. In the case of Job, we are told that Job was tested by Satan in what was a bet between him and God to establish if Job was an upright man or not. Although Job proclaimed that his redeemer (God) lives at the end of his ordeal, one cannot help but wonder if he is not the victim of some power play between God and Satan. Job's story does not give people living with HIV/AIDS any help on how to understand their disease. For one thing, most people infected with the virus innocently have not lived to proclaim that their redeemer is alive, although one could argue that they could learn a lesson from Job's patience.

In the case of the man who was born blind, Jesus told the disciples that this happened for the glory of God. The idea again is that certain things, including human tragedy, bring glory to God. One cannot conclude that God operates that way all the time. Furthermore, one might want to do a little probing to ask how God is glorified through a such tragic situation. The real question here is: Would God knowingly inflict pain like the HIV/AIDS pandemic in order to get glory? I doubt it! In both stories, we are dealing with individuals, although in the case of Job, he lost his entire family and animals. However, with HIV/AIDS, we are talking about the suffering of millions of people. It seems to me safe to say that we have no strong biblical models on which to construct a theology of HIV/AIDS.

Perhaps the only way one could link illness to sinfulness in the Bible is the general sense in which the Christian tradition emphasizes that this world is a fallen world. Since we live in a less than perfect world , we are constantly subjected to different kinds of problems. These in turn affect our health. Furthermore, the activities of others in a fallen world can cause us to become ill. When we are confronted with these realities, one cannot say conclusively either that God is punishing people for sins they might have committed or that these things happen so that God would be glorified. Illness is just one of the things people experience as they live in a fallen world. On the other hand, Christians still face tough questions when it comes to illness that results from sexual contact, especially when that sexual contact takes place outside the bonds of marriage. The temptation, as I have pointed out already, is to conclude that these illnesses, especially HIV/AIDS, are punishment from God because the Bible prohibits fornication. The problem here is that we are dealing with the spread of the disease in high-risk situations. In such high-risk situations, someone may indeed suffer because he or she has engaged in "high-risk behavior." But we certainly do not have any basis for a conviction that the millions of people living with HIV/AIDS are being punished for their sins.

Biblical scholars have several questions to address if they are to come up with a theological understanding of this particular disease. Does the Bible give us enough information to conclude that God actually inflicts people with a disease like HIV/AIDS? To answer yes to such a question requires an epidemiological, phenomenological, and theological study of the HIV virus that might call for an examination of the first HIV infection. If one could determine who the first infected patient was and identify the kind of sin this person committed, one could then begin to speculate that HIV/AIDS is a punishment from God. Until such a determination could be made, any notion that HIV/AIDS is a punishment from God is groundless. Even if such a phenomenology of the disease were to lead a researcher to theorize that the "original" HIV virus was sent from God as a punishment for sin, such a position would not answer all our questions. For instance, which sin did God target? Why did God choose that particular sin, and why did God decide to strike with a disease that is deadly and not with any other disease that is curable? If God indeed chose to strike sinners with this particular disease, why did God ignore other sins that have greater impact on many people such as hatred, discrimination, injustice, corruption, dictatorship, and marginalization of other members in the society? What was particularly terrible about a particular sin that made God choose to inflict the world with a disease that is silently killing millions of people? Perhaps the most touching question would be to ask: Why did God not choose to punish the sinner alone without passing the effect of that punishment to thousands of babies born to infected mothers?

My point is, rather than search the Bible to justify the view that HIV/AIDS is God's punishment or to claim that there is specific information on how to address HIV/AIDS, the church ought to plead ignorance. In pleading ignorance, Christians are not claiming that one cannot know anything about HIV/AIDS. Instead, such a position states only that one does not know the origin of the HIV/AIDS virus and that to attribute it to God would be playing God. This position does not mean that people ought to use their ignorance of the disease's origin to justify careless behavior. Most communities around the world actually have information on how HIV is transmitted and how it is spreading throughout Africa: the majority of infections in Africa come from heterosexual sexual contact.

In pleading ignorance about the origin of AIDS, neither the church nor individuals can plead ignorance to steps one can take to avoid spreading the disease. The church in Africa cannot tell its young people to go on, enjoy life, and live as if nothing is wrong. The church has a responsibility in teaching responsible sexual behavior. The church needs to work in partnership with public health specialists, physicians, and researchers who work with infectious diseases. In doing so, the church ought also to continue to unmask the oppressive structures that have made the spread of the disease possible. It is imperative that the community encourages individual responsibility, mindful of the fact that HIV/AIDS occurs in a context where structural injustice exists. Therefore, the Christian church that calls for individual responsibility also has a great obligation to advocate for social justice.

The church as a community ought to read the Bible and other sacred texts of its tradition with humility. Christians ought to be cautious about what they say about the origins of HIV/AIDS. It seems to me that for the Christian community and people living with HIV/AIDS, reading the Bible in the light of the pandemic is useful for a number of reasons. First, close meditation on such a troubling experience reflects the *koinonia* (community, fellowship, partnership). As a *koinonia*, the church shares the word of God together. God uses these ancient texts to give examples of perseverance to individuals and religious communities. Although the texts do not give any specific guidance for dealing with an illness like HIV/AIDS, they remind members of the church that they have a responsibility to care for one another in times of difficulty. The biblical narratives remind the community of the struggles other people have gone through in their spiritual journey, and invite readers to copy the examples of faith and courage demonstrated by those who have suffered greatly. The narratives of the Bible also provide Christian communities with additional resources and supporting materials for an ethical engagement with the world. Furthermore, the Bible reminds Christians, as a *koinonia*, that the body of Christ is a worldwide communion, and that, when one part of the body suffers, all parts suffer.

Reading the Bible together as a church also gives hope to people who know that here on earth death still has its sting. People living with HIV/AIDS know that they could be living with a terminal disease if there is no vaccine in place soon. Yet this is a terminal disease that moves slowly, as if using that pace to remind one that death is still a threat in this material world. In the experiments with Bible reading engaged in by Dube in Botswana and West in Pietermartizburg, people living with HIV/AIDS have received support, encouragement, and hope to live their lives in full without fear. They have said no to desperation.

This is also the message given by The AIDS Support Organization (TASO), one of the first African-based non-governmental organizations dedicated to educating people about HIV/AIDS. It is a challenging thing to live every day knowing that you have in your body a deadly virus that will continue to destroy your immune system and that some day, barring the discovery of a vaccine, that virus will overcome your immune system and you will succumb to death. Yet in such a state, people around the world have turned to the narratives of the Bible to find hope and confidence to make each day count.

Several years ago Ron Russell-Coons of the Metropolitan Community Church in San Francisco talked of finding hope in the Word of God. He quoted Saint Paul's Second Letter to the Corinthians where Paul admonished people: "So we do not lose heart. Even though our outward nature is wasting away, our inward nature is being renewed day by day. For this slight momentary affliction is preparing us for an eternal weight of glory beyond all measure" (2 Cor 4:16-17).[87] For many people infected in Africa who know that they will die if a vaccine is not discovered during their lifetime, nothing can be more comforting from the Christian tradition than knowing that inwardly they can be renewed each day. As the physical expression of the *imago dei* wastes away, the only encouragement they can have is to know that God can and does provide inner renewal to all of God's children. However, in order for that assurance to take root, it is necessary that the community that is called to gather in the name of God act now in multiple ways to provide a welcoming and nurturing space for all people living with HIV/AIDS in Africa and around the world.

Chapter 5

The Church, Globalization and HIV/AIDS

<hr>

We are all human, and the HIV/AIDS epidemic affects us all in the end. If we discard the people who are dying from AIDS, then we can no longer call ourselves people. The time to act is now. We can make a difference.

—Nelson Mandela[1]

An effective AIDS vaccine remains the world's best chance to reverse this relentless epidemic. But the search for a vaccine must not come at the expense of our immediate response . . . we must do it as part of a truly comprehensive response.

—Mitchell Warren[2]

The remarks by Nelson Mandela invite the international community to respond to HIV/AIDS in the age of globalization.[3] In this chapter, I explore the concept of globalization and its relationship to HIV/AIDS and argue that the Christian community worldwide needs to respond to global changes and advocate for a "truly comprehensive response," as Mitchell Warren argues, to the AIDS crisis: new forms of treatment, research and development of vaccines, and international collaboration in fighting against the disease in the African context. In the first section, I discuss the idea and inescapability of globalization, and then examine the international response to HIV/AIDS. I next argue that the *imago dei* provides a ground for the Christian community in Africa to scale up its response to HIV/AIDS by fighting for universal access to treatment. I will then argue that the Christian community should support the search for new treatments and for a vaccine, listen critically to cure claims, and support debt relief for African countries to enable the funding of HIV/AIDS programs. My larger objective is to challenge all communities of discourse to work together at a time of great stress in the human community. Churches must intensify their fight against HIV/AIDS because they recognize that human beings are created in the image of God. Jeffrey Sachs and Sonia Sachs have said: "Africa is the place where we will confront our own humanity, our morality, our purposes as individuals and as a country."[4] All the peoples of the global community share a common humanity, although cultures, symbols of faith, and political systems differ.

The Prospects and Problems of Globalization

The Christian community in Africa needs to adopt a critical yet supportive stance toward globalization, a concept that refers to concrete historical processes, socioeconomic realities, and more recent linkages and interconnectedness within the human family. Globalization is real, a promising development to some but deceitful, oppressive, and perilous to those who have looked in vain for the profits of this new revolutionary praxis of the free market and other social relations.[5] It is an expansive praxis of modernity and postmodernity that promotes interdependence in order to enhance market profits and global well-being.[6]

Supporters of globalization flaunt the success of free market competition and technological developments in a global village where liberal economic and political doctrines dominate. Economic liberalization, which facilitates globalization, has dissolved artificial economic frontiers and created a global marketplace where transnational production and financing of goods and services determine economic activity and hold out the promise of economic recovery in poor countries. Advances in technology have simplified complex economic transactions across the globe. Amartya Sen has argued: "The predicament of the poor across the world cannot be reversed by withholding from them the great advantages of contemporary technology, the well-established efficiency of international trade and exchange, and the social as well as economic merits of living in open, rather than closed societies."[7] Thus, an important aspect of globalization is the new technology that has promoted international trade and encouraged an open and beneficial free market economy.

While the articulations of these processes are recent, international connections, with their attendant concerns, have been with us for a while.[8]

Christian communities in Africa cannot ignore globalization; it is all around us, represented by the growing McDonaldization and MTVization whose "infotainment" extends popular and consumer culture from the West to the world. Globalists support the internationalization of business on grounds that it promotes efficiency in production, creates opportunities for people to improve living standards, and promotes democratic ideals around the world. One impact of globalization is evident in recent migrations from countries in the south to the north, a trend that accelerated in the last decades of the twentieth century because of severe economic decline in the developing world. Recent migrations confirm Anthony Giddens's view that globalization is an intensification of social relations.[9] Finally, technology has intensified globalization by facilitating international communication. The CNNization of the world has created a global television audience and computer technology in a digital age has dramatically compressed the world to the click of a computer mouse. One can now communicate and do business around the world without leaving one's home.[10]

Economic liberalization has produced economic growth in India, China, Mexico, Vietnam, and in Uganda. The global economy has grown tremendously at a time when world population has doubled in less than 100 years.[11] The United Nations Development Program, (UNDP) estimated the global economy in 1998 to be at U.S. $30 trillion.[12] The Gross Domestic Product (GDP) of the world has quadrupled, standards of living have risen in many countries, and more people today have sufficient income to buy a variety of consumer goods. While these benefits have come to many nations, the nations of Africa and other areas of the developing world have been largely left out. Poverty has actually risen in the least developed countries. In 1998, UNDP estimated that about 841 million people were malnourished, 880 million without adequate health services, one billion did not have adequate shelter, 1.3 billion people did not have access to safe drinking water, two billion did not have electricity, and 2.6 billion did not have good sanitation.[13] Around the world, poverty has increased the prevalence of child labor in a variety of industries, including sex work. The rise of poverty has also increased mortality rates in many countries. It is estimated that 50,000 people die each day of illnesses related to poverty, the common ones being measles, pneumonia, and diarrhea.[14] If globalization means economic growth and well-being, then the people who live in the least developed countries have not experienced that growth.

In Africa, President Thabo Mbeki of South Africa has championed globalization and called on African states to embrace it so that they will not be left behind.[15] Economist S. Ibi Ajayi argues that Africa's economic isolation has resulted in its political marginalization.[16] African states must accordingly practice open trade to maximize their comparative advantage and have access to foreign direct investment and new technologies. These initiatives may succeed if African states institute sound economic policies, use untapped economic resources profitably, stabilize transaction costs in global trading, and restore Africa's competitive position. It will take some time for such changes to take place, however, because of the debt burden, economic decline, and the economic problems associated with the HIV/AIDS pandemic.

Globalization is not linked to a particular institution, but the World Bank (WB), the International Monetary Fund (IMF), and the World Trade Organization (WTO) influence and provide ideological support for the effort. Critics charge that globalization is an imperial project aimed at the conquest of goods, culture, and even symbolic capital.[17] The agenda of globalization has forced the heavily indebted poor countries to comply with the reforms designed by the WB and the IMF.[18] Critics contend that growth generated by markets has also created unfair distribution of income between the rich and poor countries. Prioritizing market freedoms ignores the possibility that a market-driven agenda could be used to constrain human freedoms where they infringe on profits. Furthermore, a market-driven economy promotes accumulation and consumption, and exaggerates self-interest at the expense of communal interests. Finally, critics charge only transnational corporations—especially large pharmaceutical companies that control the drugs that hold the key to survival for many, including people living with HIV/AIDS in the developing world—have benefited from free markets.[19] These transnational corporations dictate policy in rich countries and control the resources of poor countries.[20]

Christian communities should maintain a critical stance toward global economic developments because, although the market may indeed hold the key to global growth, it has not worked so far for many African countries. Foreign Direct Investments (FDI) in Africa have declined despite the fact that macroeconomic policies have attempted to liberalize the economy. African countries lack capital because of a low savings rate. Many African states depend on the export of primary products. These hurdles have undercut Africa's ability to compete in the new global economy on an equal footing.[21] African states have a long road to go before they stabilize their macroeconomic environment, invest in human capital and develop an economic infrastructure that would strengthen the private sector and enable them to benefit from global trade.[22]

Since the gap between the rich and poor countries has actually widened, Simeon Ilesanmi has argued that "globalization as both a facilitator of material prosperity and a response to its unequal distribution, constitute the core of the globalization debate."[23] Current capitalist economic arrangements favor the rich nations and work against the poor nations. Since 1995 the World Bank has demonstrated in various ways that Africa's economic condition, now compounded by the HIV/AIDS crisis, is a serious challenge to world order.[24] The debt burden of most countries in sub-Saharan Africa has exploded and they now spend more than 5 percent of the GDP, an estimated $12 billion, on debt servicing alone. Spending on social services such as education, health care, and child welfare has declined substantially; the death rate for children under five in Sierra Leone is 335 per 1,000. The irony is that parts of Africa are richly endowed with natural resources, but with little industrialization, unfair trading practices, and control of the oil wealth by large oil multinationals that have joined some African leaders in promoting corruption, African countries have seen their fortunes decline in the age of globalization. Many countries cannot provide basic health care because the health infrastructure has crumbled. There are serious implications here for the idea, logic, and praxis of globalization.

Finally, the Christian community should maintain critical engagement with globalization to check the imposition of cultural hegemony on the rest of the world through media magnets like MTV, ESPN, and especially CNN, which some observers call the sixteenth member of the United Nations Security Council because it reaches most places in the world and shapes world opinion. K. C. Abraham laments that globalization is a form of cultural imperialism seeking to "create a mono-culture . . . [through] the undermining of economic, cultural and ecological diversity, the nearly universal acceptance of a technological culture has developed in the West and the adoption of its inherent values. The indigenous culture and its potential for human development are vastly ignored."[25]

Christian communities should take seriously the criticisms of globalization, while recognizing that it is to some degree inescapable. Africans, for example, are caught up in the global spirit through popular culture. I spent the summer of 2003 in Bamenda, Northwest Province, where my sister Caroline Bongmba Nfor and her husband were my hosts. When I discussed music with my nieces and nephews, they wanted me to talk with them about Britney Spears and her music. They keep up with the details of her life. This is not a one-way street—African musicians have paraded across Western stages regularly since Cameroonian musician Manu Dibango introduced

African music to the West through his famous song, "Soul Makossa." Mega stars like King Sunny Ade, Ali Farka Toure, Mory Konte, Youssou N'Dour, and groups like Ladysmith Black Mambazo from Africa have toured the United States to critical acclaim.[26]

Global popular culture has affected the discourse on HIV/AIDS because artists have recorded songs on the subject. Of the many songs that have been recorded perhaps no single piece better reflects the global nature of HIV/AIDS than that by Congolese musician François Luambo Makiadi, also know as Franco: "Attention Na SIDA" (Beware of AIDS), which he composed and recorded in 1987, five years after the first reported cases of HIV/AIDS.[27] In the sixteen minutes that Franco warns the Congolese society and the world about the dangers of HIV/AIDS, he appeals to youths, parents, religious leaders, politicians, researchers, and governments of the rich and poor countries to join in the fight against the disease. The lyrics are in Lingala and French, and in his dialogical rendition, Franco articulates his message in French and the chorus in somber timbre sings: "Protect yourself as I protect myself, save yourself as I save myself, AIDS strikes all nations, AIDS strikes all races, AIDS strikes all ages, mothers let's beware, fathers let's beware."[28] Franco sings that this disease frightens everybody, even physicians. Today Africa is being blamed again, this time for having infected the world with HIV/AIDS. HIV/AIDS separates people from one another, and people desert their friends because of AIDS.[29] Franco warns youth, the life force of society, to protect themselves by avoiding dangerous sexual habits and having sexual relations with multiple partners. He admonishes parents not to be ashamed to talk to their children about AIDS. He calls on religious leaders not to regard AIDS as a punishment like that of Sodom and Gomorrah, but instead to pray to God to deliver humanity from this terrible disease. They should use their pulpits to preach what society needs to understand about this disease. Franco calls on researchers not to waste time debating their discoveries but to search for a cure like the geniuses of the past: Fleming, Pasteur, and Curie. He calls on governments of the world to help poor countries fight HIV/AIDS and not to proliferate arms, which are used to kill. Arguing that the real struggle in the world is the fight against AIDS, Franco states that this one struggle must mobilize us.

Globalization and the HIV/AIDS Pandemic

Critics of globalization argue that it has had a negative impact on health and health care because the global economic imbalance has caused poverty in developing countries and depleted resources needed for primary health care.[30] A. J. McMichaels and Robert Beaglehole have argued that the growing income differential among nations has weakened labor. Job insecurity has increased and wages have dropped and threatened the entire health care system. Industrial growth has caused environmental degradation and spread pollutants that have in turn contributed to the spread of diseases. Many processed foods intended to meet urban demands have also contributed to obesity, infectious diseases, and mental illnesses.[31] Further, negative effects of globalization, or what Diaz-Bonilla and others have called "spillover," include global warming, cross-border pollution, financial crises, crime, and the spread of HIV/AIDS.[32] World leaders have not delivered the promises of globalization to a world that is being devastated by the HIV/AIDS pandemic. African leaders have failed to create a climate that could nurture the ideals of globalization and a humane system of governance.[33] The rhetoric and praxis of globalization needs to be reconsidered because what has emerged is an "othering" and neglect of the poor countries that have been hit hardest by HIV/AIDS.[34] In a statement which underscores the fact that the work of liberation is not over yet, Margaret Farley has argued: "[I]f ever there was a situation in which the principle of Preferential Option for the Poor was relevant and crucial, it is difficult to think of one more dramatic than the AIDS pandemic in the South."[35] HIV/AIDS is a threat to global security from a social, economic, and medical standpoint. It is perhaps the most severe threat to food security that Africa has ever faced because it is taking away the productive capacity of African countries. The only entities that have benefited from the HIV/AIDS pandemic are the pharmaceutical companies who have already made billions of dollars and will earn more money from future sales of drugs or a future vaccine.

Global military spending has expanded greatly in the years that HIV/AIDS has become a threat to the human community. The current war in Iraq could cost hundreds of billions of dollars, but American President George Bush pledged only 15 billion dollars to fight AIDS in Africa. Although funds like the William J. Clinton Foundation and the Bill and Melinda Gates Foundation have contributed money for antiretroviral drugs, annual military spending is estimated in trillions of dollars. The Stockholm International Peace Research Institute reported in June 2004, that the U.S.-led invasion of Iraq has caused military spending to rise by 11 percent to $956 billion dollars, with the United States accounting for about 47 percent of that amount.[36] It is reported that United States military spending was $466 billion in fiscal year 2004, China, $65 billio , followed by Russia with $50 billion, and France with $45.5 billion. In Africa the top military spender was Algeria with $1.87 billion reported in 2001, followed by South Africa with $1.79 billion in 2001. Ethiopia reported $800 million in 2000; Sudan, $581 million in 2001; Nigeria, $374.9 million in 2001; Zimbabwe, $350.6 million in 2001; Botswana, $135 million in 2001; Uganda, $121.3 million in 2001; and Cameroon, $118.6 in 2000 and 2001. Even if these figures were for all the twenty years that the international community has lived with the scourge of HIV/AIDS, the numbers would still be inhumane.

UNAIDS as a Sign of Hope

Despite the shortcomings of globalization, HIV/AIDS has also mobilized the human community as no other emergency has since World War II. In June of 2001, member states of the United Nations (UN) held a special session to work out a comprehensive response to HIV/AIDS. The Declaration of Commitment, which called for greater access to treatment and care of people living with HIV/AIDS, also called on government leaders around the world to promote the use of antiretroviral drugs.[37] Delegates also pledged to strengthen health-care systems and remove barriers to antiretroviral drugs such as "affordability and pricing, including differential pricing, and technical and health-care system capacity."[38]

The Joint United Nations Programme on AIDS (UNAIDS) has become the new symbol of international compassion because it is dedicated to providing "leadership and advocacy, strategic information, tracking, monitoring and evaluation of the epidemic and responses to it, civil society engagement and partnership development; mobilization of resources to support effective response."[39] One of the most significant efforts of the international community in confronting HIV/AIDS is the International HIV/AIDS Conference, now held under the auspices of UNAIDS along with many other sponsoring organizations. Although it is expensive to attend the International AIDS Conference, AIDS activists, physicians, researchers, and policymakers have shared critical information at these meetings. The first international conference on HIV/AIDS was held in Atlanta, Georgia, April 15–17, 1985, four years after the disease was first diagnosed.[40] At the second international conference in Paris, June 23–25, 1986, it was reported that a new drug called AZT (3 azidothymidine also called Zidovudine and Tetrovir) had decreased the rate of opportunistic infections, and slowed down mortality. The U.S. Food and Drug Administration approved the drug in March of 1987. At the fourth international conference held in Stockholm, Sweden, June 13–17, 1988, Belgian researchers reported that HIV-III had been discovered in a pregnant woman in Cameroon, but this news was greeted with skepticism by other researchers. At the fifth international conference in Montreal, Canada, June 4–9, 1989, Dr. Jonas Salk reported that initial tests of his vaccine demonstrated that it was safe; however, there was very little data for members of the scientific community to reach any conclusions. At the AIDS conference in Durban in 2001, South African President Mbeki remained defiant about his doubts that the HIV virus causes AIDS, a claim that placed the leader of the most influential African country on a controversial path with AIDS activists and the medical community. The 2004 international conference, held in Bangkok, Thailand, focused on access to treatment, leading more force to the declaration of the Special UN General Session on HIV/AIDS of 2001. The 2006 International AIDS Conference in Toronto brought together researchers and leaders in the fight, like President Clinton, and Bill and Melinda Gates, to discuss the UNAIDS's new priority, universal access to health care.

Although UNAIDS has brought many organizations together and has now become one of the leading sources for information and statistics on HIV/AIDS, it has not succeeded in stemming the tide and spread of HIV/AIDS. Nor do its accomplishments reflect the global capacity to fight the disease. For example, the Global AIDS Policy Group estimated that in 1990–1991 between $7.1 billion and $7.6 billion was spent on HIV/AIDS, with about 95 percent of those dollars spent in the developed world on care and research and only 5 percent spent in the developing world, where the majority of people living with HIV/AIDS reside. In 1994 Jonathan Mann reported fragmentation in the international community and a decline in funding, personnel shortage, overlapping mandates, political intrigues, bad management, poor accountability, high overhead costs, and a bogged-down United Nations system. The situation has not changed very much because spending on HIV/AIDS is still a problem for many African countries. An earlier World Bank study, based on the estimate that about 11 million people were living with HIV/AIDS, pointed out that if all were to receive AZT, it would cost between 101 and 160 billion dollars, not counting the cost of implementing such a wide range therapy program.[41] There are no funds to undertake such a massive program. Christian communities and activists should continue to call attention to the need because it would actually be cost-effective to provide therapy to people living with HIV/AIDS, since it would offset the cost of treating HIV-related illnesses.[42]

Addressing the summit of African heads of government at Abuja, Nigeria on April 26, 2001, UN Secretary General Kofi Annan called for a global financial commitment to fight HIV/AIDS. Annan told the heads of government: "We need money. The war on AIDS will not be won without a war chest, of a size far beyond what is available so far. Money is needed for education and awareness campaigns, for HIV tests, for condoms, for drugs, for scientific research, to provide care for orphans, and of course to improve our health-care systems."[43] By November of 2003 the international community pledged $4.8 billion to the United Nations Global Fund for AIDS (UNGFA), which was created at the Genoa Summit in 2001. In the same year, $1.7 billion was paid. The world is going to need much more than has been pledged and given so far. The nations of the world must reorder their priorities and treat HIV/AIDS, not terrorism, as the primary security threat to the global system. In the case of Africa, leaders should recognize that they are what the Wimbum people call *mapqui* (bereaved mothers, who are the primary mourners). They should lead the fight against HIV/AIDS and invite the global community to join them to eliminate this disease. The global community should make funds available, maintain the right balance between research, prevention, and an accelerated treatment program, and cultivate a supportive relationship with African-based researchers.

Theological Criteria for Fighting HIV/AIDS in the Global Era

The theological motif that should galvanize the Christian community to fight HIV/AIDS in the era of globalization is the *imago dei*. Some theologians have rejected globalization because it promotes market values, privatization, and the appropriation and patenting of materials from other parts of the globe without regard to values that have held those societies together for a long time.[44] However, theologians Hans Küng and M. Douglas Meeks have contributed significantly to the search for a global ethic. Küng has argued that religious traditions could shape an emerging global ethic that is religious, open, and inclusive because the world lacks "a realistic vision of the future."[45] Küng has proposed a "minimum consensus," which calls for reciprocal humane treatment of people.[46] He has called for "a culture of nonviolence and respect for life . . . solidarity, and just economic order . . . a culture of tolerance and a life of truthfulness . . . a culture of equal rights and partnership between men and women"[47] Others have criticized Küng for grounding a global ethic on a religious foundation.[48] I do not think that a religious starting point for a global ethic is limiting if the ethic that emerges promotes mutual understanding and is devoid of dogmatic impulses.

Meeks for his part has described the world as a cosmic household and called on Christians to embrace the ancient idea of *oikonomia* (*oikos* + *nomos*, literally "household management") and to pose the question, "Will everyone in the household get what it takes to live."[49] Pre-enlightenment theology,

Meeks argues, approached economics from a relational standpoint where creation, redemption, and new creation established a new human household and organized human survival (*servivre*, "living together").[50] Meeks thinks that while the Bible cannot solve the technical problems of today, its narratives offer "a way of being in the world out of which the church can make its contribution to reshaping the 'public household.' "[51] God's *oikonomia* is eschatological because Jesus died to prepare the world as a dwelling place for God, "The Christian congregation has to eschew all dualisms that denigrate the body and nature. The whole creation is aimed teleologically toward God's Sabbath in which every creature will be reconciled, justified, and glorified and thus embodied in God's eternal life."[52] Christians ought to apply their ethic to the economy and make it sacramental. They ought also to promote justice, and "the rights of nature and human embodiment over against the modern trends toward abstract power over nature and the body."[53] Members of the political community should humanize the market because the mobility of capital has disorganized capitalism and caused "the declining effectiveness and legitimacy of nation-states which are unable to control such disorganized capitalist flows; government can no longer control the economy."[54] This has forced developing countries to live in debt and depend more and more on non-governmental organizations for essential services.[55] The extremes of wealth and poverty have divided and devastated God's *oikonomia* and the rich countries should make the political decision to restructure global economic realities. In the global *oikonomia* all members are each other's keeper.

While I share some of Küng's and Meeks's perspectives, I am convinced that the church in Africa needs to ground its engagement with HIV/AIDS in the global era on the *imago dei*. The *imago dei* makes humanity partners with God in restoring the created order. The Christian community ought to promote an open, transparent relationship on economic matters so that all inhabitants of the earth seek the common good. The moral focus of many in the global community differs from that of the Christian community, but Christians have an obligation to collaborate with UNAIDS and other groups to stop the spread of HIV/AIDS and provide treatment for people living with HIV/AIDS.

From Access to Treatments to Universal Access to Health Care

One of the acts of compassion that could bring respect to the *imago dei* affected by HIV/AIDS is for the church to join the fight for universal access to health care. The road to universal access started with a worldwide campaign for access to treatment, one of the crucial methods of fighting HIV/AIDS, which emerged as a central concern of the 2004 International AIDS Conference in Bangkok. Access to treatment remains crucial; many people living with HIV/AIDS in Africa have no access to treatments because of a lack of economic resources and the complex process of producing and marketing drugs.[56] In the past, UNAIDS has estimated that the cost of preventing HIV/AIDS and caring for orphans would grow from $12 billion in 2005 to $20 billion by 2007. This estimate reflected the cost of prevention, care, treatment, orphan support, advocacy, and administrative and other policy matters. The projection assumed that about 6 million people would be taking treatments by 2007.[57] UNAIDS predicted a shortfall by a massive $6 billion. Most people living with HIV/AIDS in African cannot afford anti-infective medications to treat opportunistic infections, or anti-cancer drugs for Kaposi sarcoma and lymphoma. There is very limited medication for palliative care, let alone antiretroviral drugs that should be taken to reduce the viral load and limit the destruction of the immune system. The World Health Organization and UNAIDS have recommended drugs for treating opportunistic infections such as isoniazide and contrimoxazole; and palliatives such as analgesics, antidiarrheals and antiretrovirals. On July 12, 2006, the United States Food and Drug Administration (FDA) announced that it had approved Atripla tablets, a fixed dose combination that is used as a single tablet that can be taken once a day, to be used together with other antiretroviral drugs. The "one-pill-once-a-day" product to treat HIV/AIDS combines the active ingredients of Sustiva (efavirenz), a Nonnucleoside Reverse Transcriptase Inhibitor (NNRTI), with Emtriva (emtricitabine) and Viread (tenofovir disoproxil fumarate), two Nucleoside Reverse Transcriptase Inhibitors (NRTIs). Emtriva and Viread are also available in a fixed dose combination known as Truvada.[58] This is a significant step forward in antiretroviral treatment in the United States.

Antiretrovirals, AZT, and NVP have been used successfully to prevent mother-to-child transmission by the Cameroon Baptist Convention Health Board and in other African countries. These therapies have improved the quality of life for some people, indicating that treatment must remain an important component of the fight against HIV/AIDS. In 2006 very few people in Africa had access to the HAART regime that has shown promise in reducing the viral load in the people who have been on it. In 2002 the Global Treatment Access Campaign (TAC) group estimated that 93 percent of the 36 million people infected with the HIV virus and living with HIV/AIDS did not have access to treatment that would let them live a full and productive life.[59] Treatment sites are available now in South Africa and

Senegal as well as other countries in Africa, although less than a million people in Africa have access to antiretroviral drugs.

The focus on treatment came on the heels of tough negotiations and fights by AIDS activists in South Africa, and campaign groups, such as Treatment Action Campaign, who demanded affordable treatment. The GlaxoSmithKline pharmaceutical company announced on April 28, 2003, that it was reducing the not-for-profit prices of its HIV/AIDS drugs to the poorest countries by 47 percent.[60] These drugs were to be sold at a reduced price to governments of the least developed countries in sub-Saharan Africa, as well as to non governmental organizations and UN agencies engaged in the fight against HIV/AIDS. At the time of GlaxoSmithKline's action, legal challenges were also brought against Boerhringer Ingelheim, because it charged excessive prices and was making a huge profit from the sale of its drugs, which activists interpreted as profits from a misfortune. The drugs concerned were Glaxo's AZT (sold under the brand name Retrovir), Lamivudine (3TC), and a combination of the two (Combivir), and Boehringer's nevirapine, manufactured as Viramune. The complainants argued that a 300mg pill of AZT cost 2.58 times the economic value; a 150mg pill of Lamivudine was 4.01 times the economic value; the combined pill with 300mg AZT and 150mg Lamivudine, 2.24 times the economic value; and a 200mg nevirapine pill, 1.7 times the economic value. The syrup form of AZT (used for treating children) was 2.27 times the economic value, and the syrup form of Lamivudine 1.97 times the economic value. Furthermore, generic antiretroviral drugs were not available in South Africa at the time because of patent laws. Pharmaceutical industries controlled the markets for drugs by treating antiretroviral medicines individually and each drug regime constituted its own market.[61]

These restrictions forced Médecins Sans Frontiéres, a party to the legal complaint in South Africa, to announce before the GlaxoSmithKline initiative that it would import generic drugs into South Africa in order to challenge the protective patent laws. Generic drugs were sold in Brazil for only $1.55 a day compared to $3.20 a day charged by pharmaceutical companies.[62] The Congress of South African Trade Unions (COSATU) joined the legal action because their findings confirmed that R450 was a reasonable price for generic drugs compared to R1000 charged by pharmaceutical companies. COSATU also stated that generic drugs were effective in fighting HIV/AIDS.[63] COSATU invoked language from the anti-apartheid struggle by calling its move a defiance campaign, and also invoked the South African Constitution, which protects the right to life and human dignity. Importing life-saving drugs then was a constitutional obligation to people living with

HIV/AIDS. Médecins San Frontiéres and COSATU dismissed President Mbeki's claim that generic drugs were toxic and called on pharmaceutical companies to issue voluntary licenses to companies to produce generic drugs in South Africa. They also argued that the R1.5 million worth of nevirapine used to prevent mother-to-child transmission donated by Boehringer would serve only 355 people a year in South Africa, a very small number out of thousands of pregnant women living with HIV/AIDS. The problem with manufacturing generic drugs was that South Africa was a signatory to the WTO Treaties on Intellectual Property Rights and had an obligation to comply with these treaties, which the U.S. and other rich nations were not willing to change.

Perterson and Obileye have argued that several factors influence drug pricing, such as research, production cost, the length of clinical trials, and the cost of advertising and distribution. However, in the United States, the federal government heavily subsidizes drug research; therefore, pharmaceutical companies often exaggerate their cost of production.[64] The major pharmaceutical companies have earned far in excess of what they invested. At the time of the debate in South Africa, it was estimated that Glaxo Wellcome had earned more than $3.8 billion from sales of AZT, 3TC, and Combivir between 1997 and 1999, while Bristol-Myers Squibb earned $2 billion from d4T and ddI during the same period. These companies used monopoly rights, restrictions to generic options, cost drivers, tariffs, taxation, and differential pricing to influence the cost of drugs that people living with HIV/AIDS need.

Concerns about access to treatment led UNAIDS and the WHO to embark on the "3 by 5" project, which was a commitment by the international community to provide treatment to 3 million people living with HIV/AIDS by 2005. In 2002 less than 30,000 people in Africa were receiving antiretrovirals, and the 3 by 5 program at that time seemed like a bold move. In 2004 it was estimated that only 150,000 had access to treatment, and by 2005, it was clear that the 3 by 5 plan had not been successful. UNAIDS has now abandoned the 3 by 5 program, arguing that in order to control the growth of the pandemic the international community must provide "universal access" which includes treatment and prevention.[65] The new focus calls on countries to promote intensive campaigns to prevent the spread of HIV/AIDS alongside aggressive treatment. This combination of aggressive prevention and treatment has shown promise in Tanzania, where it has reduced the rate of infection.[66]

The initiative to provide universal access to health care underscores the fact that if countries intensify prevention, it will enhance their ability to provide affordable treatment. It is noteworthy that UNAIDS defines prevention as a "classic 'public good' intervention that requires national governments to take the lead (including resource allocation) in building a strong response to the epidemic."[67] This makes health care a national obligation that governments cannot evade, or turn over to non-governmental and other voluntary organizations to handle. National governments can carry out this mandate effectively by reducing risk situations like "poverty, gender inequality, and social marginalization of specific populations."[68] African governments must prioritize the fight against HIV/AIDS.

To do this effectively, African governments must deal with what UNAIDS has called the drivers of HIV/AIDS in order to provide equal access.[69] States should check the erosion of community bonds that has created inequalities. State leaders should model the right beliefs, principles, and valuesas they enable members of the political community to deal with issues of identity, morality, sexuality, and illness.[70] "Cultural and religious leaders have shown that they can influence belief systems to ensure that HIV and AIDS are seen in a more positive light."[71] This is important because such perceptions would go a long way in preventing discrimination and stigmatization. States should also leverage resources—"money, leadership, human capacity, institutions, and systems" all of which have been handicapped by the collapse of the state in Africa. States should also promote specialized knowledge in three areas: biomedical research, human sexuality, and the impact of HIV/AIDS on caregivers. Finally, states should address the distribution of power and authority in the community.[72] The absolutization of political, social, and economic power has hindered attempts to address HIV/AIDS and other health issues in Africa. The UNAIDS document also discusses tough choices that African states must make.[73] The international community has an obligation to people living with HIV/AIDS and other infectious diseases around the world to monitor attempts to achieve universal access so that it will not become just another slogan, like the much publicized but unsuccessful "health for all by the year 2000."

One of the responsibilities of the Christian community in tough times is to follow new trends with an open and discerning mind. Christian communities ought to be open to the drive to achieve universal access to health for two reasons. First, Christian communities in Africa have the platform to communicate and underscore the importance of prevention and treatment to the millions who flock to their churches. They should use this platform to communicate important changes and developments taking place in the global community. Members of Christian communities trust their leaders more than they trust the political leaders of their countries or other experts in international health-care issues.

Second, Christian communities provide health services in many African communities. In the crucial area of treatment and distribution of antiretrovirals, Christian organizations like the Mission for Essential Drugs and Supplies (MEDS) in Kenya have demonstrated that Christian communities can do an excellent job of organizing and managing the distribution of essential health-care supplies and drugs. MEDS now provides drugs, medical supplies, and antiretrovirals to the Kenyan Episcopal Conference and the Christian Health Association of Kenya.[74] The Health Board of the Cameroon Baptist Convention has also distributed antiretrovirals successfully. These Christian organizations should continue to collaborate with and seek funding from international and national organizations that are engaged in the fight against HIV/AIDS in Africa. Such organizations have typically maintained better standards than state-run hospitals, and have delivered health care when state health services have collapsed.

In order to advance universal access, Christian groups that operate health services in Africa need to expand their resources by looking outside their traditional funding agencies for money and resources. Vinand Nantulya, an official of the Global Fund for AIDS, has invited African churches to apply to the fund for assistance to treat AIDS, tuberculosis, and malaria, and to redefine their missionary role. In issuing his invitation to church leaders at an HIV/AIDS summit in Nairobi, Nantulya stated: "But we are concerned that you are not in the arena."[75] I am convinced that at this time of great crisis, churches and faith-based organizations could be attractive applicants for such funding because many Christian organizations operate the only functioning medical institutions in Africa and have a history of using the money they receive judiciously.

In addition to the task of raising financial resources, churches and Christian health-care providers will face challenges in navigating the complex world of biomedicine, the powerful pharmaceutical industry, UNAIDS, the World Health Organization, the World Bank, and medical experts. The task is monumental but I believe churches are up to the task. The church in Africa has faced major challenges before. The South African church stood before what appeared as the insurmountable obstacle of apartheid and spoke truth to power. The church needs now to speak truth to power again because health-care delivery systems have collapsed. There is intensive training and testing going on now in different countries on how to provide treatment when drugs become available, but in the meantime, churches could engage their own local governments on improving the state of the health-care system in their countries.

Church leaders should also remain diligent as they engage in these negotiations and confrontations with state power. One of the best ways to remain diligent is to continue to manage their own institutions according to the highest standards. This may require reforming their services to make them more efficient, upgrading training of medical staff, and providing staff with the equipment they need to succeed in their practice and in fighting against HIV/AIDS. They should manage their resources in a transparent manner. Institutions like the Baptist Health Board in Cameroon and Kijabe Hospital in Kenya have done remarkably well under very difficult circumstances, with very few resources. The road ahead calls for greater stewardship of human and financial resources. The church cannot afford the waste that takes place in public institutions; that would amount to an abuse of the *imago dei*. Christian medical institutions in Africa now face a new crisis; many of their trained staff, physicians, nurses, and laboratory technicians are migrating to greener pastures in the wake of the massive decline in economic, social, and political life in the postneocolonial state.

In pursuing funding and support from international organizations, Christian health-care leaders should partner with non-governmental, faith-based, and private voluntary organizations to compete for funds to buy drugs. Some of these groups have experience in writing and competing for grant money in the West and could work with denominational leaders to identify donors who could give money for treatments. Christian leaders also must learn how to work with major pharmaceutical companies to get them to invest in treatment. This is a challenging prospect because they would be dealing with entities whose main interest is profit, but Christian groups should not ignore them—they represent a major source of resources in the fight against HIV/AIDS.

Finally, to be effective in promoting universal access the Christian community in Africa should work with experts to understand the complex agreements and logic involved in the negotiations for access to drugs. International patent laws that grant the owners of a patent the exclusive right to set the price for the drugs complicate the struggle. Christian leaders should partner with regional organizations such as the All African Conference of Churches, the coalition of the Episcopal Conference of Bishops of Africa and Madagascar, and the Association of Evangelicals of Africa and Madagascar, to name only a few. These organizations in turn should work with and seek advice from specialized coalitions like the Ecumenical Advocacy Alliance, an international network of Christian organizations that speak out and work for justice in global trade and in the fight against HIV/AIDS as a way of living out the Christian faith.[76] Another specialized group that has been very effective in Africa is the Nairobi-based Ecumenical Pharmaceutical Network (EPN) whose work has been crucial in the struggle to prevent HIV/AIDS and provide treatments to Christian organizations in twenty-two African countries.[77] In 2004, while welcoming President George Bush's Emergency Plan for AIDS Relief (PEPFAR), EPN raised critical issues about the plan because its provisions required that beneficiaries buy only drugs approved by the United States FDA, meaning brand name drugs. EPN pointed out that PEPFAR promoted mainly American products and such a practice could kill other drug initiatives in recipient countries. Furthermore, the provisions of PEPFAR disregarded national drug legislation in different countries, lacked long-term provision for treatments, and promoted extensive use of American skills to the detriment of local expertise and resource personnel. PEPFAR's bureaucratic bottlenecks and unilateral implementation ignored strategies put in place by the United Nations and the World Health Organization. The statement argued that PEPFAR's requirements should be revised, removing the requirement that recipient countries buy only FDA-approved drugs, addressing fears of local drug management in recipient countries, consulting and working with local partners and experts, and using relevant local data to coordinate their activities with global HIV/AIDS programs.[78]

Christian health-care organizations should network with groups like the Ecumenical Advocacy Alliance and EPN who understand international issues because access to drugs is linked to two international protocols—compulsory licensing and parallel imports—which such large ecumenical groups could provide expertise in analyzing and challenging should those provisions continue to stand in the way of universal access to health care as they have in the past. These international protocols have crystallized in the discussion on the patenting of generic drugs to facilitate access to treatment for people living with HIV/AIDS in the developing world. Compulsory licensing allows a government to negotiate with a patent holder to grant a license to another manufacturer, government agency, or third party to produce generic drugs. An example would be for GlaxoSmithKline to issue a license for a company in Cameroon to produce an HIV/AIDS drug manufactured by them under a generic name and sell it in Cameroon at a lower price. The company in Cameroon would pay royalties to GlaxoSmithKline. This arrangement would be beneficial because it makes drugs available in more countries. Compulsory licensing also contributes to lower prices for drugs because the drugs are manufactured in the country whose company acquires the license. Parallel imports refer to the practice of importing drugs from one country for resale in another country. This allows the governments to import drugs from where they can get a good price and sell the drugs at the lowest cost. Both of these provisions were part of the General Agreement on Tariffs and Trade (GATT) that is overseen by the World Trade Organization.[79]

A problematic aspect of GATT protocols for African countries is the Agreement on Trade-Related Aspects of Intellectual Property Rights (TRIPS), or the so-called Marrakesh Agreements of the World Trade Organization of 1994. These agreements endorse patent laws currently in force in the United States, which give patents for at least twenty years. Developing countries who do not have the tough patent laws the United States has, argue that these laws favor large Western corporations and do not protect biodiversity in the developing nations. TRIPS endorses compulsory licensing and parallel imports but the international community has not lived up to these agreements because rich nations and the large pharmaceutical companies have argued that implementing them would violate their patent rights and hurt profits. Cuba, Honduras, Paraguay, and Venezuela launched the debate on TRIPS when they tabled a proposal with the United Nations General Council for Intellectual Property Rights regarding the traditional knowledge of indigenous peoples. At the ministerial meeting of the WTO in Seattle, these countries demanded "the carrying out of a detailed study of how to protect the moral and economic rights relating to the traditional knowledge, medicinal practices and expressions of folklore of local indigenous communities."[80] The South East Asian Nations (ASEAN) backed their proposals, arguing that TRIPS also has relevance to pharmaceuticals. They highlighted declarations and conventions drafted by the international community on the relationship of indigenous knowledge to fauna, medicine, and human and environmental sustainability since 1988.

African states have joined the TRIPS debate, advocating local control of indigenous resources, and have argued that people who live where the resources are found ought to participate in decisions about the exploration and development of biological resources. They should also participate in attempts to preserve local knowledge and promote the equitable distribution of resources. Professor J. A. Ekpere, recounts that the Organization of African Unity (OAU), now African Union (AU) Model Law, which addressed TRIPS, raised concerns central to the issue of local U.S. corporate creativity.[81] Patents sanction corporate creativity but ignore local creativity in Africa. "This inequity does not only derogate and threaten the validity of the biological resources and knowledge system of local communities and indigenous people, but the value of their technologies, innovation and practices."[82]

Africans have an obligation to protect their biodiversity and creativity. The
OAU Model Law defined and protected the inalienable rights of Africans to
resources in their countries. Its aim was to ensure that practices that alter
natural resources also promote sustainability. In other words, the pursuit of
economic goals and sustainable development are not antithetical. Further,
economic pursuits do not have to disrupt life and endanger "seed and other
planting materials; traditional medicinal plants, the basis of health care
delivery service for a majority of African people; natural fiber and dyes, the
basis of African arts and crafts."[83] These biodiversity concerns drive Africa's
protest against the patent system, which allocates exclusive rights to multinational corporations.

The OAU Model Law also addresses cultural, moral, religious, and social
values of local communities facing challenges from the growth of science, and
the excessive commercialization of therapeutic products derived from African
resources, especially in the age of HIV/AIDS. One cannot deny that corporations and pharmaceutical companies need to make a profit; they do have to
meet their bottom line in order to play an important role in the manufacturing and distribution of drugs. Cameroonian philosopher Godfrey Tangwa has
argued: "As commercial enterprises, multinational corporations cannot be
blamed for pursuing profit as such. The question, however, is whether the
nature of the catastrophe in Africa does not require imaginative emergency
measures, where such profit pursuit can be combined with more morally sensitive global cooperation aimed at helping those in dire need and towards dis-
covering and manufacturing a cheap and affordable vaccine."[84] The issue
then is the level of profitability and not the idea of profit itself. The question
all participants in the discussion on the manufacture and distribution of
drugs should rethink carefully is whether current treaties enhance the ability
of the pharmaceutical companies to produce and distribute drugs at a reasonable price to help in the fight against HIV/AIDS. This is not the case.
Issues raised by the TRIPS debate involve much more than sustainable development; they call for justice and attention to biodiversity, sociocultural values, and a sustainable praxis that protects the rights of people and allows
nature to flourish. The global community has the capacity to develop technologies that could facilitate the extraction and management of biodiversity
products in a responsible and sustainable manner. In doing this the opinions
and concerns of local people should be taken seriously.

At the local level, religious leaders should begin to familiarize themselves
with these debates so that they can work with local elders to inform people
about ways of managing biodiversity. One local example comes to mind.
The *wotango* tree (*prunus Africana*), also called the "red stinkwood" or

"African cherry," is found in several places in Africa. Its bark is believed to have a medicinal compound useful in treating prostate problems in men. This tree faces the danger of extinction in the Southwest Province of Cameroon because many people are harvesting the bark of the tree and leaving the tree to die. People harvest the bark, grind it into powder, develop an extract out of it, and export it to Europe. In some cases, they cut down the entire tree to make it easy to strip the bark. When this bark was identified thirty years ago, a French pharmaceutical company acquired the license to extract the substance. The license was terminated in 1985, and the Cameroon government gave licenses to local businesses. Bark collection has escalated out of control with no concern for regeneration.

The paramount chief of the Bakweris, His Highness Chief Sam Endeley, says that a mafia network oversees clandestine collecting, harvesting, and exporting of the bark. Thye collect these barks because there are no jobs for them in Cameroon. They further blame the Cameroon government, which they argue is corrupt, for failing to control the collection of the barks. When Plantecam, the company that processes the bark, carried out operations in the area, they raised seedlings and distributed them to local people to start their own plantations of *wotangos*.[85] Such an exercise had the potential of prolonging the life of the *wotango* tree, but the plant has been sold to the Cameroon Baptist Convention Health Board. This is a welcome development because the Health Board is using it to manufacture some treatment products and has also opened the facility to researchers from the Centers for Disease Control in Atlanta.

The threat to the *wotango* tree is just one example of the threat to bio-diversity. What is disturbing in this particular case is that locals are perpetuating the destruction. This strengthens the argument that negotiations on TRIPS and other international protocols dealing with the protection of the environment cannot remain at the level of state officials. Local religious leaders could also work with the rulers of the area to ensure that the tree is not harvested to extinction, especially on Mount Fako, where some of the barks are harvested because it is a sacred site. Resources like the *wotango* bark are sources of drugs that enhance quality of life. However, churches cannot defend human health at the expense of our common habitat with nature, whose resources are agents of life.

Support for Vaccine Research, Trials, and Listening to Cure Claims

The African church could play a key role in the fight against the HIV/AIDS pandemic in the area of research on vaccine development and drug trials.

Churches and their health institutions should support these developments and follow the debates about cure claims in their area as part of their overall effort to enhance social and economic justice. Since HIV/AIDS erupted, financial resources have been allocated for research and development of new therapies and vaccines. The Christian community must support the search for new therapies, especially research to produce a vaccine, because this is probably the best hope the global community has for preventing new infections. The cost of treatment is prohibitive and millions of people infected with the virus do not have any access to treatments.

Several organizations promote and monitor vaccine research and development, including UNAIDS, the International AIDS Vaccine Initiative (IAVI), AIDS Vaccine Advocacy Coalition (AVAC), and Alliance for Microbicide Development (AMD). Mitchell Warren describes AVAC as a community of activists from all backgrounds. It was formed in 1995 and "uses education, policy analysis and advocacy to accelerate the ethical development and global delivery of vaccines against HIV/AIDS. AVAC is committed to translating and communicating this long, complex web of activities to a wider constituency and to ensuring that the rights and interests of trial participants, eventual vaccine users and communities are fully represented and respected in the process."[86] IAVI was established to foster the development of a safe, effective, accessible and preventive HIV vaccine for use around the world, and to promote the global search for HIV vaccines.[87] Researchers have made some modest progress since 1995, and testing of some drugs and vaccines is taking place in different countries around the world. Funding for these important research activities has increased sevenfold.[88]

Advocates for a vaccine remind us that if we are going to survive the scourge of disease, we must make the twenty-first century the "biology century." Scientists tell us that the road to an effective vaccine is a long one. This is not unusual: the search for a vaccine for typhoid took one hundred and five years; haemophilus influenza, ninety-two years; pertussis, eighty-nine years; polio, forty-seven years; measles, forty-two years, and hepatitis B, sixteen years.[89] It is going to take concerted effort and enormous financial commitments by the international community to acquire an effective vaccine. The scientific community is optimistic. Current research targets cellular immune responses that depend on two immune cells, the cytotoxic T-lymphocytes (CTLs or CD8+ T-cells) or so-called killer cells that destroy infected cells in the body.[90] The other cells are CD4+ T-cells, also called helper cells, that assist the CD8+ T-cells by coordinating the immune response. The notion of immunity itself has been part of the scientific vocabulary for over a thousand years and has been used in many parts of the world.[91] While researchers argue that the global community cannot expect to eradicate HIV infections with a vaccine alone, they also indicate that if vaccines were 30–50 percent effective, they could still reduce new infections to the extent that if one quarter of the population received effective vaccines, the rate of infection could drop by half in twenty years.[92] Based on projections from UNAIDS, IAVI argues that if the level of treatment continues as it is today, it might level at 80 percent coverage by 2012. IAVI assumes that if a vaccine is available by 2015, this might be the global scenario. If there were no vaccine by 2030, annual HIV infections would stand at 10.2 million.[93] However, in a low scenario case where a vaccine were 40 percent effective and given to 20 percent of the populations, it could reduce the rate of infection to about 7 million in 2030 and prevent 19 million new infections between 2015 and 2030. In their medium scenario, IAVI estimates that if a vaccine were 60 percent effective and administered to 30 percent of the population it would reduce annual infections by 54 percent to 4.7 million by 2030, preventing 47 million infections between 2015 and 2030, the simulation period. If researchers were able to achieve a 95 percent efficacy and the vaccine were administered to 40 percent of the population, they project that it could reduce the pandemic by about 82 percent in 2030 and prevent over 71 million new infections in fifteen years—that is the total number of infections since the pandemic started nearly twenty-five years ago. In Africa, researchers predict that even at the medium level, a vaccine would prevent about 2 million infections each year.[94] If a vaccine becomes available, IAVI estimates that about 260 million people could be vaccinated in five years, although no one knows what this will cost.[95]

Unfortunately, for many, the several years wait before a vaccine is available may be too long. With the current rate of treatment, many people will succumb to HIV complications. The cost of research and implementing a vaccine program in the developing world is not yet known. IAVI estimates that the current thirty candidates for testing cost about $600 million each year. In the United States, the National Institute of Allergy and Infectious Diseases (NIAID) of the National Institutes of Health (NIH) reported in May 2000 that great progress had been made on HIV vaccine development.[96] On World AIDS Day 2005, Margaret I. Johnston and Anthony S. Fauci reported that since 2000, NIAID has spent over 2 billion dollars on vaccine research.[97] They pointed out that despite these concerted efforts worldwide, there is no vaccine yet for HIV/AIDS. On May 18, 2006, at the ninth annual HIV Vaccine Awareness Day, Fauci put a perspective on American efforts to find a vaccine when he pointed out that his organization had engaged 23,000 volunteers in the ninety-six HIV vaccine clinical trials and tested fifty-eight different vaccine candidates, but "an effective vaccine eludes us. We must continue to accelerate efforts in both basic and clinical research to design promising new vaccine candidates and to test their potential for preventing HIV infection."[98] The statement from NIAIDS is encouraging but one also gets the impression that the Institute seems to focus much of its research on influenza and flu epidemics, an indication that if the perceived threat of a flu epidemic persists, research on HIV/AIDS vaccine could receive less attention.[99]

In its June 2005 publication, IAVI indicated that accelerating the development of vaccine depends on improving the quality of the vaccine candidates being considered so that they can be ready sooner—a task that requires improved laboratory standards. A second way of accelerating vaccine development is to increase the number of candidates for consideration; the third way is to reduce the time it takes for a candidate to go through the evaluation process, a task that requires more volunteers and an efficient regulatory process.[100] The Coordinating Committee of the Global HIV/AIDS Vaccine Enterprise has estimated that the financial cost would be about $1.2 billion per year.[101] Most of the funding for vaccine research and development comes from the public sector, which accounted for 88 percent of the funding in 2004. The commercial sector, which stands to benefit the most from such a discovery, accounted for 10 percent and philanthropic organizations accounted for 2 percent.[102] The United States government, which leads the world in funding of vaccine research, committed $568 million or 86 percent of the total resources in 2004. Europe, including the European Commission, committed U.S. $39 million, others $8 million, and multilaterals (UNAIDS, WHO, World Bank) committed $2 million of 0.5 percent. These figures do not include the commitment made by the Bill and Melinda Gates Foundation of $360 million for five years.[103] Although funding targets have not been met, it is impressive that most of the funding comes from the public sector. The commercial sector invested about $468 million, and even in that area most of the companies also received funding from state agencies such as NIH in the United States, Agence Nationale de Recherches sur le Sida in France, IAVI, and the South African AIDS Vaccine Partnership. Of the $687 million committed in 2004, 44 percent was devoted to preclinical research, 23 percent was spent on basic research, 22 percent on clinical research, 10 percent on cohort and site development, and 1 percent was spent on advocacy and policy development.[104]

In Africa, only South Africa has committed substantial economic resources to research. While research is taking place in Africa, there is very limited funding, and scientists working in Africa do not often have access either to good research tools or adequate equipment. Agencies that support research at the international level must increase their collaboration with African scientists and provide financial support for research currently taking place in Africa and other developing countries. Research funding in Africa lags behind not only in HIV/AIDS but other diseases as well; most funds are directed toward diseases that affect people in wealthy countries. Less than 1 percent of research funds worldwide are used to research diseases like diarrhea, tuberculosis, malaria, and pneumonia, which continue to cause mortality at all levels in the developing world. It is estimated that out of 1393 new drugs approved and marketed from 1975 to 1999, only sixteen were developed for tropical diseases.[105]

Western researchers get most of the funding; such a practice eliminates many potential researchers and could delay the discovery of new therapies or vaccines. The global community ought to support research on all fronts, including developing countries. The Christian community in Africa, which is involved in health care, could lend its voice to the conversation and encourage governments to join the South African government in committing more resources to vaccine research and development.

Research funding is not the only issue, however. Drug trials also pose ethical questions, which the church could join other communities of discourse to resolve. HIV/AIDS vaccine research and trials started in the early 1990s.[106] The first sixteen trials of the antiretroviral drug known as AZT, funded by the American government, the National Institutes of Health, and UNAIDS raised serious issues for researchers, health experts, and ethicists.[107] These included recruitment of participants, confidentiality, informed consent, ensuring that the experiment does not harm participants, and distribution of the benefits of the research. There were additional questions about the obligation of researchers to participants in the developing world, where such participants might expect to be compensated for their role in the research. For example, a vaccine trial started in Uganda in 1999 with fifty volunteers.[108] Pontiano Kaleebu recounts that relevant questions were raised about safety, compensation in the case of harm, intellectual property issues, and clade—the genetic subtype of HIV virus used in making the vaccine, because it was from North America. "Ironically, in the end this trial yielded some of the first evidence that HIV vaccines can induce immune responses that work across clades."[109] The Ugandan researchers worked closely with government leaders, took public concerns into consideration and emphasized scientific knowledge during the entire trial.[110] The second trial that was launched in 2003 did not encounter many problems because by then the procedure was streamlined and a Community Advisory Board (CAB) was set up. Volunteers were drawn from individuals who wanted to contribute to the search for a vaccine; some had lost loved ones to HIV/AIDS. Although there have been challenges, Kaleebu believes that such research and trials are possible in developing countries. There have been failures in vaccine trials, but researchers are committed to research and development because that is the only way forward.

The ethics of recruiting volunteers to be involved in the testing of the vaccine remains complicated because in some cases there is no data describing the risk involved. C. Tacket and R. Edelman have called attention to what they describe as "vaccine induced immunotoxicity or antibody-induced enhancement of infection."[111] The international community follows the Nuremberg Code, which states that participation in any medical research and trial ought to be based on the free choice of the individual. The Nuremberg Code was affirmed by the Helsinki Declaration of 1964, which placed the interest of the individual above the interest of science and society. In Africa, the Dakar Declaration regulates medical research and drug trials. It states: "the interest of research subject or communities should be paramount. Research should be based on free and informed consent, be non-intrusive, and the results should be made available to the community for timely and appropriate action."[112]

There are legitimate concerns about drug trials in Africa because many people living with HIV/AIDS could be driven by desperation to participate in clinical trials in the expectation that they might be getting drugs. Questions about the ongoing availability of the drugs or vaccines after the trials conclude remain important. Other issues include the notion of informed consent, which is a very Western approach to potential problems. An approach which stresses individualism is out of step with the communitarian spirit of African peoples. The question of desperation cannot be dismissed easily because many people in Africa would be willing to try something that holds promise. While Africans might be willing to participate in trials because of the need to find treatment, what might motivate drug companies, who market their products at prices that Africans cannot afford, to carry out clinical trials in Africa? P. Wilmhurst has argued that pharmaceutical companies want trials in Africa because they benefit from "lower costs, lower risk of litigation, less stringent ethical review, the availability of populations prepared to give unquestioning consent, anticipated underreporting of side effects because of lower consumer awareness, the desire for personal advancement by participants, and the desire to create new markets for drugs."[113]

The church in Africa could play a significant role in addressing potential concerns through its network of medical services. First, church leaders and medical staff could use their resources to educate people about the importance of vaccine testing and drug trials. Second, leaders could help people to understand the terms of participation, including basic ideas like giving consent. Third, leaders could work with local, state, and international researchers and pharmaceutical firms to ensure full compliance with all the conventions on drug testing and trials. Finally, church leaders could play an advocacy role to ensure that pharmaceutical companies make their drugs affordable to people living with HIV/AIDS. Christian organizations and other religious groups that deal with health issues can contribute to the discussion because the research and trials have a direct impact on the *imago dei*.

Vaccine and drug trials remain a sensitive issue in Africa. Keymanthri Moodley, using *ubuntu* (oneness, community) ethics has argued that in Africa, a communitarian approach to the question of trials and testing might be a better way to approach the question of consent than a Western individual approach.[114] Thus in drug trials in Africa, a community elder or family might actually give consent rather than the individual participants. This does not mean that procedures such as consent forms would be ignored, but that they would be signed after an elder has given his or her approval. Moodley rightly points out that there is a great danger that some African participants may be coerced. "Subtle and unexpected elements of coercion can reside in the perceptions (real or imagined) held by patients recruited into a research project in a medical care setting."[115] In such a context, individual competence to make reasonable consent decisions may not always apply if the individual is not educated. This leaves research subjects in Africa open to exploitation and paternalism.

HIV/AIDS vaccine trials pose other problems for researchers. For example, it is difficult to determine the efficacy of the vaccine in patients who are already on some kind of drug.[116] Researchers do not really know the outcome of using either genetically altered or kill virus or live-attenuated HIV-1 vaccine.[117] Susan Craddock has argued that these trials then have to take place in developing countries with high prevalence rates and less stringent measures. In such a context, even proposed changes to the Helsinki Declaration do not protect the participants; although they make provision for researchers to provide participants with drugs in countries where prophylactics and drugs are not available.[118] Trials would have to be assessed on whether infections occurred or how the drug affected the viral load. Where infection occurred, researchers would have a moral obligation to provide antiretroviral drugs and in such a case it would be difficult to measure the efficiency of the vaccine.[119]

Other potential problems include post-immunization consequences for the people participating in the trial. In some cases, their spouses may refuse to have sex with them. There is of course a possibility that a volunteer will get a placebo and concern that once immunized, a participant might actually engage in more risky behavior. One important concern about trials is the anticipated benefits of research. Moodley argues that justice demands that the anticipated benefit and the burdens of research be distributed equally. Therefore, Africans cannot be principal subjects of research when they are not likely to be principal beneficiaries of the research. Africans would have a disproportionate share of the burdens and research risks.[120] The Helsinki Declaration requires that outcomes of research should benefit the host community or country, a principle that has already been violated in South Africa following trials of antiretroviral treatment for pregnant women.

I believe Moodley's contribution to the debate lies in his claims that drug trials are important in South Africa and ought to bring together individual autonomy and community concerns because the participation of the community could enhance trial participation. I am sympathetic to Moodley's views that community leaders should play an important role in the decision-making process. However, individual African communities should discuss and decide if they will support the idea that the individual should give up his or her right of consent in preference to the decision of leaders of the community. I think that with good education each person could make the decision to participate or not, without feeling a communal obligation to take part in a trial because the leaders have supported such trials. The Christian community ought to continue to offer education in these matters, making members of the community aware of the importance of drug trials but making sure that individuals reserve the right to give their consent or to choose not to participate.

Two cases from Africa highlight some of the ethical issues discussed by scientists and legal experts. I refer specifically to cure claims that have come up in Kenya and Cameroon.[121] Some research scientists and traditional healers have claimed that they have discovered either a cure or a vaccine that has worked effectively in reducing the viral load in AIDS patients. A report describing a cure claim in Kenya was titled "At last a miracle drug against AIDS."[122] The miracle drug called Kemron, which was touted as a possible cure for AIDS, was a form of interferon-alfa. Dr. Davy Koech, an immunologist who at the time was director of the Kenya Medical Research Institute (KEMRI) first made the claim that this drug could cure AIDS at the eleventh annual meeting of KEMRI. Their pilot project had tested the medication on a hundred patients and it reduced opportunistic infections and greatly improved the health of the patients. The drug also reduced fatigue and loss of appetite. Christian health-care workers have an obligation to follow these claims carefully in order to educate people about what is taking place.

In Cameroon, Professor Victor Anoma Ngu also claimed that he was working on a drug that had proven effective in reducing the viral load in some of the patients suffering from AIDS.[123] Ngu discussed his findings at international meetings but received a mostly negative response. The WHO Global AIDS programme has declined to fund his research because Ngu's "methods of antigen preparation and its standardization were not fully described, and that the study did not have sufficient scientific basis."[124] Ngu was not deterred by this skepticism and continued his research, developing a vaccine which he tried on some patients. He presented his findings at a Bioethics Congress in London in September 2000 in a paper co-authored with Godfrey Tangwa. They claimed that HIV antigens whose envelope has been destroyed cannot infect a person and hence could be an effective vaccine. Ngu further claimed that he had tested it on some patients and it helped their immune system respond by killing the virus, confirming that it could be effective as a vaccine. Ngu and Tangwa claimed that if the vaccine were produced, it could cost a mere 10 cents per vaccine. Ngu went ahead and named his discovery the VANVAHIV vaccine, although scientists in Cameroon and the West remained skeptical, and no Western agency had supported the project.[125]

Ngu has described his discovery, VANVAHIV, on his Web site as a therapeutic preventive auto-vaccine that was tested on a normal person to determine if it could destroy the HIV virus. The vaccine is specific because it uses a patient's own blood. Professor Ngu did not get authorization from the government because people were skeptical about his findings. He claimed that he had administered the vaccine on patients who volunteered because this was their last resort. Ngu has not discussed the issue of the consent of the participants and he has not indicated if the participants signed any consent forms. One could perhaps argue that if there were consent forms, they were private, and not a matter of public record. Ngu is a respected scientist and it is hard to imagine him engaging in such a project without following these procedures.

Ngu claims that the results were promising because the vaccine reduced the viral load and the CD4 count increased. He also claimed that he has used this vaccine since 1989 to treat his patients. By 2004, Ngu still wanted to work out an agreement with the Cameroon government, but at the time the

vaccine was still only available at his Clinique de L'espoir in Essos Yaoundé.
He has also argued that the cost is reasonable; patients have to pay for six
months of treatment in advance, but treatment is offered only after a battery
of tests to determine if the patient might need to strengthen his or her
immune system before the treatment starts. In Ngu's account we have not
only claims that the patients have volunteered, but also the product has
shown some signs of success and stands to benefit the public because the cost
of the medication is not prohibitive. Furthermore, Ngu is not a foreign
researcher seeking to exploit poor Cameroonians. He is a distinguished
Cameroonian professor of health and former minister of health. The extent
to which he has fully complied with the Nuremberg Code and Helsinki
2000 has not been part of the discussion so far. However, he has claimed that
if people come to him at an early stage of the infection, his drugs can help
reduce the viral load.

The cure claims by Professor Ngu have received considerable attention
in the Cameroonian community and abroad for several reasons. Some have
called on the Cameroon government to support Ngu's efforts on humani-
tarian grounds, arguing that with a seroprevalence rate of nearly 12 percent,
Cameroon urgently needs drug intervention. People living with HIV/AIDS
need relief and Ngu's research could perhaps provide it. Second, others have
supported Ngu's efforts on nationalistic grounds, taking pride in the research
of the eminent Cameroonian scientist. On the internet discussion group,
Camnetwork, some have further localized this nationalist pride by pointing
out that Professor Ngu, who attended Sasse College, a Catholic secondary
school in the Southwest Province, has single-handedly brought more fame to
his former school than is enjoyed by all the other private schools in the country. Still other discussants highlight broader issues such as the crisis of
research funding in Africa and attribute this state of affairs to racist attitudes
on part of the funding agencies. The validation of an AIDS vaccine that
could change the lives of millions of people would be a huge breakthrough
and an important commercial event and the West in particular would not
want such honor, fame, and riches to go to an African.

There are some in the medical community in Cameroon, however, who
remain critical of Professor Ngu's claims because he has not demonstrated
how he came about his findings. On the claim that he has found a cure, one
Cameroonian scientist has argued: "The medical words 'treat,' 'cure,' 'vaccine,' are increasingly subjects of horrendous malapropism on this frustrat-
ing public health danger. I suppose due to sales rating, sensationalism is
prioritized above even truth in the increasingly competitive print press market back at home."[126] Others worry that Professor Ngu has neglected estab-

lished scientific procedures by deciding to test his vaccine on human subjects. Still others have asked that Professor Ngu's research be published in peer-reviewed scientific journals.

This debate continues even though the Cameroonian health establishment has criticized Ngu to the point of ridicule. Others wonder if his initial publications might have pointed to a possible breakthrough, if not a cure.[127] In early 2001, the debate was ignited again by a story written for the online edition of Panafrican News Agency by Cypriaque Ebole Bola, reporting that Professor Ngu, a former Cameroonian Minister of Health claims to have developed a vaccine that prevents and cures HIV-related infections.[128] The story indicated that Ngu has been working on this vaccine for twelve years and even tried it on infected people at his Clinic of Hope in Yaoundé. The vaccine consisted of a preparation that also included the patient's own type virus, and Professor Ngu claimed that it generated immunity reaction and eliminated residual HIV.

What some Cameroonian scientists still worry about is the fact that Professor Ngu, one of the most ethical individuals in a very corrupt political environment, claims that he administered his drug directly to patients; there is no clear indication that he followed international standards for the testing of new vaccines. Ngu has stated: "I give my product directly to patients to show that it provokes reactions that kill the virus . . . this is the proof that it could prevent infection in a healthy person. I am ready to confirm this hypothesis before my fellow physicians." I think Professor Ngu is rightly disappointed that the Cameroon government has not supported his research into development of a vaccine. While his critics worry that he has tried his vaccine on human subjects, one does not have enough information to determine if he has broken the Nuremberg Code, which stipulates that biomedical research should be based on "freedom of individual choice with no element of coercion or constraint." Given the desperate situation most people living with HIV/AIDS are in, one could raise questions about the degree to which their health situation has compromised their freedom. It is too early to say how this debate will end. It could be that Professor Ngu is onto something very promising. His critics may have to work with him to see if his findings represent a genuine breakthrough or would lead to one in the fight against HIV/AIDS. For now, his trials and his claims remain controversial.

Cure claims as well as developments in vaccine research in Africa highlight the importance of collaborative research. International collaboration does not rule out competition and I do not suggest that research should be bundled up under one supervisory agent. Collaboration between Western and African scientists could make research more cost-effective and lead to the development of effective therapies sooner. Savings from such collaboration could be passed on to the consumers, especially to patients in Africa and the rest of the developing world where the pandemic has struck hardest. Although international collaboration is necessary, contributions of all scientists involved in any collaborative projects should receive recognition for their work. British and Kenyan researchers worked together on the Majengo, where some Nairobi sex workers believed to have been exposed to the HIV virus have also been resistant to it. It has been claimed that the British researchers eventually registered and got a patent for the vaccine developed through this study without including the Kenyans who had worked with them on the project for seven years.[129] While we do not have all the facts of this case, the narrative raises questions on the ethics of doing research internationally. The basic questions are: who gets credit and recognition, and how is this research going to benefit the community where it was carried out?

It would be to the advantage of the global community if agencies that fund international research increase funding for researchers who work in Africa. Some of the agencies might start with seed money for small-scale research projects and then expand contributions as they show promise. Such small initiatives would give international researchers a greater opportunity to work with indigenous scientists, providing not only useful oversight but also critical questions and feedback that would advance the search for new therapies. Funding agencies could use their influence to facilitate better communication and respect between researchers so that scientists from the developing world are not marginalized and sidelined from important developments in HIV/AIDS medicines, especially when they have contributed to such developments. These issues are not easy to resolve, because research is also considered an issue of national interest. However, national governments and research institutions need to work closely with researchers to facilitate good communication, exchange of information, accountability, ways of testing and ascertaining the quality of drugs, regulatory issues, distribution, and the possibility of manufacturing some of the drugs in Africa to reduce cost of production.[130] Physicians who work for church-related hospitals in Africa should lend their voice to debates like this, collaborating with local researchers and in that way providing a place for peer review in the countries where such research is taking place.

The Global Era Requires Critical Collaboration with Non-governmental and Faith-based Organizations

One of the clearest evidence of globalization is the presence of new agencies, some of them homegrown, in nearly all parts of Africa. Non-governmental organizations are important players in the fight against HIV/AIDS. Non-governmental organizations have grown up in the era of a policy shift toward New Policy Agenda, which mirrors neoliberalism in minimizing the role of the state in economic development and emphasizing the role of non-state actors—both non-governmental and private voluntary organizations. In countries where data is available, both of these organizations receive funding from Western agencies and use these funds for a variety of activities.[131] Western governments see them not only as partners in the development industry, but also as viable alternatives to the state governments in Africa, many of which they consider corrupt and inept. The ambiguity surrounding non-governmental organizations makes it difficult to pass judgment on them and their activities. They traverse a variety of spaces and link the West and the developing world in indirect as well as direct ways. There are transnational bodies that offer a different kind of approach to the same product development. They have become an indispensable player in the wake of the decline of the postcolonial state.

While non-governmental organizations have accomplished many things, it is sometimes difficult to know if they are pity oriented or compassion oriented. African elites have welcomed non-governmental organizations and in some cases tried to manipulate and profit from them as they have done with structures of the state. Africans themselves have started their own non-governmental organizations to fight HIV/AIDS and to promote development. Several major international organizations are engaged in the fight against HIV/AIDS in Africa and the rest of the world. These organizations include the World Bank, the WHO, UNAIDS and all its affiliated organizations, The Overseas Development Agency (ODA), UNICEF, and USAID. In addition to these, there are well-known organizations such as Médicines Sans Frontières (MSF), numerous AIDS advocacy organizations such as Global Treatment Access, and faith-based organizations such as World Vision International and Samaritan's Purse, who are all working at different levels to combat HIV/AIDS.[132]

In Kenya, the Catholic Secretariat and the Christian Health Association of Kenya (CHAK) pushed through an initiative that culminated in the formation of a non-governmental AIDS consortium in 1990. This initiative brought together about 150 organizations to focus on HIV/AIDS at the local and national level since many of the non-governmental organizations have worked in outlying areas. The Kenyan consortium works together with the government to formulate policy and a wide range of education programs using drama, arts, and conducting informative workshops for people living with HIV/AIDS, in addition to providing counseling to HIV-positive people and their families. Shorter and Onyancha argue that in the Kenyan case, the most successful engagement of the consortium involves capacity building through networking and dissemination of information.[133]

One could make several generalizations about the nature of the international cooperation taking place in Africa and elsewhere. First, the presence of non-governmental organizations continues the internationalization of the HIV/AIDS pandemic, demonstrating that the global community can and should work together. Second, non-governmental organizations do not all speak with one voice. Probably the most contentious issue has been the presence of conservative political and religious voices that have taken a strong position against certain family planning education. Conservative religious groups, whose concerns are guided by the divisive abortion rights debate in the United States, have influenced the Bush administration to withdraw funding from family planning programs around the world. Some of these programs have been important avenues for educating women in reproductive care. These days, reproductive health in the developing world cannot be separated from the HIV/AIDS pandemic. American-based non-governmental organizations should work with the U.S. administration to reprioritize women's reproductive health in developing countries. This is an urgent matter, because in 2004 the United States Department of Health, Welfare, and Education for the first time did not send delegates to the international family planning meeting.

Third, non-governmental and international organizations could reshape the debate on universal access in the fight against HIV/AIDS. These organizations have the resources—personnel, money, literature, and social influence in the West—that African governments and religious groups do not have. Médicines Sans Frontières (MSF) has played a major role in articulating and lobbying for the acquisition of generic drugs in South Africa and other parts of the world. They have not only carried on their own campaign, but also worked with the South African government to lobby major pharmaceutical companies to make major shifts in distribution. Their work in this regard is a brilliant testimony to what could be accomplished if non-governmental organizations and national governments work together. Because of the ideological positions that President Mbeki has taken regarding some of the drugs, there were some impediments to full cooperation with South African leadership. However, MSF worked with local South African organizations like COSATU to make the case for access to generic drugs, which are available at reasonable cost from Brazil.

Fourth, non-governmental organizations could and often do act as lobby and pressure groups. Many of them come from the West and can speak the language of the political and corporate world. Leaders of these organizations have other connections that they can use to spread their message and raise awareness about the issues that Africans face with HIV/AIDS. Non-governmental organizations offer a slim hope that globalization may indeed have a human face. For many people in the developing world, institutions such as the World Bank and big capitalist conglomerates are the faces of globalization. Non-governmental organizations work on more limited budgets, but budgets that are large enough to make a difference; they have the potential to demonstrate values that humanize globalization.

Finally, African churches need to forge a critical working relationship with non-governmental and international organizations such as UNAIDS, the World Bank, and UNICEF, WHO, and the United Nations. To do this effectively, African churches and faith-based organizations may have to work with international religious institutions such as the World Council of Churches, the World Lutheran Federation, the Anglican Communion, or the Baptist World Alliance, to mention only a few organizations.[134] Church groups in Africa need to team up with international Christian organizations for two reasons. Such relationships could help churches pull resources together and avoid the duplication of services. The struggle against HIV/AIDS is going to take billions of dollars, and this is money local Christian communities alone cannot come up with. Collaboration with international organizations could expand the pool of resources available for churches and faith-based organizations. Such collaboration is also important so that members of Christian organizations will continue to share information with all those involved in the fight against HIV/AIDS. The findings of researchers are important for all people who are involved in some form of advocacy on behalf of people living with HIV/AIDS. This sharing of information should not be restricted to occasional literature from the WHO, UNAIDS, or the UNAIDS conference, which is typically attended by only a few people from the church's hierarchy. African churches and international organizations need to see each other as important partners in the battle against HIV/AIDS.

One of the benefits of collaborative work with non-governmental organizations would be to allow the members of the local community to assume more responsibility and free the non-governmental experts to coordinate their services. Such cooperation is crucial in cases where the non-governmental organization is working with widows and orphans. Members of the local communities might be involved in setting up local support networks, or working through churches to provide services, thus ensuring that the widows and orphans would not be treated as if they belonged to a foreign agency. Churches should also work with non-governmental organizations that church leaders can serve as watchdogs for those that are caught up in corruption.

In some cases, the individuals who run a homegrown non-governmental organization may control it as if it were a personal fiefdom. It provides them with a personal link to the West, and serves as a means of accumulation for them. It offers access to information from overseas and funding to travel to annual UNAIDS conferences and consultations. These contacts are crucial but if they become an end in themselves, a non-governmental organization has lost its raison d'etre. American students working with a Christian non-governmental organization in East Africa reported that during their visit in the summer of 2003, a member of a Christian organization was using the organization for his own personal benefit.[135] The individual, who was a relative of the pastor in charge, used the organization to make connections with a wealthy woman in the West who herself provided financial support for the organization. This is where the church can step in, not only to raise a critical voice but also to work with the organization to refocus its mission on the actual victims of the HIV/AIDS pandemic.

Furthermore, it is important that churches work together with non-governmental organizations to address some of the social imbalance that contributes to the spread of HIV/AIDS. While education and prevention remains crucial because they could prevent further infections, working to build social services that will train young people to be self-sufficient is an indispensable task of the church. Christian non-governmental organizations with connections to resources not often available to denominations could use these resources to build home economics centers, training in agriculture, or training that would prepare the youths to become entrepreneurs. A good example is the Christian Organization Research and Training in Africa (CORAT AFRICA), based in Nairobi. This organization specializes in health-care services—focusing on administration, finances, accountability—and emphasizes a Christian disposition that integrates values such as "love, stewardship, integrity, humility, and a Christian understanding of human nature."[136] World Vision, which sponsors development programs around the world, is also involved in the AIDS project in greater Nairobi. It promotes awareness of HIV/AIDS and trains social workers to assist in prevention programs. It provides financial support for people living with HIV/AIDS to get medical examinations, paying hospital fees for some of the patients; World Vision also works with orphans and provides meals for them. Perhaps the most important aspect of its ministry in my view is the provision of vocational training in business, bookkeeping, credit management, and small projects that can bring income to participants. This organization also provides education for orphans and coordinates placement of orphans into homes.

African churches must continue to work with the international community on debt relief. International Christian organizations, including the Roman Catholic Church, have advocated for debt relief for several years.[137] The All Africa Conference of Churches (AACC) has also advocated debt relief. The AACC has gone on record stating that the debt crisis creates "fertile ground for the exploitation of labor, the plundering of Africa's material resources and broadening the gap between rich and poor, urban and rural communities."[138] Member churches of the AACC also deplore the rampant corruption that exists in African countries because it sucks away the wealth and resources of the African people. The future generation will carry a debt burden that has not been incurred for development, but to feed greedy individuals. It is therefore necessary that African churches continue to condemn the international system which facilitates this vicious borrowing cycle. In light of the massive suffering brought by the scourge of HIV/AIDS, it is imperative that the international community does something concrete about the debt burden of many African states. A large number of people infected with the HIV/AIDS virus today live in countries designated by the United Nations as the poorest in the world. Many of these countries spend more money on debt financing than on their own health-care systems. The massive campaign mounted by a variety of organizations has so far resulted in debt relief for twenty-six countries. Even those who have qualified have gone through very stringent procedures.

Christian organizations should embrace and promote the Debt-for-AIDS swaps. The UN Declaration of Commitment on HIV/AIDS, adopted by member states in June 2001, called on member nations to adopt the "Debt-for-AIDS swaps" initiative which grants debt relief to countries on condition that they use their resources to finance HIV/AIDS programs.[139] Debt swap was defined as as "the cancellation of external debt in exchange for the debtor government's commitment to mobilize domestic resources (local currency or another asset) for an agreed purpose."[140] This is a complex arrangement, which allows the creditor to accept less money in return for some project, and the local currency of money that is to be used to accomplish that purpose is the redemption price. Debt swaps are managed in a

variety of ways including equity swaps, debt buy-backs, debt for nature
swaps, and debt for development swaps. These swaps in principle can affect
all debts, even multilateral debts, especially after the Heavily Indebted Poor
Countries (HIPC) initiative of 1999, which encouraged the writing off of
multilateral debt, but the transaction is often a swap of the debt for policy
conditionality to be implemented in the HIPC. Debt swaps can reduce the
debt and debt service of a country, affect future balance of payments, bring
in additional funds, and the money from debt swaps could be used to
involve civil society groups to work on development projects.

The creditor often recovers part of the non-performing loans. In the case
of debt between governments, the debtor can use the funds saved from the
swap for a project that the creditor approves. Several countries now want to
participate in debt swaps and use the money to help solve the mounting
problems created by the HIV/AIDS crisis. As of March 2003, twenty-six
countries have benefited from debt relief through the program, but Stefan de
Vylder points out that since the cost of scaling up HIV/AIDS intervention
is astronomical (estimated at $15 billion by 2007) debt relief, however help-
ful, cannot go very far. It might serve only as an indication that the global
community needs to do more in scaling HIV/AIDS intervention in the areas
affected most.[141]

There is still a strong case for considering debt relief. On August 15,
2000, Nigerian President Olusegun Obansanjo wrote a touching letter to
Mr. Adrian Rogers, then president of the Southern Baptist Convention, the
largest Protestant denomination in the United States with extensive mission
work in Nigeria, and appealed to him to speak on behalf of debt relief.
Referring to the principles of jubilee found in Leviticus, Obasanjo stated:

> My people cannot hallow the fiftieth year. And we enter a new millen-
> nium, not in a spirit of new beginning but a millstone of debt grinds our
> country and its people into endless poverty. Nigeria borrowed $5 billion
> from western creditors in 1978. Since then, we have paid back $16 bil-
> lion. It may surprise you to know that we still owe $31 billion! This is
> largely due to compound interest and interest rate fluctuation. Prophet
> Isaiah railed against this form of economics when he chastised the credi-
> tors, "You add house-to-house and field-to-field until there is room for no
> one but you." (Isaiah 5:8). Jesus appealed to the creditors to be "merciful
> as your father is also merciful."[142]

President Obasanjo later promised that if his country received debt relief he
would step down and most of the money would be used to fight
HIV/AIDS.[143] After many years and numerous campaigns the finance ministers of the world's richest countries agreed on June 11, 2005 to write off

more than $40 billion in debt owed by African countries to international financial institutions including the World Bank, the International Monetary Fund (IMF), and the African Development Bank. The American-based organization ONE, the Campaign to Make Poverty History made up of leading humanitarian and non-profit organizations, worked with the United States government asking the administration to provide leadership in canceling the debts. ONE hailed the June 11 decision by the world's richest countries, adding that the money can be used to build schools, health clinics, and roads.[144] Churches and organizations that have worked on debt relief, especially in the Jubilee project, must not slow their efforts now.

I have argued that globalization can be a promise and peril. The international community has responded in a massive way to the challenges of HIV/AIDS. However, there is still a lot to be done to defeat the disease. The church should critically appropriate the benefits of globalization to advocate for access to treatments, vaccine trials, and examination of cure claims, and should work with non-governmental, faith-based, and private voluntary organizations to scale up the global response to HIV/AIDS.

Conclusion

The Challenge of Individual Responsibility and Global Obligation

HIV/AIDS has now affected individuals and families around the world, but it has caused more devastation in Africa than elsewhere. It is a private and public tragedy. I have argued that the Christian community in Africa has an obligation toward people living with HIV/AIDS because humanity is created in the image of God. Members of the Christian community are enjoined to love and show compassion to all who suffer. The Christian community should work to create a social climate where certain virtues could enhance the quest for the good and well-being of others. I conclude this book by addressing the dialectic of individual responsibility and global obligation and the distinct but complementary roles of secular and religious communities. HIV/AIDS demands responsibility from all members of the human family. By "responsibility" I refer specifically to actions that would prevent the spread of HIV/AIDS and assist the people who are affected.

At a personal level, there are things that each individual must do as he or she engages in responsible action. One's first obligation is to be aware of his or her status so as to refrain from actions that would put others at risk. If an individual finds out that he or she is seropositive, that person should act in a responsible way by making sure that he or she refrains from actions that would transmit the virus to a child, a young woman, or a spouse. This means abstaining form sexual intercourse or using a protective device if one engages in sexual intercourse. It also means informing one's sex partner about the situation so that the partner is not taken unaware. Failure to communicate candidly about one's status could lead to the infection of one's

171

partner. Such behavior violates the ethics of justice. The personal and individual dimension of the HIV/AIDS crisis is very important and calls for vigilance and the use of good judgment by everyone.

There are also social dimensions to responsible action. Communities of discourse such as churches, religious groups, ethnic associations, professional groups, non-governmental, and other international organizations demonstrate responsible action by providing education, counseling, and support to members of the community. This begins with providing updated information on how one can minimize the risks of infection. Educational materials should lay out the many ways a person can become infected and address human sexuality, which is the main mode of infection for people in Africa. Such information ought to celebrate human sexuality but also include explicit information about the advantages of safe sex and the dangers of having multiple partners or risky sexual encounters with strangers.

I have argued that churches have a responsibility not only to their members but to all people, because all have the *imago dei*. The first responsibility of Christian communities is to educate people to prevent new transmissions, by talking openly about all the issues that create risk situations: poverty, risky sexual behavior, gender discrimination and marginalization at all levels of society, poor health-care infrastructure, and a lack of appropriation of state resources to fight the pandemic. Church leaders have an obligation to work in a consistent manner to address gender roles. Margaret Farley has argued that "patterns of relationship, self-understanding, sex roles, and gender differentiations ought to change . . . because over all they have been inadequate, based on inaccurate understandings of human persons, preventive of individual growth, inhibitive of the common good, conducive to social injustices, and in the Christian community not sufficiently informed by or faithful to the teachings of Christ."[1] Church leaders also have a special responsibility to people living with HIV/AIDS which requires that they communicate with state leaders on ways of preventing the spread of HIV/AIDS and providing universal access to health.

Church leaders should use all avenues open to them to educate and warn people about the dangers of HIV/AIDS, including worship services and educational initiatives. In all areas of community life, Christian communities should condemn stigmatization and discrimination against people living with HIV/AIDS and foster a culture of acceptance because all people are created in the image of God. This acceptance ought to be concretized in acts of love and compassion. For example, churches should be prepared to provide financial support, food, and child care to families affected by HIV/AIDS. Churches should also provide or serve as a clearing house for assistance to children who have been orphaned by HIV/AIDS, so that as many as possible can stay in school. Church members could offer to cultivate and plant crops in the farms of people affected by HIV/AIDS so that families would have the food they need for the year. Caring might also involve shifting the budget priorities of the church to provide for the financial needs of families that have been affected. There is no greater responsibility at this time than to adopt church life and finances to deal with the greatest catastrophe the African church has ever faced.

Churches also have a responsibility to provide counseling and support to people living with HIV/AIDS and their families. HIV/AIDS kills slowly and those affected struggle with the illness for many years, during which time they experience the pain and anxiety of living with a deadly disease. People living with the HIV virus need counseling to help them learn to live with the disease. I have argued that Bible studies are useful in this context because they offer individuals and their families narratives of hope and a witness of divine power even at very difficult times. Churches also have a responsibility to fight on behalf of the afflicted for access to treatment for their condition. While prayers and Bible reading remain important, the new frontier of responsibility in the fight against HIV/AIDS is to advocate for the millions of people living with HIV/AIDS who need access to treatment and good health care. In order to do this, churches should work with local governments, international organizations, and drug manufacturers to ensure that people living with HIV/AIDS have the treatments they need. Churches should also care for widows and orphans.

Governments in Africa have a tremendous responsibility to their people. Their responsibility in the present crisis is to make HIV/AIDS their first priority. As guardians of the good, African governments should create a social, political, and economic climate in which individuals can act in a responsible manner, since HIV/AIDS is an emergency that directly affects the individual's ability to pursue the good. Part of the state's responsibility is to educate its people to take personal responsibility for their own lives, to live and act in a way that would eliminate the risk of infection, and to protect other people. African governments should make every effort to reform the health-care infrastructure of their countries, to eradicate poverty, and to remove the structural imbalance that promotes discrimination against women and children in society. African states must avoid frivolous spending on arms, but instead devote their resources to fighting HIV/AIDS. They must provide treatment for their own people, and not depend entirely on the international community. They should make condoms available to meet the needs of the sexually active population. They should work with the international community to secure compulsory licenses to produce generic drugs in their countries or regions.

State leaders also have a responsibility to create a climate of tolerance where the rights and dignity of each person will be respected. Most African countries have signed the International Declaration of Human Rights and the African Charter of Rights and Freedoms. They have agreed to protect individual liberties and freedoms and have also agreed to guard the economic rights of people by creating an enabling environment where they can pursue meaningful economic activities that could minimize the risk of poverty and disease. The fight against HIV/AIDS can only succeed if all people recognize that every human being has rights and dignity that should not be violated. State leaders should plan how they are going to deal with food shortages as more people who are in their productive years succumb to the HIV virus and can no longer work to feed their families. Responsible leadership entails rigorous planning that will ensure sufficient food and ongoing services to the many people affected by the HIV/AIDS crisis.

State leaders have a responsibility to carry out a vigorous debate on the reality and nature of poverty in developing countries, especially at a time when private capital has increased in some countries, enabling them to experience economic growth, but declined in African countries. Such a conversation must engage policymakers at all levels, challenging them to rethink economic priorities that have so far yielded nothing other than debt, poverty, and destitution, which in turn have created risk situations for many people. Africans themselves should be involved in a vigorous dialogue about the priorities of their nations. African countries will never solve the problems of poverty if leaders think that the only way to solve problems is to talk with international financial institutions, without involving their own people in the planning and reordering of priorities. If international proposals to end economic decline did not work because of the top down approach by the World Bank and the IMF, then national programs that are mainly top down orders from government leaders will likely suffer a similar fate. All sectors of the political community must be involved in planning and working for a recovery of the economy.

The Challenge of Local and Global Responsibility

The history of HIV/AIDS is filled with discourses of distance. The first discourse of distance emerged when people thought that HIV/AIDS was a gay disease. Then Africans engaged in discourses of distance by claiming that it was a Western gay disease that did not affect them. Subsequently, Western nations and some individuals in the West began to blame Africa for HIV/AIDS. The discourses of distance were further strengthened by the fact that in Africa local efforts to fight the disease heightened extraversion and dependency created by the socioeconomic decline of the postneocolonial state. Finally, some researchers have also been engaged in discourses of distance, by restricting research or discriminating against African researchers. But it is time to balance local and international responsibility.

Leaders must realize that HIV/AIDS involves the triad of rural, urban/national, and global communities. The local community often experiences the worst of the disease in Africa because many people who have been infected in urban areas go home to wait for their final days. Let us take the case of James who attended one of the church-related secondary schools in Cameroon and later attended Yaoundé University. When he completed his education, he remained in Yaoundé to work with the government. James married in the early 1990s but did not live with his wife for a long time because she became ill; she eventually died of HIV/AIDS complications. His in-laws accused him of infecting their daughter with the virus. He took a test but it was negative. However, a later test indicated that he was HIV-positive. He continued to live in Yaoundé until it was clear that he could no longer fight the disease. He then asked his friends to take him to his home town in the Northwest Province where he suffered for a long time before he lost the battle to AIDS.

When people living with HIV/AIDS return to the rural areas, they take with them a tremendous burden and members of their families in the rural areas then assume a huge responsibility to provide for them out of their meager resources. When an individual dies, families in the rural areas often lose not only a loved one, but in many cases the person they had depended on for financial support. The frequent funerals continue to frighten people and cause panic. Since the infection rates in the rural areas are also alarming, it is clear that intervention strategies must include careful planning about what to do in the rural areas where the burden of HIV/AIDS is felt most keenly.

The rates of infection are rising in India and other parts of Asia. Whatever the mode of transmission, most people know that the global community is vulnerable to HIV/AIDS, and that many contract it sexually. Global vulnerability to HIV/AIDS demands global responsibility. The work of UNAIDS and other non-governmental, private voluntary, and faith-based organizations, along with state governments—in a world where financial and national security interests have fractured the world into all kinds of groups—demonstrate that the human family can still take a stand against an enemy like HIV/AIDS. UNAIDS reports that the international community has not reached its target of providing treatment to 3 million by the year 2005, and has changed its global strategy from a specific program like "3 by 5" to universal access to health care. Proclamations on this new strategy are not enough: the governments of the world must pledge to work together to eradicate this disease, providing the financial resources for medicines and for research into new drugs and vaccines.

African churches and governments have a responsibility to fight for greater access to treatments by people living with HIV/AIDS. Several things are necessary if the global community is going to take full advantage of this situation. All parties to treatment must communicate with each other. These parties include medical researchers, pharmaceutical firms, financial institutions, policy makers, health-care providers, and consumers. Decisions about research and drug development must not be motivated by financial concerns alone. Research and development of new drugs is expensive but very often it is the cost of marketing new therapies that drives up the cost and puts the new drugs out of the reach of those who need it most. Therefore, drug pricing should consider the interest of the consumer, and with HIV/AIDS, we are talking about over 40 million people who will need the drugs for a long time. That is a large market by any standard. People who need drugs will take a large quantity and stay on medication for a long time, allowing manufacturers to recover the cost of production and add to their already growing profit margin. A crucial question to ask is Who is the consumer?

The consumer is not some abstract entity but a concrete human being or his or her representative. The first type of consumer is the state. The state as a consumer is responsible for the health and welfare of the members of its political community. For that reason, the state is interested and has to take an active part in the acquisition and distribution of drugs to citizens. This responsibility of acquiring medicines is often fraught with intrigues and political maneuvering. The debate within South Africa, where some government leaders have raised doubts about the viability of certain drugs on the market, indicates that the state could be a problematic consumer.

In many parts of the world, the state has acted like an irresponsible consumer because it has provided few funds for HIV/AIDS. Many countries have shifted their responsibility as consumers to non-governmental and other voluntary organizations. Since states are consumers, policy makers should be proactive. They should allocate money to provide the drugs that the poorest members of the community need. One of the most important tasks any government has in a time of crisis is defending the most vulnerable members of its community. There is no greater vulnerability today than HIV/AIDS. States should carry out their responsibility with transparency.

They should maintain a strong, viable health-care system that will make sure that opportunistic infections will be treated efficiently.

The second set of consumers is the non-governmental, private voluntary, and faith-based organizations, and a host of organizations working for access to drugs and treatment for people living with HIV/AIDS. The proliferation of these organizations is a testament to the goodwill of the human family. The activities and responsibilities of these organizations include education, lobbying, volunteering in HIV/AIDS campaigns, and raising money to provide treatment. They are important clients for drug companies, especially when they engage directly in the acquisition and distribution of drugs. Organizations like Médicins Sans Frontières have acted in an exemplary manner. They have actualized what Levi Strauss once described as "a vision of humanity without frontiers,"[2] and given a new face to relief. While they may be subjected to the politics of their respective countries, they in some ways transcend organizations like the United Nations whose failures in Rwanda and the Democratic Republic of Congo have left many wondering about the state of international security. The non-governmental and international organizations are important consumers of new drugs and could set the example for national governments on how to be good consumers of new therapies.

The activities of these groups offer a new articulation of global responsibility that is not dictated by national security interests. They offer alternative values that are not governed primarily by "the bottom line." They have the capacity to document and communicate human need to the world. They have proven that they can manage resources better than many politicians in local situations do. As consumers of drugs and new therapies, non-profit organizations could help change the fight against HIV/AIDS. Non-governmental and other international organizations have their problems, and some of them must learn how to listen better, learn, and work with locals in planning the most effective ways to combat HIV/AIDS. In spite of their shortcomings, however, they are important consumers, which the international drug manufacturers cannot ignore.

The third consumer is the individual, a human being with flesh and blood. This individual may be wealthy, like Magic Johnson, and have enough money to afford medicines that can prolong his or her life. This individual may also hold a powerful and influential position in his or her country. But many of the individuals are poor, destitute, and have no one to turn to for help. The individual consumer might be someone you know—your son, daughter, brother, or sister; your mother, father, wife, husband, aunt, or coworker. Regardless of how one is related to the consumer, he or she must be treated with dignity. For millions of people the consumer who needs

HIV/AIDS drugs is a breadwinner—a lover, a friend, a spouse, or community leader.

Therefore, the consumers of existing and new therapies are local people, but they are part of the global community of individuals, states, and organizations that are actively engaged in the fight against HIV/AIDS. HIV/AIDS has created a global market where all are invited to sell and buy, but for now only certain people can afford to shop in that market. This would not be a problem if this market were made up of luxury goods. It is, instead, a market filled with essential life-prolonging drugs and new forms of therapy. The international community has a responsibility to the more than 40 million people living with HIV/AIDS around the world to ensure that market values do not spell doomsday for millions of people. If the global community wants to end the catastrophe that continues to unfold in local villages and urban centers around the world, leaders and state governments have a new responsibility to start an urgent conversation about therapeutic drugs.

HIV/AIDS and the New Sense of Obligation

For some people it seems reasonable to talk about individual responsibility and even community responsibility within communities where many people are directly affected by HIV/AIDS. In those communities, some might argue, it is easy to see why everybody has a responsibility to stop the spread of this disease and help people living with HIV/AIDS. Even though I have talked about international and global responsibility, the question for some people is, does the international community have an obligation to provide assistance where others have not assumed their responsibility? Do communities that do not have a great HIV/AIDS burden have an obligation to do something about it? To put it bluntly, why should someone feel obligated to help those who are suffering, especially in cases where it is clear that certain choices and cherished cultural practices might have contributed to their problems?

First, from a Christian perspective, all people are created in the *imago dei* and for that reason Christians have an obligation to show love and compassion. Some Christians would also argue as I do that since this disease is battering the image of God, the rest of the human family has an obligation to protect the *imago dei*. Second, the international community has an obligation to eradicate HIV/AIDS on altruistic grounds. In the discussion on compassion, I argued that the idea that one should show compassion only to someone who is suffering "innocently," undercuts a spirit of altruism. In a world where Hobbesian realities point to competitive individuals and competitive states who push national security interests, even in communities where it is clearly argued, it takes a village to raise a child, one still wonders if altruism is still something one could hold on to. In such a world, it seems to me that one could perhaps agree with Hobbes, however reluctantly, that if Jesus did not command the giving of alms, he would still give alms to a beggar to relieve both his pain and that of the beggar; self-interest may indeed be a part of the structure of altruism. But there is still a place for assuming a sense of obligation to do something helpful about HIV/AIDS without ulterior motives. For the Christian, such a sense of obligation is constitutive of being part of the global community of faith. Others would find different reasons to get involved, but I am convinced that most people still feel sympathetic toward those who suffer and move to assist them. Where this exists, we tend to see it as an altruistic spirit. Others, convinced of the common bonds we share as a human community, assume that we each have a moral obligation to stop the spread of the HIV virus because it threatens our common good. The devastation and economic destabilization it has caused undercuts human efforts to build a strong and viable international community. Writing in *Internal Medicine News*, Jeffrey Sachs has argued:

> Why should we tackle these problems? One answer is that we're talking about real people. There was a time when saying that millions of people could be saved was enough to spur our nation to action. I'm not sure why that answer seems not to be enough any more, yet I can't imagine the need for any more of an answer. We in the developed world have become so callous about the lives of the poor that we have unknowingly put our own lives at terrible risk. Letting fulminating infectious disease continue on a continent is not a good idea. We can imagine a disease spreading from Africa around the world, like AIDS. We can imagine other diseases also emerging from a continent full of unintended public health emergencies.[3]

One could argue that Sachs himself wants the West to intervene out of self-interest because he is concerned that diseases that arise in Africa might spread to the West. However, Sachs also argues that intervention is necessary because the lives of millions of people are at risk and he does not see any more reason for intervention that that reality. The international community has an obligation to act now before HIV/AIDS destroys a large segment of the human family.

A Critical Note on Secular and Religious Approaches

HIV/AIDS has raised serious questions about human nature and reminded the human community just how vulnerable we are even in a world of great technological advances. In addition, it has raised serious questions about divine power and forced human beings to reflect on how divine power works at a time of helplessness. Regardless of these problems, it seems to me that to fight HIV/AIDS effectively, the global community must avoid pitting the secular and religious dimensions of life against each other. I use the secular here to refer to all ways of perceiving and relating to the world without depending on symbolic forces.

The secular world includes the lived spaces in which different beings live an active and productive life. It is a creative world, and therefore a world of invention that is open to numerous possibilities. Those possibilities require different methods of ordering the world, and the processes of ordering are often complex, elusive, and temporal. In this secular space, the human community has a limited capability to control the possibilities the world opens. However, as human beings with limitations, people are aware of the fact that they do not have the capacity to control all of the possibilities that unfold before them. Yet one of the marks of the human spirit is the drive to search, understand, and relate to what may resist understanding or continue to remain elusive. It is this yearning to understand that creates new knowledge and in turn offers humanity the possibility of exploring to the very limits of our world. Openness to these possibilities requires that human beings constantly maintain a disciplined attitude toward science and all forms of human knowledge. Where humans may not be able to manage and control certain things like the HIV/AIDS virus, human ingenuity has taught us that certain interventions can minimize its effects. Humans have used those lessons to create products that slow down the spread of viruses and other threats to human health.

This is one way of rethinking the debate on condoms. Condoms are human products that stop the transmission of semen and fluids from one individual to another. As human products, they have limitations. However, they work if they are used properly. Condoms then are part of the concrete world, products that owe their existence to the world that is not necessarily grounded on symbolic forces. Condoms are a valid and a necessary part of the human world and could make the experience of that world more meaningful for many people. People would be helping to destroy that world if they were to brush aside the use of condoms largely because our interpretation of the world depends mainly on symbolic forces.

Many people have fetishized condoms. Some see condoms as the secular symbol of a loose, uncontrollable human sexuality. According to this perspective, the condom is a human product which only points to the fact that humanity has failed to discipline its sex drives. It might be helpful to reflect on this again. Those who have advanced this argument have stated that because the condom is available someone is likely to engage in sexual activity. One wonders if this is not a naïve view of sexual impulses because sexual drives respond to different issues and not merely the presence of condoms. Sexual desires are on the increase even in places where there might be a limited supply of condoms to remind people about the possibility of engaging in sexual intercourse. Sexuality in Africa and elsewhere is shaped by many other issues than the availability of condoms alone.[4]

Condoms have also been fetishized by those who claim that it is a foreign product that is being dumped on Africa to deprive Africans of having sex in the "African" way. Condoms make sexual intercourse artificial and unnatural. There are many questions that one could raise here, but one that bothers most people is why should natural sexual contact be privileged when that natural contact could pass on fluids that could lead to illness and death. Why has sexual intercourse become the final zone of authentic bodily contact between people? Is this authentic natural contact "natural" when it could lead to death? The question that baffles many people is, why are many Africans and their religious leaders pushing for so-called "natural sex," knowing that it could lead to millions of deaths? Why can they not see that the premature death of girls as young as 11, or of a mother who has several children, is an unnatural result of the "natural" act of someone who has compromised the lives of these women? Why is the "natural" connection of a man's sexual organ far more important than the life of a woman? Why have men or women for that matter (if there are women who buy this "natural sex" argument) so fetishized the idea of real flesh-to-flesh sexual intercourse at the expense of life when experts state that sexual intercourse with condoms is equally pleasurable? My argument is that embracing a secularity that affirms human products like condoms actually affirms and supports life. Members of the scientific community and the public health specialist who argue that condoms are one way of combating deadly sexual diseases deserve support and encouragement. Therefore, to the extent that they could save life, condoms blur the distinction between secular and religious values that must be considered in dealing with the HIV/AIDS pandemic.

I was recently in Ethiopia and talked with members of DKInternational who work in family planning and the social marketing of condoms. The process is based on the concept of "applying commercial franchise procedures on health products."[5] I found out that what makes their project successful is not only that they work with reputable organizations like USAID but that they employ meaningful concepts to market their product. They use mass media marketing and work with a diverse number of outlets. They provide support for sporting events, mobile film units where films are shown with contraceptive ads, promote their product on boat sails, shopping bags, casual clothing, caps, and key chains. They have also sponsored academic, cultural, and intellectual activities to pass on their message about contraceptives. I think what is central to their success is that condoms are marketed as part of a general contraceptive and family planning program.[6] This approach in social marketing of condoms is gaining support in Ethiopia and other parts of the world. An early study of social marketing of health and contraceptive products demonstrated that it was a more effective way of getting the population interested in these products than using mainly drug stores and clinics.[7]

The other side of the dialectic, which one must consider, is the religious perspective. By religious, I refer in broad terms to the perspective that our world has its origin in divine power. This perspective holds that the world and its people have some divine origin, even if they do not subscribe to a view that the world was created by God at a certain time. In this book, I have drawn from the Christian perspective of the world to argue that human beings are created in the image of God. The *imago dei* proposes a fundamental view of human equality that coheres with much of the secular proclamations of human equality today. The texts of creation also speak eloquently about the fact that human beings are embodied beings and, as such, there is dignity in the human body. This body remains dignified even under the ravages of deadly disease.

Humans who subscribe to the Christian worldview are invited or commanded to a life of *imitatio Christi* as they relate to other human beings who are, like them, created in the image of God. Such a life issues out in love and compassion to those who suffer because they deserve our love and compassion by merely being part of the human family. Living a life of love and compassion calls for a praxis that empowers people as individuals and as members of their communities to live up to their full potential as human beings. Such a praxis involves more than prayers and the organization of healing ministries, however central these are to religious life in the community. It also involves an engagement in activities that would empower people to break destructive patterns. Christians have an obligation to celebrate and promote responsible sexuality. The burdens of HIV/AIDS have changed previous views of responsible sexual behavior. Safe sex practices that would protect the health of both partners should be seen as acts of love, compassion, and devotion. Safe sex practices offers individuals an opportunity to fulfill their obligations to the body, which is created in the image of God, assuming those sexual acts are based on mutual respect and freedom. In a world of HIV/AIDS, secular and religious views can work together as partners to save life. The ABC (Abstain, Be Faithful, Use a Condom) campaign demonstrates this perspective.

Similarly, one cannot dismiss the attention given to abstinence as merely Puritan and claim that those who promote it are out of touch with reality. There is indeed a certain denial involved in the message about abstinence because many in the church do not want to face the truth that as human beings Christians love and desire sex. Not all the social taboos, prohibitions, and sermonizing about sex have reduced human desires and cravings for sex. It is perhaps from this perspective that many people think that religious people and church leaders who have carried out a relentless campaign for abstinence are out of touch with reality. They may indeed be out of touch with reality because sex is not only a way of affirming our common humanity, but many people consider it an important outlet for recreation.

However, the real question for anyone who thinks about these things today is, if millions are dying because they have engaged in unprotected sex, do we really have a complete picture when we argue that those who call for abstinence are out of touch with reality? Does it make sense to regard the call for abstinence in the wake of massive deaths from sexually transmitted diseases, including HIV/AIDS, as a puritanical spirit and repressive attitude? Can one look into the eyes of a mother who has lost nearly all her children to HIV/AIDS and say that the church is being unreasonable in preaching abstinence?

In light of the danger posed by HIV/AIDS, my position is now that the Christian church can and should promote the use of condoms as a safe sex method without compromising its position on life and sexual morality. However, I am convinced that the church and the rest of the communities engaged in the fight against HIV/AIDS have a lot to learn from each other. Members of the church must confess that abstinence alone is not working and must open their eyes to see the broad social situation that has created and continues to nurture the world of HIV/AIDS. The rest of the global community must recognize that as useful as they are, condoms are only part of an overall strategy that ought to make room for abstinence if the fight against HIV/AIDS is to succeed. If one thing is clear to many researchers and public health officials today, it is the fact that in the third decade of the fight against HIV/AIDS, condoms and abstinence are central to success and must continue to play a significant role; and both must be supported by the church, because we live in a fallen world. This position is not a capitulation to the condom industry. It is a reasonable position in a world where millions are likely going to die from HIV infection since there is no vaccine to protect someone from getting the virus.

Notes

Introduction

1 H. R. Englehardt Jr. "The Bioethics of Care: Widows, Monastics, and a Christian Presence in Health Care," *Christian Bioethics* 11 (2005): 1–10, p. 9. I have added "visions" in place of Englehardt's original word "conceits." Moral perspectives of today are not merely conceits.

2 Taken from the Christian hymn, "Under His Wings" by William Cushing, printed in *Sing Joyfully*, ed. Jack Schrader (Carol Stream, Ill.: Tabernacle Publishing, 1989), 483.

3 Alexander Irwin, Joyce Millen, and Dorothy Fallows, *Global AIDS: Myths and Facts, Tools for Fighting the AIDS Pandemic* (Cambridge: South End Press, 2003), 15. P. A. Treichler reports those who have come up with other explanation of HIV/AIDS in Africa listing the causes as "unadmitted homosexual or quasi-homosexual transmission, unadmitted drug use, the practice of anal intercourse as a method of birth control, the widespread use of unsterilised needles, a history of immune suppression and infectious diseases, scarification, clitoridectomy, circumcision . . . and violent, excessive, or exotic sexual practices" (Treichler, *How to Have a Theory in an Epidemic: Cultural Chronicles of AIDS* [Durham, N.C.: Duke University Press, 1999], 253–54).

4 The inspiration for the concepts "reveal" and "conceal," which I do not develop here, comes from Brown, who argues that extensive studies of gay men and HIV/AIDS both reveals and erases them. See M. Brown, "Ironies of Distance: An Ongoing Critique of the Geographies of AIDS," *Environment and Planning D: Society and Space* 13 (1995): 159–83.

5   See R. M. Anderson, R. M. May, and A. R. McLean, "Possible Demographic Consequences of AIDS in Developing Countries," *Nature* 33 (1988): 228–34.

6   See David Sanders and Abdulrahman Sambo, "AIDS in Africa," in Kenneth R. Overberg, ed., *AIDS, Ethics, and Religion* (Maryknoll, N.Y.: Orbis Books, 1994), 40–52.

7   Lisa Sowle Cahill, *Theological Bioethics: Participation, Justice, and Change* (Washington D.C.: Georgetown University Press, 2005), 45. Elsewhere, Cahill proposes a theory of human rights that is based on the belief that God has created a person free, intelligent, with a sense of purpose, and is social by nature, who thus bears rights. See her essay, "Toward a Christian Theory of Human Rights," *Journal of Religious Ethics* 8.2 (2001): 277–301.

8   The Yoruba conception of reality includes the view that all things created by *Olodumare*, the Supreme Being, are important and that one needs to treat all of the created order with respect and dignity.

9   Gordon Kaufman has argued that Christians might do well to think of themselves as biohistorical beings. Kaufman suggests that this calls for rethinking the concept of creation as creativity. See his "The Theological Structure of Christian Faith and the Feasibility of a Global Ecological Ethic," *Zygon* 38.1 (2003): 153–54.

10 Charles Villa-Vicencio, *A Theology of Reconstruction: Nation-Building and Human Rights* (Cambridge and New York: Cambridge University Press, 1992), 276, 279, 283.

11 See here P. A. Treichler, *How to Have a Theory in an Epidemic*; B. G. Schoepf, "Inscribing the Body Politic: Women and AIDS in Africa," in P. A. Lock and M. Kaufert, eds., *Pragmatic Women and Body Politics* (Cambridge: Cambridge University Press, 1991), 98–126; R. Chirimuuta and R. Chrimuuta, *AIDS, Africa and Racism* (London: Free Association Books, 1989); Q. Gausset, "AIDS and Cultural Practices in Africa: The Case of the Tonga (Zambia)," *Social Science and Medicine* 52 (1993): 509–18.

12 This visit is reported in the church's publication, *God's Voice in the Synagogue* (2001).

13 Karl Barth, *Dogmatics in Outline*, trans. G. T. Thomson (London: SCM Press, 1949), 147.

14 Agrippa G. Khathide, "Teaching and Talking About Our Sexuality: A Means of Combating HIV/AIDS," in Musa Dube, ed., *HIV/AIDS and the Curriculum: Methods of Integrating HIV/AIDS in Theological Programmes* (Geneva: World Council of Churches, 2003), 1; Donald Messer, *Breaking the Conspiracy of Silence: Christian Churches and the Global AIDS Crisis* (Minneapolis: Fortress, 2004).

15 Sheryl Bainbridge has argued: "The most basic tenet of the Jewish faith that pertains to prevention of HIV/AIDS is the value of present life . . ." ("The Second Decade of AIDS: A Call for Jewish and Christian Communities of Faith to Respond and to Collaborate With Public Health," *Religious Education* 39.2 [1998]: 244). On the priority of the personal see also Elias Kifon

Bongmba, "The Priority of the Other: Ethics in Africa—Perspectives from Bonhoeffer and Levinas," in John W. de Gruchy, ed., *Bonhoeffer for a New Day* (Grand Rapids: Eerdmans, 1997), 190–208.

16 S. Conner and S. Kingman have argued: "Despite the sexual liberation that has marked the latter half of the twentieth century, sex is still a surreptitious activity, so the hypothetical designers of a modern plague can take advantage of the age-old taboos associated with sex." Quoted in Shula Marks, "An Epidemic Waiting to Happen? The Spread of HIV/AIDS in South Africa in Social and Historical Perspective," *African Studies* 61.1 (2002): 16.

17 Solomon R. Benatar, "The HIV/AIDS Pandemic: A Sign of Instability in a Complex Global System," *Journal of Medicine and Philosophy* 27.2 (2002): 171.

18 Benatar argues: "Morality here requires an institutional component embracing attention to public health and the management of resources. Interpersonal relationships are broadened to encompass the concept of civic citizenship with primary responsibilities complementing the primary rights of individuals and the correlative duties of others in order to achieve rights in practice" (171).

19 Josephine Gitome, argues that in the case of Kenya, the churches reach a weekly audience of about 14 million out of the national population of 25 million. See "The Church's Response to AIDS in Africa," in Mary Getui and Emmanuel Obeng, eds., *Theology of Reconstruction: Exploratory Essays* (Nairobi: Acton, 1999), 200.

20 S. Heald, "Its Never as Easy as ABC: Understandings of AIDS in Botswana," *African Journal of AIDS Research* 1.1 (2001): 1.

Chapter 1

1 Ecumenical News International reported this remark made by the Anglican archbishop of Kenya on June 21, 2005. See http://www.eni.ch/ (accessed June 21, 2005). The archbishop's words are adopted from the *Anglican Book of Common Prayer*, Service of Morning Prayer: "We have left undone those things which we ought to have done. And we have done those things which we ought not to have done. And there is no health in us." I thank my editor at Baylor who suggested that I refer to the source of the archbishop's comments.

2 Kathleen M. MacQueen, "The Epidemiology of HIV Transmission: Trends, Structure and Dynamics," *Annual Review of Anthropology* 2 (1994): 509–26.

3 Helen Singer Kaplan, *The Real Truth About Women and AIDS* (New York: Simon & Schuster, 1987), 146.

4 HIV/AIDS has killed more than 25 million people. See UNAIDS, http://www.unaids.org/en/HIV_data/Epidemiology/default.asp (accessed May 20, 2006).

5 UNAIDS, *AIDS Epidemic Update and Special Report on Treatment*, 2005. See the "Global Summary of the AIDS Epidemic, December 2006," http://www.unaids.org/en/HIV_data/2006GlobalReport/default.esp. (accessed November 24, 2006).

6   Ibid., 20–25.
7   United States National Intelligence Council (NIC), *The Next Wave of HIV/AIDS: Nigeria, Ethiopia, Russia, India, and China* (Washington, D.C., September 2002), 8.
8   Medical Research Council, *The Impact of HIV/AIDS on Adult Mortality in South Africa*, Research Report (September 2001), 6.
9   Liz Walker, Graeme Reid, and Morna Cornell, *Waiting to Happen: HIV/AIDS in South Africa: The Bigger Picture* (Boulder and London: Lynne Rienner, 2004), 14, 15.
10 Philip Setel, Milton Lewis, and Maryinez Lyons, eds., *Histories of Sexually Transmitted Diseases and HIV/AIDS in Sub-Saharan Africa* (Westport, Conn.: Greenwood Press, 1999).
11 Cornelius B. Pratt, Louisa Ha, and Charlotte A Pratt, "Setting the Public Health Agenda on Major Diseases in Sub-Saharan Africa: African Popular Magazines and Medical Journals, 1981–1997," *Journal of Communication* 52.44 (2002): 899.
12 Catherine Raissiguier, "Women from the Maghreb and Sub-Saharan Africa in France: Fighting for Health and Basic Human Rights," in Obioma Nnaemeka and Joy Ngozi Ezeilo, eds., *Engendering Human Rights: Cultural and Socioeconomic Realities in Africa* (New York: Palgrave Macmillan, 2005), 111.
13 Pratt, Ha, "Setting the Public Health Agenda," 899.
14 The realism of Robert Mapplethorpe's art, which he might have intended to convey a different message, might ironically have contributed to the images of African sexuality in the Western world. Some people fear traveling to Africa because they think that they will be infected with the HIV virus.
15 Jean Goens, *De la Syphilis au Sida* (Paris: Presses interuniversitaires européennes, 1995).
16 Michael Latham, "AIDS in Africa: A Perspective on the Epidemic," *Africa Today* 40.3 (1993): 39–53.
17 See Peter Dirk Uys, "AIDS is a Laughing Matter," *The Guardian*, August 3, 2001. http://www.guardian.co.uk/comment/story/0,3604,531453,00.html. Donald Messer recounts that when he mentioned this statement at a lecture, a woman told him that a South African couple who were vacationing in Amsterdam, announced: "You know, in South Africa, we won't have a black problem much longer; it is being taken care of by AIDS." See Donald E. Messer, *Breaking the Conspiracy of Silence: Christian Churches and the Global AIDS Crisis* (Minneapolis: Fortress, 2004), 10.
18 Phillip Winn, "Personal Suspects and the Framing of Africa: Who's to Blame for AIDS?" *Mot Pluriels* 1.3 (1997). http://motspluriels.arts.uwa.edu.au/MP397pw.html.
19 See the stories compiled by Elaine Landau, ed., *We Have AIDS* (New York: Franklin Watts, 1990). These narratives not only deal with sexuality as the main cause of the infection but include stories of hemophiliacs who became infected through blood transfusions and individuals who believe they became infected because of professional negligence by a medical staff or institution.

20 Derek Jerman, *At Your Own Risk* (London: Hutchinson, 1992); Modern Nature (London: Vintage, 1992).

21 One of the best-known examples in the literature is "Patient Zero" who reportedly spread the disease in its early stages in the United States through his numerous sexual relations. In Donga Mantung Division of the Northwest Province, people speculated that the rate of HIV prevalence in the region increased dramatically when the government deployed contingent troops from the army and gendarmerie, following disturbances in Ndu between 1991 and 1992.

22 Furthermore, as Winn and others have observed, the reference to Africa is often loaded with images of zoophilia attributed to an African sexuality many believe is out of line with norms—norms here being Western standards of sexuality. "Le sida, qui a transité par le sang des singes verts, est une maladie de sorciers, d'envouteurs" (Winn, "Personal Suspects"). Hervé Guibert, whose AIDS memoir has been widely distributed, also hints that Africa is the origin of AIDS. The statement "C'est un machin qui doit nous venir d'Afrique," has been attributed to Michel Foucault who many take to be Guibert's character, Muzil. See Hervé Guibert, *A l'ami qui ne m'a pas sauvé la vie* (Paris: Guillimard, 1990), 17.

23 Leonard Horowitz, *Emerging Viruses: AIDS and Ebola—Nature, Accident or Intentional?* (Rockport, Mass.: Tetrahedron, 1997).

24 In another context in Africa, a villager told Ed Hooper, who was doing research in the Kyotera in Rakai District of Uganda, that AIDS came to their region because traders from Lukunyu took money from Bakerebwe people in Tanzania to buy goods for the Bakerebwe but failed to buy the goods and did not return the money. The traders later became sick and attributed their illness to the Bakerebwe who are known to be witches. In another area, Hooper was told that people are sexually unrestrained and it is possible for a man and his brother to have sexual relations with the same woman: it was for that reason that illnesses came to the area. Referring specifically to HIV/AIDS, this individual also speculated that border traders liked to enjoy spending time in bars with women, and that soldiers who fought in the 1979 war brought it with them from different countries. See Laurenti Magesa, "Aids and Survival in Africa: A Tentative Reflection," in J. N. K. Mugambi and A. Nasimiyu-Wasike, eds., *Moral and Ethical Issues in African Christianity: A Challenge for African Christianity* (Nairobi: Acton, 1999), 198.

25 L. Gordis, *Epidemiology* (Philadelphia: W. B. Saunders, 2000).

26 Several Web sites give detailed descriptions of the different types of HIV strains in language that is accessible to the general reader. See, for example, http://www.avert.org/hivtypes.htm (accessed June 2006).

27 Michael Gottlieb, *Morbidity and Mortality Weekly Report*, June 6, 1981.

28 Anne Larson, "The Social Epidemiology of Africa's AIDS Epidemic," *Africa* 83 (1990): 5–30, 7.

29 Larson, "Social Epidemiology," 9

30 S. Watney, "Risk Groups or Risk Behaviors," in J. Mann and D. Tarantola, eds., *AIDS in the World II: Global Dimensions, Social Roots, and Responses* (New York: Oxford University Press, 1996), 431–32. See also K. J. Rothman and S. Greenland, *Modern Epidemiology* (Philadelphia: Lippincott Williams & Wilkins, 1998).

31 *The Daily Nation*, March 24, 2001.

32 T. Wilton, *EnGendering AIDS: Deconstructing Sex, Text and Epidemic* (London: Sage, 1997).

33 In this regard, the United Nations Population Fund (UNFPA) in its 2004 report argues that cultures are not only historical realities, but constitute a space for development, a context for human rights, and are dynamic and interactive. See United Nations Population Fund, *Culture Matters: Working with Communities and Faith-Based Organizations: Case Studies from Country Programmes*, 2004.

34 Benatar, "The HIV/AIDS Pandemic," 170.

35 Anne V. Akeroyd, "Coercion, Constraints, and 'Cultural Entrapments': A Further Look at Gendered and Occupational Factors Pertinent to the Transmission of HIV in Africa," in Ezekiel Kalipeni, Susan Craddock, Joseph R. Oppong, and Jayati Ghosh, eds., *HIV and AIDS in Africa: Beyond Epidemiology* (Oxford: Blackwell, 2004), 94.

36 Akeroyd, "Coercion," 89.

37 A. M. Brandt has argued: "the [AIDS] epidemic has been shaped not only by powerful biological forces, but by behavioral, social and cultural factors as well" ("AIDS: From Social History to Social Policy," in E. Fee and D. M. Fox, eds., *AIDS: The Burdens of History* [Berkeley: University of California Press, 1998], 148).

38 E. Reid has pointed out that such a focus on risk groups has also created distancing discourses, which has increased denial and blame. See "Approaching the HIV Epidemic: The Community's Response," *AIDS Care* 6.5 (1994): 551–57.

39 Larson argues: "It is also indisputable that features of African social life encourage multiple sexual partners and frequent partner change that makes Africans especially vulnerable to a deadly sexually transmitted disease" ("Social Epidemiology," 16). See also J. C. Caldwell, Pat Caldwell, and Pat Quiggin, "Disaster in an Alternative Civilization: The Social Dimension of AIDS in Sub-Saharan Africa," *Health in Transition Working Papers*, no. 2 (Australian National University, Canberra, 1989); J. C. Caldwell and Pat Caldwell, "The Cultural Contest of High Fertility in Sub-Saharan Africa," *Population and Development Review* 13 (1987): 419–21.

40 *World Urbanization Prospectus: The 1996 Revision* (New York: United Nations Department of Economic and Social Affairs, Population Division, 1998).

41 Eliya Msiyaphazi Zulu, F. Nii–Amoo Dodoo, and Alex Chika–Ezeh, "Sexual Risk-Taking in the Slums of Nairobi, Kenya 1993–98," *Population Studies* 56 (2002): 312–13. The authors report that economic desperation often leads some of the women to engage in risky behavior for as little as 15 cents.

42 Zulu et al., "Sexual Risk-Taking," 321.

43 M. Carael and S. Allen, "Women's Vulnerability to HIV/STD in Sub-Saharan Africa: An Increasing Evidence," in Paulina Makinwa and An-Magritt Jenson, eds., *Women's Position and Demographic Change in Sub-Saharan Africa* (Leige: International Union for the Scientific Study of Population [IUSSP], 1995), 201–22.

44 M. Brockerhoff and Ellen Bennan, "The Poverty of Cities in Developing Countries," *Population and Development Review* 24.1 (1998): 75–114.

45 Ann Larson, "Social Context of Human Immunodeficiency Virus Infection in Africa: Historical and Cultural Basis in East and Central African Sexual Relations," *Reviews of Infectious Diseases*, September/October 1989; Colin Murray, *Families Divided: The Impact of Migrant Labor in Lesotho* (Cambridge: Cambridge University Press, 1981); Alan Ferguson, "Women's Health in a Marginal Area of Kenya," *Social Science and Medicine* 23 (1986): 17–29; Alanagh Raikes, "Women's Health in East Africa," *Social Science and Medicine* 28 (1989): 447–59.

46 P. W. Setel, "Comparative Histories of Sexually Transmitted Diseases and HIV/AIDS in Africa: An Introduction," in P. W. Setel, M. Lewis, and M. Lyons, eds., *Histories of Sexually Transmitted Diseases and HIV/AIDS in Sub-Saharan Africa* (Westport, Conn.: Greenwood Press, 1999).

47 K. Kiragu, "Youth and HIV/AIDS: Can We Avoid Catastrophe?" *Population Report Series L, no. 12.* Population Information Program, Bloomberg School of Public Health (Baltimore: The John Hopkins University, 2001).

48 Aylward Shorter and Edwin Onyancha, *The Church and AIDS in Africa: A Case Study of Nairobi City* (Nairobi: Paulines Publications, 1998), 23.

49 C. Akukwe and M. Foote, "HIV/AIDS in Africa: Time to Stop the Killing Fields," *Foreign Policy in Focus* 6.15 (2001); C. Combe, "HIV/AIDS Impact on the Educational Sector in South Africa," presentation to Senior Experts Conference on HIV/AIDS and Education in ECOWAS, March 19–23, 2001, Elmina, Ghana.

50 Shorter and Onyancha, 24.

51 This meeting took place at the Baptist Center in February of 2003.

52 Phillip Winn, "Personal Suspects and the Framing of Africa: Who's to Blame for AIDS?" *Mot Pluriels* 1.3 (1997). http://motspluriels.arts.uwa.edu.au/MP397pw.html.

53 The background here is the work of Sigmund Freud.

54 Musa W. Dube, "Culture, Gender, and HIV/AIDS: Understanding and Acting on the Issues," In Dube, ed., *HIV/AIDS*.

55 Beverley Clark, "Sex and Death: Spirituality and Human Existence," *Feminist Theology* 2.2 (2004): 237–52, 240. Clark quotes from Augustine, *City of God*, trans. R. W. Dyson (Cambridge: Cambridge University Press, 1998), 555.

56 Clark, "Sex and Death," 240.

57 Carter Heyward, "The Power of God-with-us." This essay was first published in *The Christian Century*, and is reprinted on religion-online at http://religion–online.org/cgi-bin/relsearchd.dll/showarticle?item_id=440.

58 Beverley Clark, *Sex and Death: A Reappraisal of Human Mortality* (Cambridge: Polity Press, 2002), 9.

59 Plato, *Symposium*, trans. W. Hamilton (New York: Penguin Classics, 1951), 80, 202a, 202b; 92; 210b.

60 Statement by the Ecumenical News International: owner-eni-summary @wccx.wcc-coe.org.

61 Quoted in Allan M. Brandt, *No Magic Bullet: A Social History of Venereal Disease in the United States Since 1880* (New York: Oxford University Press, 1985), 180.

62 Jerry Falwell, "AIDS: The Judgment of God," *Liberty Report* (April 1987), 5.

63 Njongonkulu Ndugane in "Quote, Unquote," *The Christian Century*, December 18–31, 2002, p. 15.

64 http://www.wcc–coe.org/wcc/what/mission/ny–statement.html.

65 In the United States, the archbishop of Cincinnati, who gave support to a priest who was suffering from AIDS, when asked how the priest got AIDS, responded: "I don't know. That is between him and his doctor." See Newell J. Wert, "The Biblical and Theological Basis for Risking Compassion and Care for AIDS Patients," in Overberg, ed., *AIDS, Ethics and Religion*, 235.

66 Zulu et al., "Sexual Risk-Taking," 316.

67 Josephine Gitome, "The Church's Response to AIDS in Africa," in Getui and Obeng, ed., *Theology of Reconstruction*, 201.

68 Hendrew Lusey Gekawaku, *The Church Confronted with the Problem of HIV/AIDS: Analysis of the Situation in Five Countries of Central Africa: Cameroon, Chad, Congro/Brazaville, Democratic Republic of Congo, Gabon* (Geneva: World Council of Churches, 2003), 10. The list of faith-based organizations that received funding includes Catholic Dioceses in Eséka, Bafia, Mbalmayo, Sangmélima. Ebolowa, Obala; Eglise Presbytérienne du Cameroon; Eglise Evangélique du Cameroon; Eglise Evangélique Luthérienne du Cameroon; Oeuvre Médicale des Eglises Evangéliques du Cameroon; Presbyterian Church in Cameroon; Cameroon Baptist Convention; Union des Edlises Adventistes en Afrique Centrale; Christ de la Nouvelle Alliance; Conseil Supérieur Islamique du Cameroon; Mission des Eglises Evangéliques du Cameroon.

69 Quoted in Gekawaku, *The Church Confronted*, 12.

70 Emmanuel M. Katongole, "Postmodern Illusions and the Challenge of African Theology," *Modern Theology* 16.2 (2000): 237–54.

71 Rand Stoneburner and Daniel Low-Beer, "Population-Level HIV Declines and Behavioral Risk Avoidance in Uganda," *Science* 304 (2004): 714–18.

72 Brooke Grandfest Schoepf, "Uganda: Lessons for AIDS Control in Africa," *Review of African Political Economy* 98 (2003): 556. His remarks, which are quoted from Schoepf, were originally made in a *Washington Post* article in 2003. See www.washingtonpost.com/wp-dyn/articles/A61981–2003 May15.html. Studies in the United States indicated that if used correctly, condoms were effective in preventing infections from HIV/AIDS. See Jon Fuller, "AIDS

Prevention: A Challenge to the Catholic Moral Tradition," *America* 175 (1996): 13–20.

73 Marie Laga, Michel Alary, Peter Piot et al., "Condom Promotion, Sexually Transmitted Diseases Treatment, and Declining Incidence of HIV–1 Infection in Female Zairian Sex Workers," *The Lancet* 344 (1994): 246–48.

74 This conversation took place at the Presbyterian Church Center, Ntamulung Bamenda in the Northwest Province, Cameroon during the summer of 2003.

75 Reported by the Ecumenical News International, a news service of the World Council of Churches, April 20, 2005. See http://www.eni.ch.

76 Schoepf, "Uganda," 560.

77 Schoepf, "Uganda," 561.

78 Cited on http://www.nationmedia.com/dailynation/nmgcontententry.asp?category_id=1&newsid=11426.

79 Studies on condom use in the United States and elsewhere have shown that appropriate use of condoms can help prevent the spread of HIV/AIDS. James Keenan has discussed a study that appeared in the *New England Journal of Medicine*, involving 124 couples of whom one partner was infected. After two years and about 15,000 acts of intercourse, with use of condoms, no healthy partner had been infected. See James F. Keenan, "Applying the Seventeenth-Century Casuistry of Accommodation to HIV Prevention," *Theological Studies* 60 (1999): 492–512, 505. However, it is important to point out that even this success must be placed in context; the "100% Condom Program" that was tried in Thailand did not give women full protection because some of the women were still at risk. See P. H. Klimarx, T. Palanuvej, K. Limpakarnjanarat et al., "Seroprevalence of HIV Among Female Sex Workers in Bangkok: Evidence of Ongoing Infection Risks After the 100% Condom Program was Implemented," *Journal of Acquired Immune Deficiency Syndrome* 21.4 (1999): 313–16.

80 *The Many Faces of AIDS: a Gospel Response* (Washington D.C.: USCC Publishing Services, 1987); *Called to Compassion and Responsibility: A Response to the HIV/AIDS Crisis* (Washington DC: USCC Publishing Services, 1989).

81 See responses to the USCC bishops' position in "Reaction to AIDS Statement," *Origins* 17.28 (1987): 489–93; "Continued Reaction to AIDS Statement," *Origins* 17.30 (1988): 516–22; Keenan, "Seventeenth-Century Casuistry"; James Keenan, "Prophylactics, Toleration, and Cooperation: Contemporary Problems and Traditional Principles," *International Philosophical Quarterly* 28 (1988): 201–20; James Drane, "Condoms, AIDS, and Catholic Ethics," *Commonweal* 189 (1991): 188–92.

82 See report on Congresswoman Barbara Lee at http://www.rferl.org/features articleprint/2004/07/9e5bab2f-e5d9-4d51.

83 The first of a series of books to be published from this conference is edited by Isabel Apawo Phiri, Beverley Haddad, and Madipoàne Masenya (Ngwana' Mphahlele), *African Women, HIV/AIDS and Faith Communities* (Pietermaritzburg, South Africa: Cluster Publications, 2003).

84 Isabel Apawo Phiri, "African Women of Faith Speak Out in an HIV/AIDS Era," in Phiri et al., *African Women*, 8–14.

85 Alan Fleming, "South Africa and AIDS—Seven Years Wasted," *Nursing RSA* 8.7 (1993): 18–19. For a discussion of South Africa's AIDS policies, see Olive Shisana and Nompumelelo Zungu-Dirwayi, "Government's Changing Responses to HIV/AIDS," http://www.interfund.org.za/pdffiles/vol4_three/Chapter%207.pdf (accessed June 20, 2005). See also O. Shisanam N. Zungu-Dirwayi, and W. Shisana, "AIDS: A Threat to Human Security" (Background paper, Harvard University Global Equity Initiative, 2002); Adam Sitze, "Denialism," *The South Atlantic Quarterly* 103:4 (2004): 769–811.

86 Minister of Health, Parliamentary Debate, House of Assembly, April 19, 1988, 6332.

87 Nelson Mandela, Speech on World AIDS Day, December 1, 1994. See http://www.anc.org.za/ancdocs/history/mandela/1994/pr941201.html (accessed June 20, 2005).

88 See http://www.aegis.com/news/afp/1999/AF991114.html (accessed June 20, 2005). See also Jacques Pauw, *Into the Heart of Darkness: Confessions of Apartheid's Assassins* (Johannesburg: Jonathan Ball, 1997), 70–71; Bronwen Roberts, "Apartheid Forces Spread AIDS," *Mail and Guardian*, November 12, 1999.

89 G. M. Oppenheimer and R. A. Padgung, "AIDS: The Risks to Insurers, the Threat to Equity," *Hastings Center Report* 16.5 (1986): 18–22; B. D. Schoub et al., "Epidemiological Considerations of the Present Status and Future Growth of the Acquired Immunodeficiency Syndrome Epidemic in South Africa," *South African Medical Journal* 70.4 (1988): 153–57; R. Schall, "Statistical Analysis of HIV Prevalence," *South African Medical Journal* 78.6 (1990), 373; C. J. van Gelderen, "Insurance and Compensation in the Event of HIV Infection," *South African Medical Journal* 81.6 (1992): 33.

90 Sitze, "Denialism," 790. For a working class analyses of the end of apartheid, see Julian Kunnie, *Is Apartheid Really Dead? Pan-Africanist Working-Class Cultural Critical Perspectives* (Boulder: Westview Press, 2000).

91 Daniel J. Smith, "HIV/AIDS in Nigeria: The Challenges of a National Epidemic," in Robert I. Rotberg, ed., *Crafting the New Nigeria: Confronting the Challenges* (Boulder and London: Lynne Rienner, 2004), 200.

92 President Reagan did not say the word AIDS until May 31, 1987—six years after the disease became a problem in the United States. The slogan "SILENCE=DEATH" which was designed by gay activists in New York and later adopted by ACT UP was aimed at calling attention to the wall of silence that had been erected in America about HIV/AIDS, but it was also directed specifically against President Reagan's silence. See Raymond A Smith and Kevin E. Gruenfeld, "Symbols," in Raymond A. Smith, ed., *The Encyclopedia of AIDS: A Social, Political, Cultural, and Scientific Record of the HIV Epidemic* (London: Fitzroy, 1998).

93 Gekawaku, *The Church Confronted*, 6.

94 Gekawaku, *The Church Confronted*, 6.
95 Gekawaku, *The Church Confronted*, 9.
96 Shorter and Onyancha, *Church and AIDS in Africa*, 29.
97 See E. R. Walrond, "Regional Policies in Relation to the HIV/AIDS Epidemic in the Commonwealth Caribbean," in G. Howe and A. Cobbley, eds., *The Caribbean AIDS Epidemic* (Kingston: University of West Indies Press, 2000).
98 Kristin Peterson, "HIV/AIDS and Democracy in Nigeria: Policies, Rights and Therapeutic Economies," Ph.D. dissertation, Rice University, 2004, 73.
99 See Shorter and Onyancha, *Church and AIDS in Africa*, 24–25.
100 See Shorter and Onyancha, *Church and AIDS in Africa*, 25.
101 See http://www.psi.org/news/0604d.html.
102 Smith, "HIV/AIDS in Nigeria," 199.
103 Ronald Bayer, "Public Health Policy and the AIDS Epidemic: An End to HIV Exceptionalism?" *The New England Journal of Medicine* 234.21 (1991): 1500–1504. This article is reprinted in Overberg, ed., *AIDS, Ethics and Religion*. Citations here are from *AIDS, Ethics, and Religion*.
104 In the debate about disclosure, the United States Centers for Disease Control (CDC) supported reporting, with measures taken to ensure confidentiality. The delegates of the American Medical Association supported this position.
105 In 2004 it was estimated that about 23 million people in Africa were infected with the virus. See the study jointly sponsored by UNAIDS, UNFPA, UNIFEM: *Women and HIV/AIDS: Confronting the Crisis* (Geneva and New York: UNAIDS, UNFPA, UNIFEM, 2004), 1, 2.
106 Treatment Action Campaign: http://www.tac.org.za/ (accessed June 12, 2005).
107 P. Piot, "Violence Against Women," presentation to the United Nations Commission on the Status of Women, Forty-Third Session: Panel on Women and Health, March 3, 1999. See http://www.unaids.org/unaids/speeches/ny3march99.html.
108 Stephen Lewis, UN Secretary General's Special Envoy on HIV/AIDS in Africa, July 2002. Quoted in "Policy Paralysis: A Call For Action on HIV/AIDS-Related Human Right Abuses Against Women and Girls in Africa," *Human Rights Watch* (December 2003): 1.
109 T. Barnett and A. Whiteside, *AIDS in the Twenty-First Century* (Hampshire: Palgrave Macmillan, 2002), 154.
110 *Women and HIV/AIDS: Confronting the Crisis*, 4. See M. Hunter, "The Materiality of Everyday Sex: Thinking Beyond 'Prostitution,'" *African Studies* 61 (2002): 99–120.
111 *Human Rights Watch* (December 2003), 4.
112 A few of these agreements include: Convention on the Elimination of All Forms of Discrimination Against Women (CEDAW), 1979; The Vienna Declaration of the World Conference on Human Rights, Declaration and Programme of Action, 1993; International Conference on Population and Development (ICPD) Programme of Action, 1994; Fourth World Conference on Women (Beijing) Declaration and Platform for Action, 1995; 2000

Millennium Declaration and Development Goals; UN General Assembly Special Session (UNGASS) on HIV/AIDS, Declaration of Commitment, 2001.

113 See *The Herald* (Zimbabwe), Thursday, July 24, 2003, p. 16.

114 UNAIDS, 2001.

115 *Women and HIV/AIDS,* 47, 48.

116 For further studies of masculinity see C. Campbell, "Migrancy, Masculine Identities and AIDS: The Psychosocial Context of HIV Transmission on the South African Gold Mines," *Social Science and Medicine* 42.2 (1997), 273–81; Keith Breckenridge, "The Allure of Violence: Men, Race and Masculinity on the South African Gold Mines, 1900–1950," *Journal of Southern African Studies* 24.1 (1998): 669–93.

117 Akeroyd is correct in pointing out that more studies should be done of masculinities and male sexuality in Africa. One of the key contributions to date is C. Shire's "Men Don't Go to the Moon: Language, Space and Masculinities in Zimbabwe," in A. Cornwall and N. Lindisfarne, eds., *Dislocating Masculinities: Comparative Ethnographies* (London: Routledge, 1994), 147–58.

118 Walker et al., *Waiting to Happen,* 31.

119 Kathleen F. Norr, Beverly J. McElmurry, Matshidiso Moeti, and Sheila D. Tlou, "AIDS Prevention for Women: A Community Based Approach," in Overberg, *AIDS, Ethics and Religion,* 189–99.

120 D. James, "To Take Information Down to the People: Life Skills and HIV/AIDS, Peer Educators in the Durban Area," *African Studies* 61.1 (2002): 180.

Chapter 2

1 I do not employ the *imago dei* as a definitive concept that can solve all questions that baffle the human community about HIV/AIDS. Rather, I believe the *imago dei* in the biblical and theological tradition could offer perspectives on humanity which Christians might turn to in a time of crisis to think and act boldly in love and compassion, even if one cannot use the Bible for theological speculation on particular illnesses and epidemics.

2 Jon D. Levenson in an essay titled "Why Jews Are not Interested in Biblical Theology," has pointed out that it is futile for one to construct theological systems out of a complex biblical picture. I take Levenson's remarks seriously because the context of the narratives that contain the idea of the *imago dei* do not lend themselves to simple systematization, although they offer theologians and the Christian tradition an opportunity to reflect on and reconfigure human relations in each new and challenging context. See Levenson, "Why Jews Are not Interested in Biblical Theology," in Jacob Neusner, Baruch A. Levine, and Ernest S. Frerichs, eds., *Judaic Perspectives on Ancient Israel* (Philadelphia: Fortress, 1987), 281–301.

3   World Council of Churches, *Facing AIDS: The Challenge and the Churches' Response: A WCC Study Document* (Geneva: World Council of Churches, 1997), 100.

4   Christians who employ biblical motifs in difficult times ought to do so with great humility because other disciplines offer different ways of thinking about the questions raised by HIV/AIDS. For example, biomedical ethics has enriched the field of ethics and our sense of moral obligations, offering new ways of thinking about illnesses and dilemmas like HIV/AIDS. Biomedical ethicists emphasize that all concerned ought to think seriously about issues including the autonomy of the person, beneficence, non-malfeasance, and social justice. See Tom Beauchamp and James Childress, *Principles of Biomedical Ethics*, 4th ed. (Oxford: Oxford University Press, 1994).

5   Stanley Hauerwas, *Truthfulness and Tragedy: Further Investigations into Christian Ethics* (Notre Dame and London: Notre Dame University Press, 1977), 11.

6   Martha Nussbaum, *Love's Knowledge: Essays on Philosophy and Literature* (New York: Oxford University Press, 1990), 381.

7   Paul Ramsey has stated that in time of crisis some from inside the church try to speak like sectarians, hoping that it would make the churches authentic. "The sectarian option—always an option in seasons of great and long-enduring evil—seems a possibility to be welcomed. That understanding of the contemporary church's fidelity to its Lord is, indeed, an attractive possibility until one tries to think it through practically." See Paul Ramsey, *Speak Up For Just War or Pacifism: A Critique of the United Methodists Bishops' Pastoral Letter "In Defense of Creation"* (University Park: Penn State University Press, 1988), 128.

8   David Cairns, *The Image of God in Man* (New York: Philosophical Library, 1953), 18. I am indebted to Cairns for some of the materials I have used here. Their references to Eichrodt are taken from Cairns.

9   Anders Nygren, *Agape and Eros: A Study and History of the Christian Idea of Love* (London: SPCK, 1982), 1:181.

10 Cairns, *Image of God*, 18. See Gerhard von Rad, "The Divine Likeness in the Old Testament," in Geoffrey W. Bromiley, ed. and trans., *Theological Dictonary of the New Testament*, vol. 2 (Grand Rapids: Eerdmans, 1964), 390–92.

11 Cairns, *Image of God*, 51.

12 Cairns, *Image of God*, 20.

13 Frederick G. McLeod, *The Image of God in the Antiochene Tradition* (Washington D.C.: Catholic University of America, 1999), 236.

14 Cairns argues that the image of God in the New Testament refers to Christ's dignity and relationship to God, the likeness of God which one takes when he or she believes in Christ, describe our humanity, depicts existence in the love of God, reflect God's glory in Christ, and refers to renewal in believers who are to live in community.

15 Maximos Aghiorgoussis, *In the Image of God: Studies in Scripture, Theology, and Community* (Brookline, Mass.: Holy Cross Orthodox Press, 1999).

16   See Phiri et al., *African Women*.

17   Jürgen Moltman, *On Human Dignity: Political Theology and Ethics*, trans. M. D. Meeks (Philadelphia: Fortress, 1984), 25.

18   See Margaret A. Farley, "New Patterns of Relationships: Beginnings of a Moral Revolution," *Theological Studies* 30 (1975): 627–46, 628.

19   Farley, "New Patterns," 636–37.

20   Martin Heidegger, *Being and Time*, trans. John Macquarie and Edward Robinson (London: SCM Press, 1962), 49.

21   Vincent Wilkin, *The Image of God in Sex* (New York: Sheed & Ward, 1955), 10.

22   Linda Hogan, "An Irish Nun Living with Contradictions: Responding to HIV/AIDS in the Context of Church Teaching," in James F. Keenan, ed., *Catholic Ethicists on HIV/AIDS Prevention* (New York: Continuum, 2000), 45–46.

23   Lisa Sowle Cahill, *Theological Bioethics: Participation, Justice, and Change* (Washington, D.C.: Georgetown University Press, 2005), 44.

24   Lisa Sowle Cahill, "Bioethics, Theology, and Social Change," *Journal of Religious Ethics* 31.3 (2003): 376.

25   South African missiologist Tinyinko Maluleke has argued: "A theology of AIDS will seek to do more than merely inculturate; it will fearlessly and creatively engage in critique of culture . . . go beyond sheer cultural clichés so that the weapon of criticism—i.e., African culture which was used to critique western culture and western Christendom—becomes also an object of criticism. If anything, the AIDS epidemic demonstrates the fallibility of all human cultures–African cultures included" ("Towards a New Theological Education Curriculum for the Twenty-First Century in Africa: HIV/AIDS and the New Kairos," background paper in *Report on the HIV/AIDS Curriculum Development Consultation for Theological Institutions in Eastern and Southern Africa* [Nairobi: MAP International, 2000], 97).

26   Nyambura J. Njoroge, *Kiama Kia Ngo: An African Christian Feminist Ethic of Resistance and Transformation* (Legon, Ghana: Legon Theological Studies Series, 2000).

27   In his discussion Cairns point out that Irenaeus interpreted the image of God in humanity to refer to rationality and freedom. Clement of Alexandria interpreted the image mostly in spiritual terms, reflecting the relationship of the individual to Christ. Saint Athanasius held that humanity lost the image of God in the fall. Theologian Gregory of Nyssa also interpreted the *imago dei* in rational terms and argued that the human soul strives toward perfection through intellectual and rational activities which he thought was the imprint of the divine image in human beings.

28   Saint Augustine, *Joan. Evang.* 23.19.

29   Saint Augustine, *De Trinitate* 14.4.6. Cairns argues that Augustine was also the first person to define the image of God as power (*Image of God*, 75). See Cairns's discussion on the interpretation and meaning of "likeness" and the implications it had for the idea of the divinization of humanity. Catherine LaGugna has

argued that according to Augustine, the soul actually is drawn back to God by divine power: "The human being bears within itself the image of its creator, exists in a state of longing to be reunited with God, and by returning inward, ascends upward toward union with God. In Augustine's thought, God addresses the human subject within the structure of its very being . . ." (*God For Us: The Trinity and Christian Life* [San Francisco: HarperSanFrancisco, 1993], 103).

30 Reinhold Niebuhr, *The Nature and Destiny of Man*, vol. 1 (New York: Charles Scribner & Sons, 1949), 158.

31 St. Thomas Aquinas, *Summa Theologica*, 1.93.4.

32 St. Thomas Aquinas, *Summa Theologica*, 1.93.4.

33 In a sermon on Genesis 1:26-28, Calvin argued that the image was destroyed by the fall: "although some obscure lineaments of that image are found remaining in us, yet they are so vitiated and maimed that they may truly be said to be destroyed." See Cairns, *Image of God*, 132; I have followed Cairns's discussion for this section. See John Calvin, *Commentary on Genesis*, 3:1; *Institutes of Christian Religion*, 2.1.5.

34 Emil Brunner, *Man in Revolt: A Christian Anthropology*, trans. Olive Wyon (Cambridge: Lutterworth, 2002), 519–31.

35 Cairns, *Image of God*, 160.

36 Karl Barth, *Church Dogmatics* 3.1, trans. J. W. Edwards, O. Bussey, harold Knight (Edinburgh: T&T Clark, 1958), 183–87.

37 Quoted in Cairns, *Image of God*, 174. See discussion in Karl Barth, *Church Dogmatics* 3.2, trans. Harold Knight, G. W. Bromiley, J. K. S. Reid, R. H. Fuller (Edinburgh: T&T Clark, 1960), 273.

38 Cairns, *Image of God*, 196.

39 Cairns, *Image of God*, 248.

40 Leroy T. Howe, *The Image of God: A Theology for Pastoral Care and Counseling* (Nashville: Abingdon, 1995), 58–59.

41 Cairns, *Image of God*, 249. See Barth, *Church Dogmatics* 3.2, p. 273.

42 Quoted by Dr. David Satcher at the American Public Health Association's 24th Annual President-Elect Session, Washington, D.C., October 30–November 3. http://www.ihpnet.org/aphatxt.htm.

43 Jerome A. Miller, *The Way of Suffering: A Geography of Crisis* (Washington, D.C.: Georgetown University Press, 1988), 175.

44 Initially it was reported that this was a belief held by some people in South Africa. However, there are cases where similar beliefs were held during the colonial period: Kenya is a good example.

45 See Andrew B. Lustig, "Compassion," in Warren Thomas Reich, ed., *Encyclopedia of Bioethics* (New York: Free Press, 1978), 440.

46 See Martha Nussbaum, "Compassion: The Basic Social Emotion," *Social Philosophy and Policy* 13 (1996): 29.

47 See Carol Gilligan, *In a Different Voice* (Cambridge, Mass.: Harvard University Press, 1982); Nel Noddings, *Caring: A Feminine Approach to Ethics and Moral Education* (Berkeley: University of California Press, 1984); Robin West, *Caring*

for Justice (New York: New York University Press, 1997); Diana Fritz Cates, *Choosing to Feel: Virtue, Friendship, and Compassion for Friends* (Notre Dame: University of Notre Dame Press, 1997); Myra Bookman and Mitchell Aboulafia, "The Ethics of Care Revisited: Gilligan and Levinas," *Philosophy Today* 44 suppl. (2000): 169–74; Hilde L. Nelson, "Against Caring," *Journal of Clinical Ethics* 17.3 (1992): 8–15; Nel Noddings, "In Defense of Caring," *Journal of Clinical Ethics* 3.1 (1992): 15–18.

48 Lois Shepherd, "Face-to-Face: A Call for Radical Responsibility in Place of Compassion," *St. John's Law Review* 77.3 (2003): 445–514.

49 Lawrence Blum, "Compassion," in Robert B. Kruschwitz and Robert C. Roberts, eds., *The Virtues: Contemporary Essays on Moral Character* (Belmont, Calif.: Wadsworth, 1987), 230.

50 See Arthur Schopenhauer, *On the Basis of Morality*, trans. E. F. J. Payne (Providence: Berghahn Books, 1995).

51 See Max Scheler, *The Nature of Sympathy*, trans. Paul Heath (London: Routledge & Kegan Paul, 1954), 15; Friedrich Nietzsche, *The Antichrist*, trans. W. Kaufmann (Harmondsworth: Penguin Books, 1982), sec. 7; Immanuel Kant, *The Metaphysics of Morals*, trans. M. Gregor (Cambridge: Cambridge University Press, 1991), 250/456.

52 Steven Tudor rejects this emotional and psychological infection, and argues: "to see oneself as obligated to respond with compassionate sorrow to the Other's suffering is itself the result of a certain sort of work, an active attention to oneself and the Other, an attention to how the Other's situation can lay a claim upon me" (*Compassion and Remorse: Acknowledging the Suffering Other* [Leuven: Peeters, 2001], 87).

53 Martha C. Nussbaum, *Upheavals of Thought: The Intelligence of Emotions* (Cambridge: Cambridge University Press, 2001), 306. See also Martha Nussbaum, "Compassion: The Basic Social Emotion," *Social Philosophy and Policy* 27 (1996): 27–58.

54 Nussbaum, *Upheavals of Thought*, 335.

55 Noddings, *Caring*, 16.

56 Personal communication with Rachel's sister in Bamenda, Northwest Province, summer of 2003. Rachel is not her real name.

57 Shepherd, "Face-to-Face," 458, 461, 465.

58 Emmanuel Levinas, *Totality and Infinity: An Essay on Exteriority*, trans. Alphonso Lingis (Pittsburgh: Duquesne University Press, 1969), 77.

59 See Cates, *Choosing to Feel*. Cates argues that ethical caring could be motivated by a desire for our own *eudaimonia*, the *eudaimonia* of others, and for the "maintenance of a flourishing human community" (157).

60 McNeill et al. argue: "Compassion asks us to go where it hurts, to enter into places of pain, to share in brokenness, fear, confusion, and anguish. . . . Compassion means full immersion in the condition of being human" (Donald P. McNeill, Douglas A. Morrison, and Henri J. M. Nouwen, *Compassion: A Reflection on the Christian Life* [New York: Doubleday, 1983], 4).

61 Emmanuel Levinas, "Useless Suffering," trans. Richard Cohen, in Robert Bernasconi and David Wood, eds., *The Provocation of Levinas: Rethinking the Other* (London: Routledge, 1988), 158.

62 Noddings, *Caring*, 86.

63 Cates, *Choosing to Feel*, 203.

64 While the notion of friendship offers a better perspective than that afforded by Noddings, Cates also points to the limitation: we cannot befriend everybody that comes along. If we do, we will open an expanded circle and such friendships may not fulfill their aims (*Choosing to Feel*, 234).

Chapter 3

1 The virtues I discuss have been selected only because they lend themselves to thinking about HIV/AIDS. Anyone who turns to human virtues in search of rules misses the point and, in so doing, could trigger a rule-centered ethics that has been an important aspect of modernist ethics. I follow a precedent set by James Keenan to discuss hope, fidelity, care, justice, and prudence. See James F. Keenan, SJ, "Proposing Cardinal Virtues," *Theological Studies* 56 (1995): 711; See also his "Virtue and Identity," in *Concillium* 2 (2000): 69.

2 Alasdair MacIntyre, *After Virtue* (Notre Dame: University of Notre Dame Press, 1988); See also his *Whose Justice? Whose Rationality?* (Notre Dame: University of Notre Dame Press, 1988); William Joseph Woodhill, *The Fellowship of Life: Virtue Ethics and Orthodox Christianity* (Washington D.C.: Georgetown University Press, 1996); Joseph J. Kovta, *The Christian Case for Virtue Ethics* (Washington D.C.: Georgetown University Press, 1996); and Cates, *Choosing to Feel*.

3 MacIntyre, *After Virtue*, 111.

4 Charles Larmore has suggested that what MacIntyre objects to in the modern liberal view is its claim that "the norms of justice apply to 'the relationship of human beings as such'" (*Patterns of Moral Complexity* [Cambridge: Cambridge University Press, 1987], 441). Larmore questions further: "But did not Christianity also aim its message at a universal audience? In his (MacIntyre) discussion of Augustine, he says just that, though without retracting his earlier indictment of modernity: 'the law of the *civitas Dei* is by contrast (with Aristotle) a law for all (mankind),'" See also recent writings on the justification of virtues in Craig Dykstra, *Vision and Character* (New York: Paulist Press, 1981); Donald Capps, *Deadly Sins and Saving Virtues* (Minneapolis: Fortress, 1987); Lee H. Yearly, "Recent Work on Virtue," *Religious Studies Review* 16 (1990): 2; Keenan, "Cardinal Virtues," 711; and Keenan, "Virtue and Identity," 69.

5 Bujo Bénézet, *African Christian Morality at the Age of Inculturation* (Nairobi: Paulines Publications, 1990); *African Theology in Its Social Context*, trans. John O'Donohue (Maryknoll, N.Y.: Orbis Books, 1992); idem, *The Ethical Dimension of Community: The African Model and the Dialogue between North*

and South (Nairobi, Kenya: Paulines Publications, 1998); see also Augustine Shutte, *Ubuntu: An Ethic for a New South Africa* (Pietermaritzburg, South Africa: Cluster Publications, 2001).

6   Carol Gilligan, *In a Different Voice: Psychological Theory and Women's Development* (Cambridge, Mass.: Harvard University Press, 1982).

7   Kathryn Tanner, "The Care That Does Justice: Recent Writings in Feminist Ethics and Theology," *Journal of Religious Ethics* 24.1 (2001): 171–91, 174.

8   Seyla Benhabib, *Situating the Self* (New York: Rutledge, 1992); Owen Flanagan, *Varieties of Moral Personality: Ethics and Psychological Realism* (Cambridge, Mass.: Harvard University Press, 1991); Susan Moller Okin, *Justice, Gender, and Family* (New York: Basic Books, 1989).

9   Stanley Hauerwas, *A Community of Character: Toward a Constructive Social Ethics* (Notre Dame: University of Notre Dame Press, 1981); James McClendon Jr., *Ethics: Systematic Theology*, vol. 1 (Nashville: Abingdon, 1986); Gilbert Meilaender, *The Theory and Practice of Virtue* (Notre Dame: University of Notre Dame Press, 1984).

10   James Gustafson, *Ethics from a Theocentric Perspective*, vol. 1 (Chicago: University of Chicago Press, 1982); Robert Sokolowski, *The God of Faith and Reason: Foundations of Christian Theology* (Notre Dame: University of Notre Dame Press, 1982).

11   Keenan has argued: "virtues are traditional heuristic guides that collectively aim for the right realization of human identity. . . . The historical dynamism of the virtues applies . . . to the anthropological vision of human identity" ("Virtue and Identity," 74). Keenan has explored cardinal virtues of justice, prudence, fortitude, and temperance. He has replaced temperance with fidelity and self-care ("Proposing Cardinal Virtues").

12   Gwendolyn Mikell has argued that the emerging African feminist is concerned with "bread, butter, culture, and power issues" (4). Women will continue to bring their own resources to the fight for liberation, but they will also turn to other places for additional resources that will improve the human condition. She has also argued that if women have shown complicity by subscribing to ideologies of domination, they have done so as a pragmatic choice for themselves and their children. See Gwendolyn Mikell, *African Feminism: The Politics of Survival in Sub-Saharan Africa* (Philadelphia: University of Pennsylvania Press, 1997), 5, 16. For a discussion of the ways in which African women negotiate existence and identity, see Obioma Nnaemeka, "Nego-Feminism: Theorizing, Practicing, and Pruning Africa's Way," *Signs: Journal of Women in Culture and Society* 29.2 (2003): 257–85; Obioma Nnaemeka, "Mapping African Feminisms," in Andrea Cornwall, ed., *Readings in Gender in Africa* (Bloomington: Indiana University Press, 2005), 32. See also Nnaemeka's introduction to *Sisterhood, Feminisms and Power: From Africa to the Diaspora* (Trenton, N.J. and Asmara, Eritrea: Africa World Press, 1998).

13   Julia Driver in *Uneasy Virtue* has argued that determining if human actions are good or bad on the basis of agent, personal traits, states of mind, or the will as

Kant's approach in the *Groundwork*, and what she also calls "character motivation" fails. Driver advances a consequentialist approach that takes into account a diversity of virtues and notes that some virtues cannot be linked to mental states. She defends the idea of partiality articulated by feminist thinkers who point out the diverse ways in which women respond to embodied persons and complex human relationships. See Julia Driver, *Uneasy Virtue* (Cambridge: Cambridge University Press, 2001); See also her "The Conflation of Moral and Epistemic Virtue," in *Metaphilosophy* 34.3 (2003): 367–83, 368. Normy Arpaly on her part has argued that praise or blame cannot be assigned only on grounds that people act in a rational manner as defined in virtue ethics. She argues that some decisions made on the spur of the moment or based on one's gut feelings may be worthy of praise if the individual actor's will, motivation, and heart are in the right place. See Normy Arpaly, *Unprincipled Virtue: An Inquiry into Moral Agency* (New York: Oxford University Press, 2002).

14 See Aristotle, *Nicomachean Ethics* 1134a35–b1, 1138a–5–11, 1094a24–28, b5–11, 1102a5–13, 1103b2–6, 31–34; *Politics* 1282b1–6, 1287a16–32; see also Donald Morrison, "Politics as a Vocation, According to Aristotle," *History of Political Thought* 22 (2001): 221–41; Susan D. Collins, "Moral Virtue and the Limits of the Political Community in Aristotle's *Nicomachean Ethics*," *American Journal of Political Science* 48.1 (2004): 47–61. I am indebted to Don Morrison and Susan Collins for some of these insights.

15 See Rosalind Hursthouse, *On Virtue Ethics* (Oxford: Oxford University Press, 1999); see also Bernard Williams, *Ethics and the Limits of Philosophy* (Cambridge, Mass.: Harvard University Press, 1985), 8–11, 35–37.

16 John C. Caldwell, Pat Caldwell, and Pat Quiggin, "The Social Context of AIDS in Sub-Saharan Africa," *Population and Development Review* 15.2 (1989): 185–234.

17 Hursthouse, *On Virtue Ethics*, 177.

18 Margaret A. Farley, "Fragments for an Ethic of Commitment in Thomas Aquinas," in David Tracy, ed., *Celebrating the Medieval Heritage,* Supplement of *Journal of Religion* 58 (1978): 40–45.

19 Aristotle wrote three treatises on ethics: *Eudemonian Ethics, Magna Moralia,* and *Nicomachean Ethics*. Some scholars think that *Eudemonian Ethics* and *Nicomachean Ethics* were earlier works that were named after their editors. One of Aristotle's earliest discussions of ethics appears in the Protrepticus where he focuses on the norms of good conduct. He makes no distinctions between practical and theoretical wisdom, which is called at this early stage *phronesis*. In the *Nicomachean Ethics* Aristotle describes *phronesis* as practical wisdom and sophia as theoretical wisdom. Both are necessary for one to attain intellectual virtues.

20 John Cooper indicates that Aristotle's word *philia* does not have the same meaning of ordinary intimacy as we know it today. See John Cooper, "Aristotle on Friendship," in Ameila Oksenberg Rorty, ed., *Essays on Aristotle's Ethics* (Berkeley: University of California Press, 1980), 301. Cooper also draws from Aristotle's definitions in *The Rhetoric* in his discussion of friendship and hatred

and Cooper concludes that the central idea of *philia* "is that of doing well by someone for his own sake, out of concern for him (and not, or merely, out of concern for oneself)" (302).

21 Cooper, "Aristotle on Friendship," 211.

22 Cooper, "Aristotle on Friendship," 213.

23 Cooper, "Aristotle on Friendship," 215.

24 Cooper, "Aristotle on Friendship," 218.

25 Eleanor Humes Haney, "What is Feminist Ethics? A Proposal for Continuing Discussion," *Journal of Religious Ethics* 8.1 (1990): 118–19.

26 Maria Cimperman, *When God's People Have HIV/AIDS: An Approach to Ethics* (Maryknoll, N.Y.: Orbis Books, 2005), 48.

27 Cimperman, *God's People*, 49.

28 There is extensive literature on Christian sexuality in Africa. For a brief sample see for instance, Walter Trobisch, *The Collected Works of Walter Trobisch* (Downers Grove, Ill.: InterVarsity, 1987). Most of his work was published in the context of his encounter with youths in Cameroon as a pastoral counselor. Elsewhere, there is enormous literature on sexuality in the Christian tradition. See Kevin Kelley, *New Directions in Sexual Ethics: Moral Theology and the Challenge of AIDS* (London: Geoffrey Chapman, 1998); Keenan, *Catholic Ethicists*; James B. Nelson, *Embodiment: An Approach to Christian Sexuality and Christian Theology* (Minneapolis: Augsburg, 1978); James B. Nelson and Sandra P. Longfellow, eds., *Sexuality and the Sacred: Sources for Theological Reflection* (Louisville: Westminster John Knox, 1994); United States Council of Catholic Bishops, *The Many Faces of AIDS: A Gospel Response*, A Statement of the Administrative Board (Washington D.C.: United States Catholic Conference, 1987); Vincent J. Genovesi, *In Pursuit of Love: Catholic Morality and Human Sexuality* (Collegeville, Minn.: Liturgical Press, 1996); Christian Gudorf, *Body, Sex, and Pleasure: Reconstructing Christian Sexual Ethics* (Cleveland, Ohio: Pilgrim Press, 1994).

29 Okin, *Justice*. I am indebted to Kathryn Tanner for this discussion. See Tanner, "Care that Does Justice," 174–76.

30 Tanner, "Care that Does Justice," 176.

31 See Michael Slote, *Morals from Motives* (Oxford: Oxford University Press, 2001), 4, 5, 29–30, 36–37, 63–73.

32 Bad self-love is an incorrect view of the self, and good self-love is the correct view of self. It can lead to virtue and costly sacrifice. See Slote, *Morals from Motives*, 255–56.

33 Slote, *Morals from Motives*, 245.

34 Slote, *Morals from Motives*, 246.

35 Keenan, "Proposing Cardinal Virtues," 727.

36 See Margaret Farley, "Feminism and Universal Morality," in Gene Outka and J. Reeder, eds., *Prospects for a Common Morality* (Princeton: Princeton University Press, 1993), 170–90; idem, "A Feminist Version of Respect for Persons," *Journal of Feminist Studies in Religion* 9 (1993): 182–98.

37 Cimperman, *God's People*, 51–52.

38 Aristotle, *Nicomachean Ethics* 1129a3–11.

39 Aristotle, *Nicomachean Ethics* 1130a32–b5.

40 Aristotle, *Nicomachean Ethics* 1130a3–5.

41 St. Thomas Aquinas, *Summa Theologiaem*, ed. Thomas Gilby (London and New York: Blackfriars, 1975), 31.

42 Theological perspectives on justice are rooted in the biblical traditions, especially the prophetic writings of the Hebrew Bible. However, Christians do not have a monopoly on the idea of justice and ought to articulate their views in conversation with other religious and moral communities that have similar values. Nobel Prize-winning economist Amartya Sen has pointed out that the Moghal Emperor Akbar encouraged interfaith dialogue in the 1590s, and other religious communities have taught respect for the ideas of others. See Amartya Sen, "What's the Point of Democracy?" *American Academy of Arts and Sciences Bulletin* 57.3 (2004): 9.

43 John Rawls, *A Theory of Justice* (Cambridge, Mass.: Harvard University Press, 1971), 7.

44 John Rawls, *Political Liberalism* (New York: Columbia University Press, 1993), 113.

45 Rawls, *Theory of Justice*, 62.

46 See, for instance, the critique by John Langan: "Rawls, Nozick, and the Search for Social Justice," *Theological Studies* 38 (1977): 346–58.

47 Benhabib, *Situating the Self*, 158–70.

48 Tanner, "Care that Does Justice," 181.

49 Amartya Sen, "What Do We Want from a Theory of Justice?" presentation at Rice University, February 2006, unpublished manuscript.

50 Sen, "What Do We Want." Sen also draws a sharp distinction between the tran scendental approach to justice and the comparative approach that includes varied discussion on issues like "inequities of hunger, illiteracy, torture, arbitrary incarceration, or medical exclusion as particular social features that need remedying. . ." (5). He also argues that social choice theorists seem to assume tran scendental approaches to justice. See Kenneth Arrow, *Social Choice and Individual Values* (New York: Wiley, 1951); see also Amartya Sen, *Collective Choice and Social Welfare* (San Francisco: Holden-Day, 1971).

51 Sen, "What Do We Want."

52 Sen, "What Do We Want."

53 See W. G. Runciman and Amartya Sen, "Games, Justice and the General Will," *Mind* n.s. 74.296 (1965): 554–62; See also Thomas Scanlon, *What We Owe to Each Other* (Cambridge, Mass.: Harvard University Press, 1998), 5; Thomas Scanlon, "Contractualism and Utilitarianism" in Amartya Sen and Bernard Williams, eds., *Utilitarianism and Beyond* (Cambridge: Cambridge University Press, 1982); these references are taken from Sen, "What Do We Want."

54 John Rawls, *The Law of Peoples* (Cambridge, Mass.: Harvard University Press, 1999).

55 Amartya Sen, "Open and Closed Impartiality," *Journal of Philosophy* 99 (2002): 445–69.

56 L. Gregory Jones, "Should Christians Affirm Rawls' Justice as Fairness? A Response to Professor Beckley," *Journal of Religious Ethics* 16 (1988): 251–71, 260.

57 MacIntyre, *After Virtue*, 195, 203.

58 Charles Curran, *Catholic Social Teaching, 1891–Present: A Historical, Theological and Ethical Analysis* (Washington D.C.: Georgetown University Press, 2000), 189.

59 Karen Lebacqz, "Justice," in Bernard Hoose, ed., *Christian Ethics: An Introduction* (Collegeville, Minn.: Liturgical Press, 1998), 169.

60 In these relationships, one could consider justice as what J. B. Schneewind has described as "the habit of following right reason with respect to the rights of others" ("The Misfortunes of Virtue," in Roger Crisp and Michael Slote, eds., *Virtue Ethics* [Oxford: Oxford University Press, 1997], 183).

61 Stephen Hart, *Cultural Dilemmas of Progressive Politics: Styles of Engagement among Grassroots Activists* (Chicago: University of Chicago Press, 2001), 119.

62 Thomas W. Ogletree, *The Use of the Bible in Christian Ethics* (Philadelphia: Fortress, 1983), 32.

Chapter 4

1   Dr. Catherine Akale is minister with the Methodist Church in Cameroon. See full citation in Gekawaku, *The Church Confronted*, 13.

2   The situation has not changed very much in many African churches from when *The Christian Century* reported that some twenty-five church leaders interviewed by Keith Benjamin of the South African Council of Churches stated that they did not deal with the crisis. See Sarah Ruden, "AIDS in South Africa: Why the Churches Matter," *The Christian Century*, May 17, 2000, p. 570.

3   Mark Anthony Damesyn, "Epidemiological Impact of Door-to-Door HIV Counseling and Testing in Rural Kenya," Ph.D. dissertation, University of California, Los Angeles, 2002.

4   Not his real name; personal communication with me in Bamenda, Northwest Province, 1996. James passed away three years after this conversation.

5   Walker et al., *Waiting To Happen*, 77, 78. See also P. Delius and C. Glaser, "Sexual Socialization in South Africa: A Historical Perspective," *African Studies* 61.1 (2002). Kevin T. Kelly has pointed out that traditional Christian ethics often hinders attempts to deal with the HIV/AIDS pandemic. See Kevin T. Kelly, *New Directions in Sexual Ethics: Moral Theology and the Challenge of AIDS* (London: Geoffrey Chapman, 1998).

6   Madeleine Boumpoto, "Sida, Sexualité et Procréation au Congo," in C. Becker et al., eds., *Vivre et Penser le Sida en Afrique. Experiencing and Understanding AIDS in Africa* (Dakar/Paris: CODESRIA/Karthala, 1999), 370.

7   See Marc Epprecht, "Reflections upon the Gay Rights Movements in Southern Africa," *Canadian Journal of Development Studies* 22 (2001): 195–212; Marc Epprecht, "Premodern and Early Colonial Africa," in G. H. Haggerty, ed.,

Encyclopedia of Gay Histories and Cultures (New York: Garland Press, 2000); idem., "Good God Almighty, What's this!: Homosexual 'Crime' in Early Colonial Zimbabwe," in Steven Murray and Will Roscoe, eds., *Boy Wives and Female Husbands: Studies in African Homosexualities* (New York: St. Martin's Press, 1998): 197–220; idem., "The Gay Oral Project: Black Empowerment, Human Rights and the Research Process," *History in Africa* 26 (1999): 25–41; idem., "The 'Unsaying' of Homosexuality among Indigenous Black Zimbabweans: Mapping a Blindspot in an African Masculinity," *Journal of Southern African Studies* 24.4 (1998): 631–51.

8   Melvin E. Wheatley, a United Methodist bishop, in an open letter to the United Methodists of the Rocky Mountain Conference of Colorado described homosexuality this way: "It is a mysterious gift of God's grace communicated through an exceedingly complex set of chemical, biological, chromosomal, hormonal, environmental, developmental factors totally outside my homosexual friend's control. His or her homosexuality is a gift—neither a virtue nor a sin. What she/he does with their homosexuality however is their personal, moral, and spiritual responsibility. Their behavior as a homosexual may therefore be very sinful—brutal, exploitative, selfish, promiscuous, and superficial. Their behavior on the other hand, may be beautiful—tender, considerate, loyal, other-centered, profound" ("Open Letter to the United Methodist Rocky Mountain Conference," Denver, Colorado, October 12, 1981).

9   J. C. Caldwell, P. Caldwell, and P. Guiggin, "The Social Context of AIDS in Sub-Saharan Africa," *Population and Development Review* 15.2 (1989): 185–233.

10   Caldwell et al., "Social Context," 187.

11   See responses to Caldwell et al. in Suzette Heald's *Manhood and Morality: Sex, Violence and Ritual in Gisu Society* (New York: Routledge, 1999). See especially chap. 8, "The Power of Sex: Reflections on the Caldwells' 'African Sexuality' Thesis," 129–45; Marie-Nathalie Le Blanc, Deidre Meintel, Victor Piche, "The African Sexual System: Comment on Caldwell et al.," *Population and Development Review* 17.3 (1991): 497–505; Beth Maina Ahlberg, "Is There a Distinct African Sexuality? A Critical Response to Caldwell," *Africa: Journal of the International Institute* 64.2 (1994): 220–42.

12   MMWR CDC Surveillance Summaries 2002; 51 (SS–4): 1–64.

13   Agrippa G. Khathide, "Teaching and Talking about Our Sexuality: A Means of Combating HIV/AIDS," in Dube, ed., *HIV/AIDS*, 1–9.

14   Khathide argues that among the Zulu a young woman who had lost her virginity before the wedding night had caused *ihlazo* (shame) for her family (2).

15   Saint Augustine, *The City of God*, book 14, chs. 16–19.

16   World Council of Churches, "Plan of Action: The Ecumenical Response to HIV/AIDS in Africa," Global Consultation on the Ecumenical Response to the Challenge of HIV/AIDS, Nairobi, November 25–28, 2001.

17   United Nations Population Fund (UNFPA), *Culture Matters, Working with Communities and Faith-Based Organizations: Case Studied from Country Programs,* 2004.

18 UNFPA, *Culture Matters*, 6.
19 UNFPA, *Culture Matters*, 7.
20 UNFPA, *Culture Matters*, 32.
21 UNFPA, *Culture Matters*, 34.
22 UNFPA, *Culture Matters*, 36.
23 Margaret A. Farley, *Compassionate Respect: A Feminist Approach to Medical Ethics and Other Questions* (New York: Paulist Press, 2002), 17.
24 Carolyn Baylies, "HIV/AIDS and Older Women in Zambia: Concern for Self, Worry over Daughters, Towers of Strength," *Third World Quarterly* 23.2 (2002): 351–75.
25 Baylies, "HIV/AIDS and Older Women," 366.
26 N. Bajos and J. Marquet, "Research in HIV and Sexual Risk: Social Relationship-Based Approach in Cross-Cultural Perspectives," *Social Science and Medicine* 50 (2000): 1533–46.
27 C. Obbo, "Women, Children and a Living Wage," in H. Hansen and M. Twaddle, eds., *Changing Uganda: The Dilemma of Structural Adjustment and Revolutionary Change* (London: James Currey, 1991); see also idem., "The Language of AIDS in Rural and Urban Uganda" *African Urban Quarterly* 6.1–2 (1991): 83–92.
28 Personal communication from a physician in Cameroon.
29 Schoepf, "Inscribing the Body Politic," 113.
30 See Stella Babalola and Pearl Nwashili, "Poverty, Adolescent Sexuality, and the Shadow of AIDS: A Study of Female Motor Park Workers in Lagos Nigeria," in Obioma Nnaemeka and Joy Ngozi Ezeilo, eds., *Engendering Human Rights: Cultural and Socioeconomic Realities in Africa* (New York: Palgrave Macmillan, 2005), 157–77.
31 Schoepf, "Inscribing the Body Politic," 558.
32 *Women and HIV/AIDS: Confronting the Crisis*, 4.
33 There is extensive literature on the state of widowhood by Africanists and I will not review that literature here. See Michael Kirwen, *African Widows: An Empirical Study of the Problems of Adapting Western Christian Teachings on Marriage to the Leviratic Custom for the Care of Widows in Four Rural African Societies* (Maryknoll, N.Y.: Orbis Books, 1979); Betty Pottash, *Widows in African Societies: Choices and Constraints* (Stanford, Calif.: Stanford University Press, 1986); Beatrice Mutongi, "Generations of Grief and Grievances: A History of Widows and Widowhood in Margoli, Western Kenya, 1900 to Present," Ph.D. dissertation, University of Virginia, 1996; Vanessa von Struensee, *Widows, AIDS, Health and Human Rights in Africa: Case Study from Tanzania*. See her discussion of widow rights in the context of illness at http://papers.ssrn.com/sol3/papers.cfm?abstract_id=569665#PaperDownload (accessed June 5, 2005); Human Rights Watch, "Double Standards, Women's Property Rights Violations in Kenya," http://www.hrw.org/reports/2003/kenya 0303 (accessed June 5, 2005); see also Elias K. Bongmba, *The Dialectics of Transformation in Africa* (New York: Palgrave Macmillan, 2006).

34 Evelynes Kawango Agot, "Widow Inheritance and HIV/AIDS Interventions in Sub-Saharan Africa: Contesting Conceptualizations of 'Risks' and 'Spaces' of Vulnerability," Ph.D. dissertation, University of Washington, 2001, p. 84.

35 Agot, "Widow Inheritance," 89.

36 Agot, "Widow Inheritance," 93.

37 Agot, "Widow Inheritance," 142.

38 Agot, "Widow Inheritance," 147.

39 Agot, "Widow Inheritance," 152–57.

40 Agot, "Widow Inheritance," 112.

41 The texts are 1 Corinthians 7:8-9, 39 and Romans 7:2.

42 The text that states that the younger brother takes the wife of his brother who dies without children is Deuteronomy 25:5-10. New Testament passages sometimes used to support the practice are 1 Timothy 5:9, 14 and 1 Corinthians 7:3, 4.

43 Agot, "Widow Inheritance," 120.

44 Agot, "Widow Inheritance," 124.

45 Hope for the Widow Ministry, Bamenda, Cameroon.

46 UNAIDS, *2004 Report on the Global AIDS Epidemic*, 62. Distinctions are made between maternal and paternal orphans based on the parent that has died.

47 UNAIDS, *2004 Report*, 61.

48 Nfor Njingti, who is coordinator for finance and administration for the new foundation, provided the information.

49 Cameroon Baptist Convention, "Chosen Children Program Family Caregivers Manual: Helping Families Change Lives," June 2005, p. 4.

50 "Chosen Children Program," 4.

51 "Chosen Children Program," 11–12.

52 "Chosen Children Program," 17.

53 "Chosen Children Program," 28–30.

54 See Dube, *HIV/AIDS and the Curriculum*.

55 Cameroon Baptist Convention Health Board, AIDS Control and Prevention Program (ACP), p. 8.

56 Cameroon Baptist Convention Health Board, "Rapid Scaling-Up of Prevention of Mother-to-Child HIV Transmission (PMTCT) in Cameroon, West Africa," 1.

57 "Rapid Scaling-Up," 1.

58 "Rapid Scaling Up," 1.

59 "Rapid Scaling-Up," 2.

60 Cameroon Baptist Convention Health Board, *AIDS Control and Prevention (ACP): Information, Education and Communication (IEC) Material on HIV/AIDS*, 11.

61 *AIDS Control and Prevention*, 16.

62 *AIDS Control and Prevention*, 17.

63 Reverend Nyansoko-ni-Nku, "The Church and the Challenge of AIDS," Moderator's Message on the Occasion of the 45th Church Day Celebration.

The Handbook: A Manual of the Presbyterian Youth Fellowship Movement of the Presbyterian Church in Cameroon (Bamenda: Church Center, n.d.), 33.

64   I have not been able to get complete verification of this program and I have not received confirmation that it is widely available in Cameroon.

65   Nyansoko-ni-Nku, "Church and Challenge."

66   Nyansoko-ni-Nku, "Church and Challenge."

67   Setah Lydia Ajeitoh, "AIDS, A Friend to All," *The Handbook: A Manual of the Christian Youth Fellowship Movement of the Presbyterian Church in Cameroon* (Bamenda: Youth Department of the PCC, n.d.), 40–41.

68   Southern African Catholic Bishops' Conference, "A Message of Hope from the Catholic Bishops to the People of God in South Africa, Botswana and Swaziland," Pretoria, 2001.

69   Philippe Denis, "Sexuality and AIDS in South Africa," *Journal of Theology for Southern Africa* 115 (2003): 63–77, p. 74.

70   Edward C. Green, "The Impact of Religious Organizations in Promoting HIV/AIDS Prevention," *The CCIH Forum* 11 (2001): 3–6. For a further discussion of Ugandan prevention, see Peter Mwaura's essay, "Pioneers in the Control of HIV/AIDS: Uganda and Senegal Show that Infection Rates can be Reduced," *African Recovery Online: A United Nations Publication* 12.4 (1999): http://www.un.org/ecosodev/geninfo/afrec/vol12no4/pioneers.htm.

71   Claudio Schuftan quotes Justin Parkhurst of the London School of Hygiene as arguing that infections rates have dropped in Uganda, but not at the rate that was reported by President Moseveni. See Claudio Schuftan, "Aids in Uganda: Is There Such a Thing as a Success Story?" *Afro Nets* 12 (2002): http://www.afro nets.org/afronets-hma/afro-nets.200209/msg00018.php.

72   Quoted in Donald Messer, *Breaking the Conspiracy of Silence: Christian Churches and the Global AIDS Crisis* (Minneapolis: Fortress, 2004), 57. See original quotation in Michael Specter, "The Vaccine," *New Yorker*, February 3, 2003, p. 56.

73   Brendan Carmody, "Religious Heritage and Premarital Sex in Zambia," *Journal of Theology for Southern Africa* 115 (2003): 79–90.

74   Carmody, "Religious Heritage," 83.

75   Carmody, "Religious Heritage," 85.

76   Carmody, "Religious Heritage," 89.

77   World Council of Churches, "Plan of Action," 3.

78   See Michael Kelly's programmatic essay, "Defeating HIV/AIDS through Education." http://www.jesuitaids.net/dateducation.htm.

79   Schoepf, "Uganda," 553–72.

80   Musa Dube, "Methods of Integrating HIV/AIDS in Biblical Studies," in Dube, ed., *HIV/AIDS and the Curriculum*, 10–13.

81   Dube has reflected on her shocking realization that if the statistics are true and everything happens as predicted, most of the students who have studied with her at the University of Botswana are not likely to be alive in a few years.

82   Dube, "Methods of Intergrating," 4. Dube has organized seminars that have brought the entire university community to focus on the pandemic. Central to Dube's impressive approach has been viewing the Bible as a historic and contemporary document. Historical approaches to biblical studies enable people to grasp the context of passages that deal with illness but also make linkages to current epidemics such as poverty, inequality, corruption, international inequities, and exploitation of the most vulnerable members of the community, such as widows and orphans. Literary readings of the biblical text invite readers to consider "narrative, ideological, psychoanalytical, feminist and post-colonial methods" in understanding the HIV/AIDS crisis. Dube cites the New Testament story of a woman who had a bleeding problem and healers could not do anything about the disease. Reading it in light of HIV/AIDS brings out different issues: feminist concerns with discrimination, stigmatization, and the absence of a cure. The narrative of Jairus bringing his daughter to Jesus, although he knew she was dead, is a story of hope. These narratives in the context of HIV/AIDS then offer hope and life. Dube also discusses social scientific and cultural anthropological methods that emphasize approaching a text on its terms.

83   Dube, "Methods of Intergrating," 20.

84   Gerald West, "Reading the Bible in the Light of HIV/AIDS in South Africa," *Ecumenical Review* 55.4 (2003): 335–44, 35.

85   Johanna Stiebert, "Does the Hebrew Bible Have Anything to Tell Us About HIV/AIDS?" in Dube, ed., *HIV/AIDS and the Curriculum*, 25.

86   However, God brought plagues on the Egyptians not to punish sin but demonstrate that God is in control. The case of Job demonstrates that illness was not always a punishment for sin. Furthermore, the Hebrew Bible also indicates that impurities caused illness. In case of infectious diseases such as leprosy, the victim was supposed to announce his or her presence to warn other members of the community.

87   Ron Russell-Coons, "We Have AIDS," in Letty M. Russell, ed., *The Church with AIDS: Renewal in the Midst of Crisis* (Louisville, Ky.: Westminster John Knox, 1990), 36.

Chapter 5

1   Nelson Mandela, "Care, Support, Destigmatization," Closing Statements at the XVI International AIDS Conference Barcelona, Spain, July 12, 2002.

2   Mitchell Warren, "An Epidemic that Rages On," in Patricia Kahn, ed., *AIDS Vaccine Handbook: Global Perspective* (New York: AIDS Vaccine Advocacy Coalition, 2005), v.

3   In this chapter I am concerned with relations between nations or states, and what I refer to variously as the community, global village, or society. For clearer distinctions see the discussion of nation, state, and society in Anthony Giddens,

The Consequences of Modernity (Cambridge: Polity Press, 1990); Roland Robertson, "Globalization: Time-Space and Homogeneity," in M. Featherstone, ed., *Global Modernities* (London: Sage, 1995), 25–44; J. A. Scholte, *Globalization: A Critical Introduction* (London: Palgrave, 2000).

4   Jeffrey Sachs and Sonia Ehrlich Sachs, "AIDS and Africa: Where is the U.S.," *Boston Globe*, February 2002.

5   John Tomlinson has described globalization as "the rapidly developing and ever–densening network of interconnections and interdependence that characterizes modern social life" (*Globalization and Culture* [Chicago: The University of Chicago Press, 1999], 2).

6   See Roland Robertson, *Globalization: Social Theory and Global Culture* (London: Sage, 1992).

7   Amartya Sen, "If It Is Fair, It's Good: 10 Truths About Globalization," *International Herald Tribune*, July 1–15 (2001): 6.

8   James H. Mittleman identifies three phases of globalization. He calls the first phase incipient globalization, which marked the shrinking of the world before the sixth century. The connective strategies during this period were conquest, trade, and migration. The second phase, bridging globalization, defined human relations and connections on economic principles. The driving force was "competitive markets oriented to[wards] profit maximization, wage labor, and the private ownership of the major means of production" (18). This shift objectified human and economic relations through territorial expansion. The third phase of globalization is what Mittelman calls accelerated globalization where competition has not only been strengthened but is "accompanied by a restructuring of production, including its spatial reorganization, which is, in turn, facilitated both by technological advances and state policies" (19). See James H. Mittleman, *The Globalization Syndrome: Transformations and Resistance* (Princeton: Princeton University Press, 2001).

9   Giddens, *Consequences of Modernity*, 64.

10   William Schweiker argues: "It is not only that we now have access to information via TV, radio, the Internet, and the market about other parts of the world, although that is important. Much more the 'compression of the world' in terms of the range of consciousness means a new moment within the imaginative project of world-making." See William Schweiker, "A Preface to Ethics: Global Dynamics and the Integrity of Life," *Journal of Religious Ethics* 32.1 (2004): 13–37, 19.

11   Shang-Jin Wei, argues that globalization is central to economic development, although he acknowledges the fact that unequal capital flow makes globalization risky business. Shang-Jin Wei, "Risk and Reward of Embracing Globalization: The Governance Factor," *Journal of African Economies* 12, AERC Suppl. 1 (2003): 72.

12   United Nations Development Program, *Human Development Report 1998* (New York: Oxford University Press), 183.

13   UNDP, *Human Development Report*, 49.

14 Simeon O. Ilesanmi, "Leave No Poor Behind: Globalization and the Imperative of Socio-Economic Development Rights from an African Perspective," *Journal of Religious Ethics* 32.1 (2004): 77. I am indebted to Professor Ilesanmi for his insights on globalization in this essay.

15 Thabo Mbeki, "On African Renaissance," *African Philosophy* 12.1 (1999): 5–10. See Elias K. Bongmba, "Reflections on Thabo Mbeki's African Renaissance," *Journal of Southern African Studies* 30.2 (2004): 289–314.

16 S. Ibi Ajayi, "Globalization and Africa," *Journal of African Economies* 12, AERC Suppl. 1 (2003): 122.

17 Schweiker argues: "The temptation to understand the movement of 'globalization,' the making of one world, as somehow simply the product of western imperialism or capitalism seems to miss the historical complexity of the reality we are trying to understand. And yet, we should not deny the novelty of our situation. Pictures of the earth as a blue green orb floating in a silent dance about the sun have only been available to the human imagination during the so-called space age. The spread of global capital has also bound people in a complex web of interdependences" (19).

18 See Elias K. Bongmba, *The Dialectics of Transformation in Africa* (New York: Palgrave Macmillan, 2006).

19 For a detailed analysis of the role of markets in globalization, see Cynthia Moe-Lobeda, *Healing a Broken World: Globalization and God* (Minneapolis: Fortress, 2002); David R. Loy, "Religion and the Market," *Journal of the American Academy of Religion* 65 (1997): 275–90.

20 Dwight Hopkins describes this kind of globalization that is driven by the monopoly of finance through capitalism as a religion. "Monopoly, finance, capitalist wealth, as god in the religion of globalization, is a power in its own right that makes its adherents bow down to it and pursue any means necessary to obtain it" (9). Hopkins argues that the theology of this religion is neoliberalism, which espouses free markets, privatization, and deregulation. See Dwight N. Hopkins, "The Religion of Globalization," in Dwight N. Hopkins, Lois Ann Lorentzen, Eduardo Mendieta, and David Batstone, eds., *Religions/Globalizations: Theories and Cases* (Durham and London: Duke University Press, 2001), 7–32.

21 "Africa has failed to attract substantial private investment because of the perception of Africa in general as a high-risk environment, even though the degree and extent of risk varies from one country to another" (Ajayi, "Globalization and Africa," 131).

22 Ajayi, "Globalization and Africa," 143–44.

23 Ilesanmi, "Leave No Poor Behind," 72.

24 World Bank, *World Development Report*, 1995, p. 122.

25 K. C. Abraham, "Together in Mission and Unity: Beholding the Glory of God's Kingdom," *Voices from the Third World* 22.1 (1999): 144–45.

26 Manu Dibango, *Three Kilos of Coffee: An Autobiography, in collaboration with Danielle Rouard,* trans. Beth R. Raps (Chicago: The University of Chicago Press, 1994). See especially the chapter "Soul Makossa."

27 Franco at le TPOK Jazz, "Attention Na Sida" in *Le Grand maitre Luambo Intepelle Le Societé dans Attention Na Sida* (Paris: Sono Disc). Franco's album *Les Rumeurs* addresses the growing speculation in Kinshasa that Franco himself was infected with the HIV virus and that he was suffering from HIV complications. Since Franco died in 1989, rumors have persisted that he died of AIDS. The late Pepe Kale, also from the Democratic Republic of the Congo, wrote and performed a song on HIV/AIDS for UNICEF.

28 See David Eaton, "Understanding AIDS in Public Lives," in Kalipeni et al., eds., *HIV and AIDS in Africa*, 279–90.

29 Luambo never stated throughout his life that he was HIV-positive.

30 See Kelly Lee, *Health Impacts of Globalization: Towards Global Governance* (London: Palgrave Macmillan, 2002); David Woodward, Nick Drager, Robert Beaglhole and Debra A. Lipson, "Globalization and Health: A Framework for Analysis and Action," *Bulletin of the World Health Organization* 70 (2001): 875–80.

31 See A. J. McMichael and Robert Beaglehole, "The Changing Global Context of Public Health," *The Lancet* 356 (2000): 495–99. http://thelancet.com/era/ LLAN.ERA.1060 (accessed November 25, 2004).

32 Eugenio Diaz-Bonilla, Julie Babinard, and Per Pinstrup-Andersen, "Globalization and Health: Opportunities and Risks for the Poor in Developing Countries," *Nord-Süd aktuell* 16.3 (2002): 417–25. See also http://www.icreier. res.in/pdf/risk.pdf (accessed November 25, 2004).

33 Richard Falk, *On Humane Governance: Toward a New Global Politics* (University Park: Penn State University Press, 1995).

34 Centers for Disease Control (CDC), "HIV/AIDS among Racial/Ethnic Minorities," *Morbidity and Mortality Weekly Report* 49 (2000): 4–11.

35 Farley, *Compassionate Respect*, 18.

36 Associated Press reporter Matt Moore wrote the story. See http://www.world revolution.org/article/1448 (first accessed June 19, 2004).

37 UNAIDS, *Report on the Global HIV/AIDS Epidemic*, 2002, p. 83.

38 United Nations General Assembly Special Session on HIV/AIDS, June 2001. See para. 55 for the full text of this declaration.

39 UNAIDS, *A Joint Response to HIV/AIDS*, 2004. In 1996 six UN agencies established the Joint United Nations Programme on HIV/AIDS, which has come to be called, UNAIDS. These were United Nations Children's Fund (UNICEF), United Nations Development Programme (UNDP), United Nations Population Fund (UNFPA), United Nations Educational, Scientific and Cultural Organization (UNESCO), World Health Organization (WHO) and the World Bank. Other organizations that are now participating in the global effort to combat HIV/AIDS are: the United Nations Office on Drugs and Crime (UNODO), International Labor Organization (ILO), World Food Programme (WFP), and United Nations Development Fund for Women (UNIFEM).

40 "Update: Acquired Immunodeficiency Syndrome—United States," *Morbidity and Mortality Weekly Report* 34 (1985): 275–76.

41 See studies by Katherine Floyd and Charles Gilks, "Cost and Financing of Providing Anti-Retroviral Therapy: A Background Paper," *World Health Organization*, April 1997; www.worldbank.org/aids–econ/arv/floyd/whoarv. pdf, p. 6 (accessed June 19, 2005).

42 Floyd and Gilks, "Cost and Financing," 7.

43 See a copy of his remarks at http://www.unaids.org/.

44 See the work of Agricultural Missions of New York (wcarroo@ncccusa.org), and also National Catholic Rural Life Conference, Des Moines, Iowa (ncrlcg@aol.com). Several papers published by SEDOS on their Web site are critical of globalization.

45 Hans Küng, *A Global Ethic for Global Politics and Economics* (New York: Oxford University Press, 1999), xiii. See also H. Küng and K. J. Kuschel, eds., *A Global Ethic: The Declaration of the World's Religions* (London: SCM Press, 1993); Hans Küng, *Yes to a Global Ethic* (New York: Continuum, 1996). Küng's claim that the world lacks a vision of the future ignores other scholarly perspectives in the debate on globalization and development. See for example Robertson, *Globalization*; Robertson, "Globalization," 25–44; Marty Chen, *A Quiet Revolution: Women in Transition in Rural Bangladesh* (Dhaka: BRAC, 1986).

46 Küng, *Global Ethic*, 110.

47 Küng, *Global Ethic*, 111. The Parliament of World Religions has defined the new global ethic as: "a fundamental consensus on binding values, irrevocable standards, personal attitudes. . . . We need mutual respect, partnership, and understanding, instead of patriarchal domination and degradation. . . . We condemn sexual exploitation and sexual discrimination as one of the worst forms of human degradation. . . . Let no one be deceived. There is no authentic humaneness without a living together in partnership." See *Towards a Global Ethic*, statement by the 1993 Parliament of the World's Religions, August 28–September 5, 1993, Chicago.

48 Some scholars from different disciplines have responded to Küng's projects in the *International Journal of Politics, Culture and Society* 13.1 (1999).

49 Douglas Meeks, "God's *Oikonomia* and the New World Economy," in Max L. Stackhouse, ed., *Christian Social Ethics in a Global Era* (Nashville: Abingdon, 1995), 112. See also M. Douglas Meeks, *God the Economist: The Doctrine of God and Political Economy* (Minneapolis: Fortress, 1989) and his essay "Global Economy and the Globalization of Theological Education," in Alice Frazer Evans, Robert A. Evans, and David A Roozen, eds., *The Globalization of Theological Education* (Maryknoll, N.Y.: Orbis Books, 1993).

50 Meeks, "God's *Oikonomia*, 112.

51 Meeks, "God's *Oikonomia*, 112.

52 Meeks, "God's *Oikonomia*, 113.

53 Meeks, "God's *Oikonomia*, 113.

54 Meeks, "God's *Oikonomia*, 117.

55 The mobility of capital and resources has been accompanied by a massive migration of people from the South to the economically viable North, further weakening the productive capacity of the Least Developed Countries (LDC). This exodus has devastated the health-care industry because many trained physicians and nurses have taken up employment in Europe, the United States, Canada, Australia, and New Zealand. Even South Africa, which seems to be doing relatively well in sub-Saharan Africa, is seeing most skilled workers leave the country to seek employment elsewhere. The impact of this exodus has not been fully grasped and will undercut all attempts at capacity building in the near future.

56 E. D. Pellegrino, "Ethics," *Journal of the American Medical Association* 263.19 (1990): 2641–42. See also his essay, "Ethics and Treatment of HIV Infection," in Overberg, *AIDS, Ethics and Religion*, 78–82.

57 UNAIDS, "Financing the Expanded Response to AIDS," http://www.unaids.org/bangkok2004/report.html.

58 See http://www.thebody.com/fda/atripla.html?m158h (accessed July 12, 2006).

59 Kris Peterson and Olatubosun Obileye, "Access to Drugs for HIV/AIDS and Related Opportunistic Infections in Nigeria," *Policy Project*, Nigeria, 2002, pp. 2–4. See http://www.globaltreatmentaccess.org, p. 2. I have used materials from the Altering Nature Project, a Ford Foundation-funded project at Rice University, chaired by Baruch Broody and Jerry McKenny, and directed by Andy Lustig. For this project, we used the study co-authored by Peterson and Obileye. I extend appreciation to my colleagues on the legal and economic team for some of this material.

60 Peterson and Obileye,"Access to Drugs," 2–4.

61 Peterson and Obileye,"Access to Drugs," 8.

62 Peterson and Obileye,"Access to Drugs," 8.

63 Peterson and Obileye,"Access to Drugs," 8.

64 Peterson and Obileye,"Access to Drugs," 20. See also Carmen Pérez and Pascale Boulet, *HIV/AIDS Medicines Pricing Report. Setting Objectives: Is There a Political Will?* (Geneva: Médicines Sans Frontiéres, 2000).

65 UNAIDS and World Health Organization, *Progress on Global Access to HIV Antiretroviral Therapy: A Report on '3 by 5' and Beyond* (Geneva, 2006), 6.

66 B. Jordan-Harder et al., "Thirteen Years of HIV–1 Sentinel Surveillance and Indicators for Behavioral Change Suggests Impact of Programme Activities in Southwest Tanzania," *AIDS* 18 (2004): 287–94.

67 UNAIDS and WHO, *Progress on Global Access*, 7.

68 UNAIDS and WHO, *Progress on Global Access*, 7.

69 UNAIDS, *AIDS in Africa* (Geneva: UNAIDS, 2005), 14.

70 UNAIDS, *AIDS in Africa*, 14.

71 UNAIDS, *AIDS in Africa*, 14.

72 UNAIDS, *AIDS in Africa*, 15

73 UNAIDS, *AIDS in Africa*, 15. These tough choices include interest of the state vs. individuals, immediate economic growth vs. investment in long-term human capital, working with traditions that promote risks, ensuring that

nation building is balanced with alliances that are pan-African, balancing freedom from outside control with appropriate relationship to the resources that
come from outside, choosing between protecting women and giving them freedoms, choosing to target prevention and treatment for a few or for all, and balancing the needs of the rural and the urban. See p. 16.

74 See World Health Organization, *The Mission for Essential Drugs and Supplies*
(Geneva: WHO, 2004).

75 Ecumenical News Digest, World Council of Churches on-line, June 19, 2004.

76 See http://www.e–alliance.ch/hivaids.jsp.

77 See http://www.epnetwork.org.

78 This summary is taken from http://www.africa.upenn.edu/afrfocus/afrfo
cus110504.html, received in an e-mail on November 5, 2004.

79 In this part I have drawn from the work in the economic section of the Altering
Nature Project at Rice University, from Peterson and Obileye, "Access to Drugs."

80 C. Raghavan, "No Investment Rules Reducing Flexibility," *South-North
Development Monitor* 45.7 (1999).

81 J. A. Ekpere, "The OAU Model Law and Africa's Common Position on the
TRIPS Review Process," 2. Professor Ekpere is former executive secretary of the
OAU Scientific, Technical and Research Commission. For the Model Law, see
http://www.grain.org/brl/oau-model-law-en.cfm.

82 Ekpere, "OAU Model Law," 5.

83 Ekpere, "OAU Model Law," 6.

84 Godfrey Tangwa, "The HIV/AIDS Pandemic, African Traditional Values and
the Search for a Vaccine in Africa," *Journal of Medicine and Philosophy* 27.2
(2002): 224.

85 See http://www.2.cnn.com/Earth/9703/18/bark/.

86 Warren, "An Epidemic," vi.

87 Bill Snow, "Why We Need Vaccine Activism Still," in Kahn, ed., *AIDS Vaccine
Handbook*, 3. See also http://www.iavi.org/ (first accessed December 1, 2005).

88 http://www.iavi.org/viewpage.cfm?aid=13 (accessed May 20, 2006).

89 See Patricia Kahn, "Where Are We in the Search for an AIDS Vaccine?" in
Kahn, *AIDS Vaccine Handbook*, 8.

90 Richard Jeffreys, "Vaccines that Trigger Cellular Immunity: What Can We
Hope For?" in Kahn, *AIDS Vaccine Handbook*, 53–54.

91 See Bill Snow, "Vaccine Basics," in Kahn, *AIDS Vaccine Handbook*, 25.

92 See the policy brief of Accelerated Vaccine Introduction Project, "Estimating
the Global Impact of an AIDS Vaccine" (November 2005), 1; http://www.iavi.
org/viewfile.cfm?fid=35239 (accessed December 1, 2005).

93 "Estimating the Global Impact," 2.

94 "Estimating the Global Impact," 2.

95 See J. Esparza, M. L. Chang, R. Widdus, Y. Madrid, N. Walker, and P. Ghys,
"Estimation of 'Needs' and 'Probable Uptake' for HIV/AIDS Preventive
Vaccines Based on Possible Policies and Likely Acceptance" (a WHO/
UNAIDS/IAVI study), *Vaccine* 21 (2003): 2032–41. I am indebted to the IAVI
policy paper for this reference.

96 See its report at http://www.niaid.nih.gov/hivvaccines/whsummarystatus.htm (accessed May 2006).

97 Dr. Margaret I. Johnston is the director of vaccine and prevention research in the division of AIDS and assistant director of HIV/AIDS vaccines at the NIAID; Dr. Anthony S. Fauci is the director of NIAID. See http://www3.niaid. nih.gov/about/directors/pdf/baltimore_sun.pdf (accessed May 20, 2006).

98 See http://www3.niaid.nih.gov/about/directors/news/HVAD2006.htm.

99 I make this observation in light of the seriousness of the global HIV/AIDS pandemic, and do not intend it as a criticism of the work of the Institute, which involves research on many other infectious diseases. The United States has also committed the largest amount of money for HIV vaccine research. See other publications on vaccine research at http://www.niaid.nih.gov/publications/vaccine.htm.

100 IAVI, "Investing in AIDS Vaccines: Estimated Resources Required to Accelerate R&D" (June 2005): 1.

101 Coordinating Committee of Global HIV/AIDS Vaccine Enterprise, "The Global HIV/AIDS Vaccine Enterprise: Sceintific Strategic Plan," *PLos Medicine* 2.2, e25 (2005): 0111–21.

102 UNAIDS, "Financing the Expanded Response to AIDS: HIV Vaccine and Microbicide Research and Development" (2005), 2.

103 UNAIDS, "Financing the Expanded Response," 4.

104 UNAIDS, "Financing the Expanded Response," 6.

105 Patrice Trouiller, Piero Olliaro, Els Torreele, James Orbinski, Richard Laing, and Nathan Ford, "Drug Development for Neglected Diseases: A Deficient Market and a Pubic Health Policy Failure," *The Lancet* 359 (2002): 2189.

106 See D. Guenter, J. Esparza, and R. Macklin, "Ethical Considerations in International HIV Vaccine Trials: Summary of a Consultative Process Conducted by the Joint United Nations Programme on HIV/AIDS (UNAIDS)," *Journal of Medical Ethics* 26 (2000): 37–43.

107 R. Bayer, "The Debate over Maternal-Fetal HIV Transmission Prevention Trials in Africa, Asia and the Caribbean: Racist Exploitation or Exploitation of Racism?" *American Journal of Public Health* 88.4 (1998): 567–70; Susan Craddock, "AIDS and Ethics: Clinical Trials, Pharmaceuticals, and Global Scientific Practice," In Kalipeni et al., eds., *HIV and AIDS in Africa*, 241–51.

108 Pontiano Kaleebu, "HIV Vaccine Trials in Uganda: Personal Experience as an Investigator," in Kahn, ed., *AIDS Vaccine Handbook*, 147.

109 Kallebu, "HIV Vaccine Trials," 147.

110 See www.aidsuganda.org for further information on the vaccine trials.

111 C. O. Tacket, and R. Edelman, "Ethical Issues Involving Volunteers in AIDS Vaccine Trials," *Journal of Infectious Diseases* 161 (1990): 356.

112 African Networks on Ethics, Law and HIV, 1994.

113 P. Wimhurst, "Scientific Imperialism," *British Medical Journal* 314 (1997): 841.

114 Keymanthri Moodley, "HIV Vaccine Trial Participation in South Africa—An Ethical Assessment," *Journal of Medicine and Philosophy* 27.2 (2002): 197–215.

115 Moodley, "HIV Vaccine Trial Participation," 203. See original study in Karim Abdool Q., S. S. Karim, H. M. Coovadia, and M. Susser, "Informed Consent for HIV Testing in a South African Hospital: Is It Truly Informed and Truly Voluntary?" *American Journal of Public Health* 88.4 (1998): 637–40.

116 Craddock, "AIDS and Ethics," 247.

117 Moodley, "HIV Vaccine Trial Participation," 205.

118 Craddock, "AIDS and Ethics," 248.

119 Craddock, "AIDS and Ethics," 206.

120 Craddock, "AIDS and Ethics," 209. See N. A. Christakis, "The Ethical Design of an AIDS Vaccine Trial in Africa," *Hastings Center Report* (June/July 1988): 31–37.

121 Kris Peterson reports other cure claims made by physicians in Nigeria. See Peterson, "HIV/AIDS and Democracy."

122 "At Last a Miracle Drug Against AIDS," *The Weekly Review*, Nairobi, February 9, 1990, 10–34.

123 V. A. Ngu, "The Viral Envelope in the Evolution of HIV: A Hypothetical Approach to Inducing an Effective Immune Response to the Virus," *Medical Hypothesis* 48 (1997) 517–21. For further information on Professor Ngu, see his Web page, http://www.vangu.8m.net/index.html.

124 Tangwa, "The HIV/AIDS Pandemic," 223.

125 Tangwa, "The HIV/AIDS Pandemic," 224.

126 Camenetwork, December 5, 2000.

127 For Professor Ngu's initial publication, see V. A. Ngu, "The Viral Envelope in the Evolution of HIV: A Hypothetical Approach to Inducing an Effective Immune Response to the Virus," *Medical Hypothesis* 48 (1997): 517–21.

128 Panafrican News Agency, 2000.

129 A. Okwemba and Makokha, "Kenyan May Lose out on 'Majengo' AIDS Vaccine," *Daily Nation*, Thursday, October 12, 2000.

130 Peterson and Obileye, "Access to Drugs," 2–4. See http://www.globaltreat mentaccess.org/.

131 The Canadian ministry Crossroads announces on its Web site that it also receives funding from the Canadian government. See http://www.crossroads. ca/missions/index.html.

132 See http://www.globaltreatmentaccess.org. Religious organizations range from small groups to large international organizations. See http://www.worldvi-sion.com.au/resources/global_issues.asp. This particular site has information on a range of global issues including HIV/AIDS.

133 Shorter and Onyancha, *Church and AIDS in Africa*, 31.

134 This might not be as much of a problem for many of the African churches as for some of the Western churches they are affiliated with. Many Western churches opposed the World Council of Church's campaign to combat apartheid. The Southern Baptist Convention, the largest Protestant denomina-tion in the United States, announced in June of 2004 that it was breaking ties with the Baptist World Alliance. American evangelical churches continue to shy

away from social action. However, in light of the global HIV/AIDS pandemic, churches have no choice but to collaborate with the global community.

135 Personal communication from students who traveled to East Africa.

136 Shorter and Onyancha, *Church and AIDS in Africa*, 34.

137 For work done by Catholic development organizations see information on the International Cooperation for Development and Solidarity (CIDSE) and Caritas Internationalis (CI), http:// www.cidse.org/pubs/finaldebteng.html.

138 All Africa Conference of Churches, "AACC Jubilee Convocation Message: Time to Rediscover the Gospel," *Tam Tam, A Publication of AACC* (January–June 2001): 27–30.

139 I am indebted to Stefan de Vylder for this summary. See *Debt-for-AIDS Swaps: A UNAIDS Policy Information Brief* (Geneva: UNAIDS, 2004). For further discussion of this topic see J. Kaiser and A. Lambert, *Debt Swaps for Sustainable Development: A Partial Guide for NGOs* (Gland, Switzerland and Cambridge, UK: International Union for Conservation of Nature and Natural Resources, 1996); L. Mercado, *Debt Swaps for Nature and Human Development: An Initiative for Turning a Problem into Opportunities in SIDS* (New York: UNDP, 2003); UNAIDS and the World Bank, *AIDS, Poverty Reduction and Debt Relief: A Toolkit for Mainstreaming HIV/AIDS Programmes into Development Instruments* (Geneva: UNAIDS, 2001).

140 Quoted in Mercado, *Debt Swaps,* 3.

141 Vylder, *Debt-for-AIDS Swaps,* 16.

142 Olusegun Obansanjo, "Letter to the Southern Baptist Convention," in *The aWake Project: Uniting Against the African AIDS Crisis,* compiled by Jenny Eaton and Kate Etue (Nashville: W Publishing Group, 2002), 76–79.

143 For organizations currently working on debt relief see: http://www.africa action.org/action/debt.htm; www.jubilee2000uk.org, www.oxfam.org.uk; www. Christian-ad.org; www.dropthedebt.org (accessed August 2004 and June 12, 2005). See the International Monetary Fund's Heavily Indebted Poor Countries (HIPC) project at http://www.imf.org/external/np/exr/ib/2001/071001.htm (accessed June 12, 2005). See also the World Bank's HIPC's Initiative at http://www.worldbank.org/hipc.

144 Some of the organizations include Bread for the World, DATA, PlanUS/Childreach, International Medical Corps, International Rescue Committee, Mercy Corps, Oxfam America, Save the Children, World Concern and World Vision. See http://ONE.org.

Conclusion

1 Farley, "New Patterns," 628.

2 Claude Levi-Strauss, *The Savage Mind* (London: Weidenfeld & Nicholson, 1966), 166.

3 Jeffrey D. Sachs, "Third World Disease: Our Problem," Internal Medicine News 38.1 (2005): 2–3. See http:/www2.einternalmedicinenews.com/scripts/ om.dll/serve?action (accessed January 12, 2005).

4   Despite some reports that abstinence was the main factor in reducing the rate of infections in Uganda, the results of a study conducted by researchers from Columbia University school of public health, John Hopkins University, and Ugandan organizations over a ten-year period in the Rakai district found that people did not really abstain; the number of people reporting engaging in sexual intercourse with two or more partners actually increased from 28 percent to 35 percent, and the percentage of young people who abstained from sex actually declined from 60 percent to 50 percent. During the period of the study, the researchers found that HIV prevalence rates declined among men and women, although it increased slightly for men between ages 15 and 24. Researchers attributed the decline to premature deaths of HIV-positive people, but the researchers also pointed out that increased condom use might have contributed to the decline. See *Medical News Today*, February 26, 2005 (accessed March 3, 2005). See also kaisernetwork.org at www.kaisernetwork.org/dailyreports/hiv, for the full report.

5   Rob Stephenson, Amy Ong Tsui, Sara Sulzbach, Phil Bardsley, Getachew Bekele, Tilahun Giday, Rehena Ahmed, Gopi Gopalkrishnan, and Bamikale Feyesitan, "Franchising Reproductive Health Services," *Health Services Research* 39.6, part 2 (2004): 2053–80.

6   See their Web site for details at http://www.dktinternational.org/article5.htm (accessed May 24, 2006).

7   Timothy R. L. Black, and Philip D. Harvey, "A Report on a Contraceptive Social Marketing Experiment in Rural Kenya," *Studies in Family Planning* 7.4 (1976): 101–8.

Bibliography

Abdool, Karim Q., S. S. Karim, H. M. Coovadia, and M. Susser. "Informed Consent for HIV Testing in a South African Hospital: Is it Truly Informed and Truly Voluntary?" *American Journal of Public Health* 88.4 (1998): 637–40.

Adams, Julia. "Ancient and Modern Morality." In *Philosophical Perspectives* 6, *Ethics* (1992): 119–36.

Abraham, K. C. "Together in Mission and Unity: Beholding the Glory of God's Kingdom." *Voices from the Third World* 22.1 (1999): 144–45.

Aghiorgoussis, Maximos. *In the Image of God: Studies in Scripture, Theology, and Community.* Brookline, Mass.: Holy Cross Orthodox Press, 1999.

Agot, Evelynes Kawango. "Widow Inheritance and HIV/AIDS Interventions in Sub-Saharan Africa: Contesting Conceptualizations of 'Risks' and 'Spaces' of Vulnerability." Ph.D. dissertation, University of Washington, 2001.

Ajayi, S. Ibi. "Globalisation and Africa." *Journal of African Economies* 12, AERC Supplement 1 (2003):120–50.

Akeroyd, Anne V. "Coercion, Consent, and 'Cultural Entrapments': A Further Look at Gendered and Occupational Factors Pertinent to the Transmission of HIV in Africa." In *HIV and AIDS in Africa: Beyond Epidemiology.* Edited by Ezekiel Kalipeni, Susan Craddock, Joseph R. Oppong, and Jayati Ghosh. Malden, Mass.: Blackwell, 2004.

Akukwe, C., and M. Foote. "HIV/AIDS in Africa: Time to Stop the Killing Fields." *Foreign Policy in Focus* 6.15 (2001).

Akyeampong, Emmanuel. "Africans in the Diaspora: The Diaspora and Africa." *African Affairs* 99 (2000): 183–215.

All Africa Conference of Churches. "AACC Jubilee Convocation Message: Time to Rediscover the Gospel." *Tam Tam, A Publication of AACC* (January–June 2001): 27–30.

Amadiume, Ifi. *Male Daughters, Female Husbands: Gender and Sex in African Societies.* London: Zed Books, 1987.

Anderson, R. M., R. M. May, and A. R. McLean. "Possible Demographic Consequences of AIDS in Developing Countries." *Nature* 332 (1988): 228–34.

Arpaly, Normy. *Unprincipled Virtue: An Inquiry into Moral Agency.* New York: Oxford University Press, 2002.

Augustine, Saint. *City of God.* Translated by R. W. Dyson. Cambridge: Cambridge University Press, 1998.

Babalola, Stella, and Pearl Nwashili. "Poverty, Adolescent Sexuality, and the Shadow of AIDS: A Study of Female Motor Park Workers in Lagos Nigeria." In *Engendering Human Rights: Cultural and Socioeconomic Realities in Africa.* Edited by Obioma Nnaemeka and Joy Ngozi Ezeilo. New York: Palgrave Macmillan, 2005. Pp. 157–77.

Bainbridge, Sheryl. "The Second Decade of AIDS: A Call for Jewish and Christian Communities of Faith to Respond and to Collaborate With Public Health." *Religious Education* 39.2 (1998): 241–57.

Bajos, N., and J. Marquet, "Research in HIV and Sexual Risk: Social Relationship-Based Approach in Cross-Cultural Perspectives." *Social Science and Medicine* 50 (2000): 1533–46.

Bancroft, Angus. "Globalisation and HIV/AIDS: Inequality and the Boundaries of a Symbolic Epidemic." *Health, Risk and Society* 3.1 (2001): 89–98.

Baptist World Alliance. "Mission in the Twenty-First Century." *International Review of Missions* 92 (2003): 613–16.

Barnett, T., and A. Whiteside, *AIDS in the Twenty-First Century.* Hampshire: Palgrave Macmillan, 2002.

Barth, Karl. *Church Dogmatics* III.I. Edinburgh: T&T Clark, 1958.

———. *Dogmatics in Outline.* Translated by G. T. Thomson. London: SCM Press, 1949.

Bayer, R. "The Debate over Maternal-Fetal HIV Transmission Prevention Trials in Africa, Asia and the Caribbean: Racist Exploitation or Exploitation of Racism?" *American Journal of Public Health* 88.4 (1998): 567–70.

Bayer, Ronald. "Public Health Policy and the AIDS Epidemic: An End to HIV Exceptionalism?" *The New England Journal of Medicine* 234.21 (1991): 1500–1504.

Baylies, Carolyn. "HIV/AIDS and Older Women in Zambia: Concern for Self, Worry over Daughters, Towers of Strength." *Third World Quarterly* 23.2 (2002): 351–75.

Beauchamp, Tom, and James Childress. *Principles of Biomedical Ethics*. 4th ed. Oxford: Oxford University Press, 1994.

Beidelman, Thomas O. *Colonial Evangelism: A Socio-Historical Study of an East African Mission at the Grassroots*. Bloomington: Indiana University Press, 1982.

Benatar, Solomon R. "The HIV/AIDS Pandemic: A Sign of Instability in a complex Global System." *Journal of Medicine and Philosophy* 27.2 (2002): 163–77.

Benhabib, Seyla. *Situating the Self*. New York: Routledge, 1992.

Benn, Christoph, and Kenneth Boyd. "Ethics, Medical Ethics and HIV/AIDS." *The Ecumenical Review* (2001): 222–32.

Berger, Peter. "Religions and Globalisation." *European Judaism* 36.1 (2003): 4–10.

Black, Timothy R. L., and Philip D. Harvey. "A Report on a Contraceptive Social Marketing Experiment in Rural Kenya." *Studies in Family Planning* 7.4 (1976): 101–8.

Blum, Lawrence. "Compassion." In *The Virtues: Contemporary Essays on Moral Character*. Edited by Robert B. Kruschwitz and Robert C. Roberts. Berkeley: University of California Press, 1987. Pp. 507–17.

Bongmba, Elias K. "Reflections on Thabo Mbeki's African Renaissance." *Journal of Southern African Studies* 30.2 (2004): 289–314.

———. "The Priority of the Other: Ethics in Africa—Perspectives from Bonhoeffer and Levinas." In *Bonhoeffer for a New Day*. Edited by John W. de Gruchy. Grand Rapids: Eerdmans, 1997. Pp. 190–208.

———. *The Dialectics of Transformation in Africa*. New York: Palgrave Macmillan, 2006.

Bookman, Myra, and Mitchell Aboulafia. "Ethics of Care Revisited: Gilligan and Levinas." *Philosophy Today* 44 suppl. (2000): 169–74.

Boumpoto, Madeleine. "Sida, Sexualité et Procréation au Congo." In *Vivre et Penser le Sida en Afrique. Experiencing and Understanding AIDS in Africa*. Edited by C. Becker et al. Dakar and Paris: CODESRIA and Karthala, 1999. Pp. 363–76.

Brant, Allan M. *No Magic Bullet: A Social History of Venereal Disease in the United States Since 1880*. New York: Oxford University Press, 1985.

Brant, A. M. "AIDS: From Social History to Social Policy." In *AIDS: The Burdens of History.* Edited by E. Fee and D. M. Fox. Berkeley, Los Angeles, and London: University of California Press, 1998. 147–71.

Breckenridge, Keith. "The Allure of Violence: Men, Race and Masculinity on the South African Gold Mines, 1900–1950." *Journal of Southern African Studies* 24.1 (1998): 669–93.

Brockerhoff, M., and Ellen Bennan. "The Poverty of Cities in Developing Countries." *Population and Development Review* 24.1 (1998): 75–114.

Brouwer, Steve, Paul Gifford, and Susan D. Rose. *Exporting the American Gospel: Global Christian Fundamentalism.* New York and London: Routledge, 1996.

Brown, M. "Ironies of Distance: An Ongoing Critique of the Geographies of AIDS." *Environment and Planning D: Society and Space* 13 (1995): 159–83.

Bujo, Bénézet. *African Christian Morality at the Age of Inculturation.* Nairobi: Paulines, 1990.

———. *African Theology in Its Social Context.* Translated by John O'Donohue. Maryknoll, N.Y.: Orbis Books, 1992.

———. *The Ethical Dimension of Community: The African Model and the Dialogue between North and South.* Nairobi: Paulines, 1998.

Cahill, Lisa Sowle. "Bioethics, Theology, and Social Change." *Journal of Religious Ethics* 31.3 (2003): 363–98.

———. *Theological Bioethics: Participation, Justice, and Change.* Washington D.C.: Georgetown University Press, 2005.

———. "Toward A Christian Theory of Human Rights." *Journal of Religious Ethics* 8.2 (2001): 277–301.

Cairns, David. *The Image of God in Man.* New York: Philosophical Library, 1953.

Caldwell, J. C., P. Caldwell, and P. Guiggin. "The Social Context of AIDS in Sub-Saharan Africa." *Population and Development Review* 15.2 (1989): 185–233.

Cameroon Baptist Convention Health Board. *AIDS Control and Prevention Program (ACP): Information, Education and Communication (IEC) Material on HIV/AIDS.* Bamenda, Cameroon: nd.

Campbell, C. "Migrancy, Masculine Identities and AIDS: The Psychosocial Context of HIV Transmission on the South African Gold Mines." *Social Science and Medicine* 45.2 (1997): 273–81.

Capps, Donald. *Deadly Sins and Saving Virtues.* Minneapolis: Fortress, 1987.

Careal, M., and S. Allen. "Women's Vulnerability to HIV/STD in Sub-Saharan Africa: An Increasing Evidence." In *Women's Position And*

Demographic Change in Sub-Saharan Africa. Edited by Paulina Makinwa and An-Magritt Jenson. Leige: International Union for the Scientific Study of Population (IUSSP), 1995. Pp. 201–22.

Carmody, Brendan. "Religious Heritage and Premarital Sex in Zambia." *Journal of Theology for Southern Africa* 115 (2003): 79–90.

Cates, Diana Fritz. *Choosing to Feel: Virtue, Friendship, and Compassion for Friends.* Notre Dame: The University of Notre Dame Press, 1997.

Centers for Disease Control (CDC). "HIV/AIDS among Racial/Ethnic Minorities." *Morbidity and Mortality Weekly Report* 49 (2000): 4–11.

Chirimuuta, R., and R. Chrimuuta. *AIDS, Africa and Racism.* London: Free Association Books, 1989.

Christakis, N. A. "The Ethical Design of an AIDS Vaccine Trial in Africa." *Hastings Center Report* (June/July 1988): 31–37.

Cimperman, Maria. *When God's People Have HIV/AIDS: An Approach to Ethics.* Maryknoll, N.Y.: Orbis Books, 2005.

Clark, Beverley. *Sex and Death: A Reappraisal of Human Mortality.* Cambridge: Polity Press, 2002.

———. "Sex and Death: Spirituality and Human Existence." *Feminist Theology* 2.2 (2004): 237–52.

Clarke, Donald S. *AIDS: The Biblical Solutions.* Nairobi: Evangel Publishing House, 1994.

Collins, Susan D. "Moral Virtue and the Limits of the Political Community in Aristotle's *Nicomachean Ethics.*" *American Journal of Political Science* 48.1 (2004): 47–61.

Comaroff, John, and Jean Comaroff. *Of Revelation and Revolution: Christianity, Colonialism, and Consciousness in South Africa.* Vol. 1. Chicago: The University of Chicago Press, 1991.

Combe, C. "HIV/AIDS Impact on the Educational Sector in South Africa." Presentation to Senior Experts Conference on HIV/AIDS and Education in ECOWAS. March 19–23 2001, Elmina, Ghana.

Commission of Appraisal, William Ernest Hocking, Chairman. *Re-Thinking Missions: A Laymen's Inquiry After One Hundred Years.* New York and London: Harper & Brothers, 1932.

Cooper, John. "Aristotle on Friendship." In *Essays on Aristotle's Ethics.* Edited by Amelia Oksenberg Rorty. Berkeley: University of California Press, 1980.

Costas, Orlando. *The Church and its Mission: A Shattering Critique from the Third World.* Wheaton, Ill.: Tyndale House, 1974.

Craddock, Susan. "AIDS and Ethics: Clinical Trials, Pharmaceuticals, and Global Scientific Practice." In *HIV and AIDS in Africa: Beyond*

Epidemiology. Edited by Ezekiel Kalipeni, Susan Craddock, Joseph R. Oppong, and Jayati Ghosh. Oxford: Blackwell, 2004. Pp. 241–51.

Curran, Charles. *Catholic Social Teaching, 1891–Present: A Historical, Theological and Ethical Analysis.* Washington D.C.: Georgetown University Press, 2000.

Damesyn, Mark Anthony. "Epidemiological Impact of Door-to-Door HIV Counseling and Testing in Rural Kenya." Ph.D. dissertation, University of California, Los Angeles, 2002.

De Vylder, Stefan. *Debt-for-AIDS Swaps: A UNAIDS Policy Information Brief.* Geneva: UNAIDS, 2004.

Delius, P., and C. Glaser. "Sexual Socialization in South Africa: A Historical Perspective." *African Studies* 61.1 (2002): 27–54.

Denis, Philippe. "Sexuality and AIDS in South Africa." *Journal of Theology for Southern Africa* 115 (2003): 63–77.

Diaz-Bonilla, Eugenio, Julie Babinard, and Per Pinstrup-Andersen. "Opportunities and Risks for the Poor in Developing Countries." (Working Paper 83) Indian Council for Research on International Economic Relations. http://www.icreier.res.in/pdf/risk.pdf.

Dowknontt, George D. *Murdered Millions.* London: 1894.

Drane, James. "Condoms, AIDS, and Catholic Ethics." *Commonweal* 189 (1991): 188–92.

Driver, Julia. "Consequentialism and Feminist Ethics." *Hypatia* 20.4 (2005): 183–99.

———. "The Conflation of Moral and Epistemic Virtue." *Metaphilosophy* 34.3 (2003): 367–83.

———. *Uneasy Virtue.* Cambridge: Cambridge University Press, 2001.

Dube, Musa W. "Culture, Gender, and HIV/AIDS Understanding and Acting on the Issues." In *HIV/AIDS and the Curriculum: Methods of Integrating HIV/AIDS in Theological Programmes.* Edited by Musa W. Dube. Geneva: World Council of Churches, 2003.

Dye, Eva N. *Bolenge: A Story of Gospel Triumphs on the Congo.* Introduction by Archibald McLean. 5th ed. Cincinnati: Foreign Christian Missionary Society, 1910.

Dykstra, Craig. *Vision and Character.* New York: Paulist Press, 1981.

Eaton, David. "Understanding AIDS in Public Lives." In *HIV and AIDS in Africa: Beyond Epidemiology.* Edited by Ezekiel Kalipeni, Susan Craddock, Joseph R. Oppong, and Jayati Ghosh. Oxford: Blackwell, 2004. Pp. 279–90.

Englehardt Jr., H. R. "The Bioethics of Care: Widows, Monastics, and a Christian Presence in Health Care." *Christian Bioethics* 11 (2005): 1–10.

Esparza, J., M. L. Chang, R. Widdus, Y. Madrid, N. Walker, and P. Ghys, "Estimation of 'Needs' and 'Probable Uptake' for HIV/AIDS Preventive Vaccines Based on Possible Policies and Likely Acceptance." *Vaccine* 21 (2003): 2032–41.

Falk, Richard. *On Humane Governance: Toward a New Global Politics.* University Park: Penn State University Press, 1995.

Falwell, Jerry. "AIDS: The Judgment of God." *Liberty Report* (April 1987): 5.

Farley, Margaret A. *Compassionate Respect: A Feminist Approach to Medical Ethics and Other Questions.* New York: Paulist Press, 2002.

———. "A Feminist Version of Respect for Persons." *Journal of Feminist Studies in Religion* 9 (1993): 182–98.

———. "Feminism and Universal Morality." In *Prospects for a Common Morality.* Edited by Gene Outka and J. Reeder. Princeton: Princeton University Press, 1993. Pp. 170–90.

———. "Fragments for an Ethic of Commitment in Thomas Aquinas." *Journal of Religion* 58 (1978): 146–47.

———. "New Patterns of Relationships: Beginnings of a Moral Revolution." *Theological Studies* 30 (1975): 627–46.

Ferguson, Alan. "Women's Health in a Marginal Area of Kenya." *Social Science and Medicine* 23 (1986): 17–29.

Flanagan, Owen. *Varieties of Moral Personality: Ethics and Psychological Realism.* Cambridge, Mass.: Harvard University Press, 1991.

Fleming, Alan. "South Africa and AIDS—Seven Years Wasted." *Nursing RSA* 8.7 (1993): 18–19.

Floyd, Katherine, and Charles Gilks. "Cost and Financing of Providing Anti-Retroviral Therapy: A Background Paper." World Health Organization, April 1997. www.worldbank.org/aids-econ/arv/floyd/whoarv.pdf.

Franco et le TPOK Jazz. "Attention Na Sida." In *Le Grand maitre Luambo Intepelle Le Societé dans Attention Na Sida.* Paris: Sono Disc.

Fuller, Jon. "AIDS Prevention: A Challenge to the Catholic Moral Tradition." *America* 175 (1996): 13–20.

Gausset, Q. "AIDS and Cultural Practices in Africa: The Case of the Tonga (Zambia)." *Social Science and Medicine* 52 (2001): 509–18.

Gekawaku, Hendrew Lusey. *The Churches Confronted with the Problem of HIV/AIDS: Analysis of the Situation in Five Countries of Central Africa; Cameroon, Chad, Congro/Brazaville, Democratic Republic of Congo, Gabon.* Geneva: World Council of Churches, 2003.

Genovesi, Vincent J. *In Pursuit of Love: Catholic Morality and Human Sexuality.* Collegeville, Minn.: Liturgical Press, 1996.

Giddens, Anthony. *The Consequences of Modernity*. Cambridge: Polity Press, 1990.

Gifford Paul. *African Christianity: Its Public Role*. Bloomington and Indianapolis: Indiana University Press, 1998.

Gilligan, Carol. *In a Different Voice: Psychological Theory and Women's Development*. Cambridge, Mass.: Harvard University Press, 1982.

Gitome, Josephine. "The Church's Response to AIDS in Africa." In *Theology of Reconstruction: Exploratory Essays*. Edited by Mary Getui and Emmanuel Obeng. Nairobi: Acton, 1999. Pp. 191–204.

Gordis, L. *Epidemiology*, Philadelphia: W. B. Saunders, 2000.

Green, Edward C. "The Impact of Religious Organizations in Promoting HIV/AIDS Prevention." *The CCIH Forum* 11 (2001): 3–6.

Grieser, Mira, Joel Gittelsohn, Anita V. Shankar, Todd Koppenhaver, Thomas K. Legrand, Ravai Marindo, Webster M. Mavhu, and Kenneth Hill. "Reproductive Decision Making and the HIV/AIDS Epidemic in Zimbabwe." *Journal of Southern African Studies* 27.2 (2001): 225–43.

Gudorf, Christian. *Body, Sex, and Pleasure: Reconstructing Christian Sexual Ethics*. Cleveland: Pilgrim Press, 1994.

Guenter, D., J. Esparza, and R. Macklin. "Ethical Considerations in International HIV Vaccine Trials: Summary of a Consultative Process Conducted by the Joint United Nations Programme on HIV/AIDS (UNAIDS)." *Journal of Medical Ethics* 26 (2000): 37–43.

Guibert, Harvé. *A l'ami qui ne m'a pas sauvé la vie*. Paris: Guillimard, 1990.

Gustafson, James. *Ethics from a Theocentric Perspective*. Vol. 1. Chicago: University of Chicago Press, 1982.

Haney, Eleanor Humes. "What Is Feminist Ethics? A Proposal for Continuing Discussion." *Journal of Religious Ethics* 8.1 (1990): 118–19.

Hart, Stephen. *Cultural Dilemmas of Progressive Politics: Styles of Engagement among Grassroots Activists*. Chicago: University of Chicago Press, 2001.

Hauerwas, Stanley. *A Community of Character: Toward a Constructive Social Ethics*. Notre Dame: University of Notre Dame Press, 1981.

———. *Truthfulness and Tragedy: Further Investigations into Christian Ethics*. Notre Dame and London: Notre Dame University Press, 1977.

Haynes, Jeff. *Religion, Globalization and Political Culture in the Third World*. New York: St Martin's Press, 1999.

Heald, S. "It's Never as Easy as ABC: Understandings of AIDS in Botswana." *African Journal of AIDS Research* 1.1 (2002): 1–10.

Hefner, Philip. "The Evolution of the Created Co-Creator." in *Cosmos as Creation: Theology and Science in Consonance*. Edited by Ted Peters. Nashville: Abingdon, 1989. Pp. 211–33.

Heidegger Martin. *Being and Time*. Translated by John Macquarie and Edward Robinson. London: SCM Press, 1962.

Hensey, Andrew Fitch. *My Children of the Forest*. New York: George H. Doran, 1924.

Hocking, William Ernest. *Rethinking Missions: A Laymen's Inquiry After One Hundred Years*. New York and London: Harper & Brothers, 1932.

Hoffman, Wendell W., and Stanley Grenz. *AIDS and Ministry in the Midst of an Epidemic*. Grand Rapids: Baker Books, 1990.

Hogan, Linda. "An Irish Nun Living with Contradictions: Responding to HIV/AIDS in the Context of Church Teaching." In *Catholic Ethicists on HIV/AIDS Prevention*. Edited by James F. Keenan. New York and London: Continuum, 2000. Pp. 41–47.

Hopkins, Dwight N. "The Religion of Globalization." In *Religions/Globalizations: Theories and Cases*. Edited by Dwight N. Hopkins, Lois Ann Lorentzen, Eduardo Mendieta, and David Batstone. Durham and London: Duke University Press, 2001. Pp. 7–32.

Horowitz, Leonard. *Emerging Viruses: AIDS & Ebola-Nature, Accident or Intentional?* Rockport, Mass.: Tetrahedron, 1997.

Howe, Leroy T. *The Image of God: A Theology for Pastoral Care and Counseling*. Nashville: Abingdon, 1995.

Human Rights Watch. "Domestic Violence, and Women's Vulnerability to HIV in Uganda." Vol. 15, 15-A. New York: Human Rights Watch, 2003.

———. "Stolen Children: Abduction and Recruitment in Northern Uganda." Vol. 15, 7-A. New York: Human Rights Watch, 2003.

Hursthouse, Rosalind. *On Virtue Ethics*. Oxford: Oxford University Press, 1999

Ilesanmi, Simeon O. "Leave No Poor Behind: Globalization and the Imperative of Socio-Economic Development Rights from an African Perspective." *Journal of Religious Ethics* 32.1 (2004): 71–92.

Irwin, Alexander, Joyce Millen, and Dorothy Fallows. *Global AIDS: Myths and Facts, Tools for Fighting the AIDS Pandemic*. Cambridge: South End Press, 2003.

Irwin, T. H. "Prudence and Morality in Greek Ethics." *Ethics* 105.2 (1995): 284–95.

Ite, Uwem E. "Turning Brain Drain into Brain Gain: Personal Reflections on Using the Diaspora Option." Edited by Paul Tiyambe Zeleza and Cassandra R. Veney.*African Issues* 30.1 (2002): 76–80.

James, D. "To Take Information Down to the People: Life Skills and HIV/AIDS, Peer Educators in the Durban Area." *African Studies* 61.1 (2002): 169–71.

Jeffreys, Richard. "Vaccines that Trigger Cellular Immunity: What Can We Hope For?" In *AIDS Vaccine Handbook: Global Perspective*. Edited by Patricia Kahn. New York: AIDS Vaccine Advocacy Coalition, 2005.

Jerman, Derek. *At Your Own Risk*. London: Hutchinson, 1992.

Jordan-Harder, B., et al. "Thirteen Years of HIV-1 Sentinel Surveillance and Indicators for Behavioral Change Suggests Impact of Programme Activities in Southwest Tanzania." *AIDS* 18 (2004): 287–94.

Kahn, Patricia, ed. *AIDS Vaccine Handbook: Global Perspective*. New York: AIDS Vaccine Advocacy Coalition, 2005.

Kaiser, J., and A. Lambert. *Debt Swaps for Sustainable Development: A Partial Guide for NGOs*. Gland, Switzerland and Cambridge: International Union for Conservation of Nature and Natural Resources, 1996.

Kaleebu, Pontiano. "HIV Vaccine Trials in Uganda: Personal Experience as an Investigator." in *AIDS Vaccine Handbook: Global Perspective*. Edited by Patricia Kahn. New York: AIDS Vaccine Advocacy Coalition, 2005. 145–52.

Kant, Immanuel. *The Metaphysics of Morals*. Translated by M. Gregor. Cambridge: Cambridge University Press, 1991.

Kaplan, Helen Singer. *The Real Truth About Women and AIDS*. New York: Simon & Schuster, 1987.

Katongole, Emmanuel M. "Postmodern Illusions and the Challenge of African Theology." *Modern Theology* 16.2 (2000): 237–54.

Kaufman, Gordon D. "The Theological Structure of Christian Faith and the Feasibility of a Global Ecological Ethic." *Zygon* 38.1 (2003): 144–61.

Keenan, James F. "Applying the Seventeenth-Century Casuistry to Accommodation of HIV Prevention." *Theological Studies* 60 (1999): 492–512.

———, ed. *Catholic Ethicists on HIV/AIDS Prevention*. New York: Continuum, 2000.

———. "Prophylactics, Toleration, and Cooperation: Contemporary Problems and Traditional Principles." *International Philosophical Quarterly* 28 (1988): 201–20.

———. "Proposing Cardinal Virtues." *Theological Studies* 56 (1995): 709–29.

———. "Virtue and Identity." *Concillium* 2 (2000): 69.

Keifert, Patrick R. "The Other: Hospitality to the Stranger, Levinas and Multicutural Mission." *Dialog* 30.1 (1991): 36–43.

Kelley, Kevin. *New Directions in Sexual Ethics: Moral Theology and the Challenge of AIDS*. London: Geoffrey Chapman, 1998.

Kelly, Michael. "Defeating HIV/AIDS through Education." http://www.jesuitaids.net/dateducation.htm.

Khathide, Agrippa G. "Teaching and Talking about our Sexuality: A Means of Combating HIV/AIDS." In *HIV/AIDS and the Curriculum: Methods of Integrating HAIV/AIDS in Theological Programmes.* Edited by Musa Dube. Geneva: World Council of Churches, 2003.

Kiragu, K. "Youth and HIV/AIDS: Can We Avoid Catastrophe?" *Population Report Series L,* no 12. Population Information Program, Bloomberg School of Public Health. Baltimore: The John Hopkins University, 2001.

Kirwen, Michael. *African Widows.* Maryknoll, N.Y.: Orbis Books, 1979.

Klimarx, P. H., T. Palanuvej, K. Limpakarnjanarat et al. "Seroprevalence of HIV Among Female Sex Workers in Bangkok: Evidence of Ongoing Infection Risks After the '100% Condom Program' was Implemented." *Journal of Acquired Immune Deficiency Syndrome* 21.4 (1999): 313–16.

Klitsch, M. "Racial Differences in Early Coitus May be Influenced by Neighborhood Context." *International Family Planning Perspectives* 26.5 (1992): 236–38.

Kovta, Joseph J. *The Christian Case for Virtue Ethics.* Washington D.C.: Georgetown University Press, 1996.

Kraemer, Hendrik. *The Christian Message in a Non-Christian World.* London and New York: Harper & Brothers, 1938.

Küng, Hans. *A Global Ethic for Global Politics and Economics.* New York: Oxford University Press, 1999.

———. *Yes to a Global Ethic.* New York: Continuum, 1996.

Küng, Hans, and K. J. Kuschel, eds. *A Global Ethic: The Declaration of the World's Religions.* London: SCM Press, 1993.

Kunnie, Julian. *Is Apartheid Really Dead? Pan-Africanist Working-Class Cultural Critical Perspectives.* Boulder: Westview Press, 2000.

LaCugna, Catherine Mowry. *God For Us: The Trinity and Christian Life.* San Francisco: HarperSanFrancisco, 1993.

Laga, Marie, Michel Alary, Peter Piot et al. "Condom Promotion, Sexually Transmitted Diseases Treatment, and Declining Incidence of HIV-1 Infection in Female Zairian Sex Workers." *The Lancet* 344 (1994): 246–48.

Landau, Elaine, ed. *We Have AIDS.* New York: Franklin Watts, 1990.

Larson, Ann. "Social Context of Human Immunodeficiency Virus Infection in Africa: Historical and Cultural Basis in East and Central African Sexual Relations." *Reviews of Infectious Diseases* 11.5 (1989): 716–31.

Latham, Michael. "AIDS in Africa: A Perspective on the Epidemic." *Africa Today* 40.3 (1993): 39–53.

Lee, Kelly. *Health Impacts of Globalization: Towards Global Governance.* London: Palgrave Macmillan, 2002.

Levenson, Jon D. "Why Jews are Not Interested in Biblical Theology." In *Judaic Perspectives on Ancient Israel.* Edited by Jacob Neusner, Baruch A. Levine, and Ernest S. Frerichs. Philadelphia: Fortress, 1987. Pp. 281–301.

Levinas, Emmanuel. *Time and the Other.* Translated by Richard Cohen. Pittsburgh: Duquesne University Press, 1987.

————. *Totality and Infinity: An Essay on Exteriority.* Translated by Alphonso Lingis. Pittsburgh: Duquesne University Press, 1969.

————. "Useless Suffering." Translated by Richard Cohen. In *The Provocation of Levinas: Rethinking the Other.* Edited by Robert Bernasconi and David Wood. London: Routledge, 1988.

————. *Otherwise Than Being: or Beyond Essence.* The Hague: Martinus Nijhoff, 1981.

————. *The Levinas Reader.* Edited by Sean Hand. Oxford: Basil Blackwell, 1989.

Loy, David R. "Religion and the Market." *Journal of the American Academy of Religion* 65.2 (1997): 275–90..

Lustg, Andrew B. "Compassion," In *Encyclopedia of Bioethics.* Edited by Warren Thomas Reich. New York: Free Press, 1975.

MacIntyre, Alasdair. *After Virtue.* Notre Dame: University of Notre Dame Press, 1988.

MacQueen, Kathleen M. "The Epidemiology of HIV Transmission: Trends, Structure and Dynamics." *Annual Review of Anthropology* 2 (1994): 509–26.

Magesa, Laurenti. "Aids and Survival in Africa: A Tentative Reflection." In *Moral and Ethical Issues in African Christianity: A Challenge for African Christianity.* Edited by J. N. K. Mugambi, A. Nasimiyu-Wasike. Nairobi: Acton, 1999.

Maluleke, Tinyinko. "Towards a New Theological Education Curriculum for the Twenty-First Century in Africa: HIV/AIDS and the New Kairos." Background paper. In *Report on the HIV/AIDS Curriculum Development Consultation for Theological Institutions in Eastern and Southern Africa.* Nairobi: MAP International, 2000.

Mandela, Nelson. "Care, Support, Destigmatization." Closing statements at the Fourteenth International AIDS Conference. Barcelona, Spain, July 12, 2002.

Marks, Shula. "An Epidemic Waiting to Happen? The Spread of HIV/AIDS in South Africa in Social and Historical Perspective." *African Studies* 61.1 (2002): 13–26.

Mbeki, Thabo. "On African Renaissance." *African Philosophy* 12.1 (1999): 5–10.

McClendon, James, Jr. *Ethics: Systematic Theology.* Vol. 1. Nashville: Abingdon Press, 1986.

McLeod, Frederick G. *The Image of God in the Antiochene Tradition.* Washington D.C.: Catholic University of America, 1999.

McMichael, A. J., and Robert Beaglehole. "The Changing Global Context of Public Health." *The Lancet* 356 (2000): 495–99.

McNiell, Donald P., Douglas A. Morrison, and Henri J. M. Nouwen, *Compassion: A Reflection on the Christian Life.* New York: Doubleday, 1983.

Meeks, Douglas. "God's *Oikonomia* and the New World Economy." In *Christian Social Ethics in a Global Era.* Edited by Max L. Stackhouse. Nashville: Abingdon, 1995. Pp. 11–26.

———. *God the Economist: The Doctrine of God and Political Economy.* Minneapolis: Fortress, 1989.

———. "Global Economy and the Globalization of Theological Education." In *The Globalization of Theological Education.* Edited by Alice Frazer Evans, Robert A. Evans, and David A Roozen. Maryknoll, N.Y.: Orbis Books, 1993.

Meilaender, Gilbert. *The Theory and Practice of Virtue.* Notre Dame: University of Notre Dame Press, 1984.

Mercado, L. *Debt Swaps for Nature and Human Development: An Initiative for Turning a Problem into Opportunities in SIDS.* New York: UNDP, 2003.

Messer, Donald E. *Breaking the Conspiracy of Silence: Christian Churches and the Global AIDS Crisis.* Minneapolis: Fortress, 2004.

Mikell, Gwendolyn. *African Feminism: The Politics of Survival in Sub-Saharan Africa.* Philadelphia: University of Pennsylvania Press, 1997.

Miller, Jerome A. *The Way of Suffering: A Geography of Crisis.* Washington, D.C.: Georgetown University Press, 1988.

Mittelman, James H. *The Globalization Syndrome: Transformations and Resistance.* Princeton: Princeton University Press, 2001.

Moe-Lobeda, Cynthia. *Healing a Broken World: Globalization and God.* Minneapolis: Fortress, 2002.

Moltman, Jürgen. *On Human Dignity: Political Theology and Ethics.* Translated by M. D. Meeks. Philadelphia: Fortress, 1984.

Moodley, Keymanthri. "HIV Vaccine Trial Participation in South Africa— An Ethical Assessment." *Journal of Medicine and Philosophy* 27.2 (2002): 197–215.

Morrison, Donald. "Politics as a Vocation, According to Aristotle." *History of Political Thought* 22 (2001): 221–41.

Murray, Colin. *Families Divided: The Impact of Migrant Labor in Lesotho.* Cambridge: Cambridge University Press, 1981.

Mussa, Michael. "Meeting the Challenge of Globalisation." *Journal of African Economies* 12. AERC Suppl. 1 (2003): 14–34.

Mutongi, Beatrice. "Generations of Grief and Grievances: A History of Widows and Widowhood in Margoli, Western Kenya, 1900 to Present." Ph.D. dissertation, University of Virginia, 1996.

Nelson, Hilde L. "Against Caring." *Journal of Clinical Ethics* 17.3 (1992): 8–15.

Nelson, James B. *Embodiment: An Approach to Christian Sexuality and Christian Theology.* Minneapolis: Augsburg, 1978.

Nelson, James B., and Sandra P. Longfellow, eds. *Sexuality and the Sacred: Sources for Theological Reflection.* Louisville, Ky.: Westminster John Knox, 1994.

Niebuhr, Reinhold. *The Nature and Destiny of Man.* Vol. 1. New York: Charles Scribner & Sons, 1949.

Nietzsche, Friedrich. *The Antichrist.* Translated by W. Kaufmann, Harmondsworth: Penguin Books, 1982.

Njoroge, Nyambura J. *Kiama Kia Ngo: An African Christian Feminist Ethic of Resistance and Transformation.* Legon, Ghana: Legon Theological Studies Series, 2000.

Nnaemeka, Obioma, "Introduction." *Sisterhood, Feminisms and Power: From Africa to the Diaspora.* Trenton, N.J. and Asmara, Eritrea: Africa World Press, 1998.

———. "Mapping African Feminisms." in *Readings in Gender in Africa.* Edited by Andrea Cornwall. Bloomington: Indiana University Press, 2005. Pp. 31–41.

———. "Nego-Feminism: Theorizing, Practicing, and Pruning Africa's Way." *Signs: Journal of Women in Culture and Society* 29.2 (2003): 257–85.

Noddings, Nel. "In Defense of Caring." *Journal of Clinical Ethics,* 3.1 (1992): 15–18.

———. *Caring: A Feminine Approach to Ethics and Moral Education.* Berkeley: University of California Press, 1984.

Norr, Kathleen F., Beverly J. McElmurry, Matshidiso Moeti, and Sheila D. Tlou. "AIDS Prevention for Women: A Community Based Approach." In *AIDS, Ethics and Religion: Embracing a World of Suffering.* Edited by Kenneth R. Overberg. Maryknoll, N.Y.: Orbis Books, 1994. Pp. 189–99.

Nussbaum, Martha C. *Upheavals of Thought: The Intelligence of Emotions.* Cambridge: Cambridge University Press, 2001.

———. *Love's Knowledge: Essays on Philosophy and Literature.* New York: Oxford University Press, 1990.

Nygren, Anders. *Agape and Eros: A Study and History of the Christian Idea of Love.* 3 vols. London: SPCK, 1982.

Obasanjo, Olusegun. "Letter to the Southern Baptist Convention." In *The aWake Project: Uniting Against the African AIDS Crisis.* Compiled by Jenny Eaton and Kate Etrue. Nashville: W Publishing, 2001. Pp. 76–79.

Obbo, C. "The Language of AIDS in Rural and Urban Uganda." *African Urban Quarterly* 6.1–2 (1991): 83–92.

———. "Women, Children and a Living Wage." In *Changing Uganda: The Dilemma of Structural Adjustment and Revolutionary Change.* Edited by H. Hansen and M. Twaddle. London: James Currey, 1991.

Okin, Susan Moller. *Justice, Gender, and the Family.* New York: Basic Books, 1989.

Okwenba, A., and Makokha. "Kenyan May Lose Out on 'Majengo' AIDS Vaccine." *Daily Nation*, October 12, 2000.

Oppenheimer, G. M., and R. A. Padgung. "AIDS: The Risks to Insurers, The Threat to Equity." *Hastings Center Report* 16.5 (1986): 18–22.

Overberg, Kenneth R., ed. *AIDS, Ethics and Religion: Embracing a World of Suffering.* Maryknoll, N.Y.: Orbis Books, 1994.

Oyeronke, Owuyemi. *The Invention of Women.* Minneapolis: University of Minnesota Press, 1997.

Paterson, Gillian. *Love in a Time of AIDS: Women, Health and the Challenge of HIV.* Geneva: World Council of Churches, 1996.

Pauw, Jacques. *Into the Heart of Darkness: Confessions of Apartheid's Assassins.* Johannesburg: Jonathan Ball, 1997.

Pellegrino, E. D. "Ethics." *Journal of the American Medical Association* 263.19 (1990): 2641–42.

———. "Ethics and Treatment of HIV Infection." In *AIDS, Ethics and Religion.* Maryknoll, N.Y.: Orbis Books, 1994. Pp. 78–82.

Pesch, Otto. *The God Question in Thomas Aquinas and Martin Luther.* Philadelphia: Fortress, 1972.

Peters, Ted. *For the Love of Children: Genetic Technology and the Future of the Family.* Louisville: Westminster John Knox, 1996.

———. *Playing God? Genetic Determinism and Human Freedom.* New York: Routledge, 1997.

Peterson, Kristin. "HIV/AIDS and Democracy in Nigeria: Politcs, Rights and Therapeutic Economies." Ph.D. dissertation, Rice University, 2004.

Peterson, Kris, and Olatubosun Obileye. "Access to Drugs for HIV/AIDS and Related Opportunistic Infections in Nigeria." Policy Project. Nigeria, 2002. Pp. 2–4. http://www.globaltreatmentaccess.org/.

Phiri, Isabel Apawo, Beverley Haddad, and Madipoane Masenya, eds. *African Women, HIV/AIDS and Faith Communities.* Pietermaritzburg, South Africa: Cluster Publications, 2003.

Pinn, Anthony B. *Why Lord?: Suffering and Evil in Black Theology.* New York: Continuum, 1995.

Piot, P. "Violence Against Women." Presentation to the United Nations Commission on the Status of Women. Forty-Third Session: Panel on Women and Health, March 3, 1999. http://www.unaids.org/unaids/speeches/ny3march99.html.

Pottash, Betty, ed. *Widows in African Societies: Choices and Constraints.* Berkeley: University of California Press, 1986.

Pratt, Cornelius B., Louisa Ha, and Charlotte A Pratt. "Setting the Public Health Agenda on Major Diseases in Sub-Saharan Africa: African Popular Magazines and Medical Journals, 1981–1997." *Journal of Communication* 52.44 (2002): 889–904.

Raikes, Alanagh. "Women's Health in East Africa." *Social Science and Medicine* 28 (1989): 447–59.

Raissiguier, Catherine. "Women from the Maghreb and Sub-Saharan Africa in France: Fighting for Health and Basic Human Rights." In *Engendering Human Rights: Cultural and Socioeconomic Realities in Africa.* Edited by Obioma Nnaemeka and Joy Ngozi Ezeilo. New York: Palgrave Macmillan, 2005. Pp. 111–28.

Ramsey, Paul. *Speak Up For Just War or Pacifism: A Critique of the United Methodists Bishops' Pastoral Letter "In Defense of Creation."* University Park: Penn State University Press, 1988.

Reid, E. "Approaching the HIV Epidemic: The Community's Response." *AIDS Care* 6.5 (1994): 551–57.

Richdbacher, Wilhelm. "*Missio Dei:* The Basis of Mission Theology or a Wrong Path?" *International Review of Missions* 92 (2003): 367.

Roberts, Bronwen. "Apartheid Forces Spread AIDS." *Mail and Guardian,* November 12, 1999.

———. *Globalization: Social Theory and Global Culture.* London: Sage, 1992.

———. "Globalization: Time-Space and Homogeneity-Heterogeneity." In *Global Modernities.* Edited by M. Featherstone, S. Lash, and R. Robertson. London: Sage, 1995. Pp. 25–44.

Rosin, H. H., and G. van Winsen. *Missio Dei, Term en Functie in de Zendingstheologische discussie.* Leiden: IIMO, 1971.

Rothman, K. J., and S. Greenland. *Modern Epidemiology.* Philadelphia: Lippincott Williams & Wilkins, 1998.

Ruden, Sarah. "AIDS in South Africa: Why the Churches Matter." *The Christian Century*, May 17, 2000.

Russell-Coons, Ron. "We Have AIDS." In *The Church with AIDS: Renewal in the Midst of Crisis.* Edited by Letty M. Russell. Louisville, Ky.: Westminster John Knox, 1990. Pp. 35–44.

Sachs, Jeffrey D. "Third World Disease. Our Problem." *Internal Medicine News* 38.1 (2005): 2–3.

Sachs, Jeffrey, and Sonia Ehrlich Sachs. "AIDS and Africa: Where is the US?" *Boston Globe*, February 2002.

Sanders, David, and Abdulrahman Sambo. "AIDS in Africa." In *AIDS, Ethics, and Religion.* Edited by Kenneth R. Overberg. Maryknoll, N.Y.: Orbis Books, 1994. Pp. 40–52.

Schall, R. "Statistical Analysis of HIV Prevalence." *South African Medical Journal* 77.1 (1990): 52.

Scheler, Max. *The Nature of Sympathy.* Translated by Paul Heath. London: Routledge & Kegan Paul, 1954.

Schneewind, J. B. "The Misfortunes of Virtue." In *Virtue Ethics.* Edited by Roger Crisp and Michael Slote. Oxford: Oxford University Press, 1997. Pp. 178–200.

Schoepf, B. G. "Inscribing the Body Politic: Women and AIDS in Africa." In *Pragmatic Women and Body Politics.* Edited by M. Lock and M. Kaufert. Cambridge: Cambridge University Press, 1991. Pp. 98–126.

Schoepf, Brooke Grundfest, "Uganda: Lessons for AIDS Control in Africa," *Review of African Political Economy* 98 (2003): 553–72.

Scholte, J. A. *Globalization: A Critical Introduction.* London: Palgrave, 2000.

Schopenhauer, Arthur. *On the Basis of Morality.* Translated by E. F. J. Payne. Providence: Berghahn Books, 1995.

Schoub, B. D., et al. "Epidemiological Considerations of the Present Status and Future Growth of the Acquired Immunodeficiency Syndrome Epidemic in South Africa." *South African Medical Journal* 70.4 (1988): 153–57.

Schuftan, Claudio. "Aids in Uganda: Is There Such a Thing as a Success Story?" *Afro Nets* 12 (2002). http://www.afronets.org/afronets-hma/afro-nets.200209/msg00018.php.

Schweiker, William. "A Preface to Ethics: Global Dynamics and the Integrity of Life." *Journal of Religious Ethics* 32.1 (2004): 13–37.

Sen, Amartya. "If It Is Fair, It's Good: 10 Truths About Globalization." *International Herald Tribune*, July 1–15, 2001.

Sen, Amartya. "What's the Point of Democracy?" *American Academy of Arts and Sciences Bulletin* 57.3 (2004): 1–9.

Setel, P. W. "Comparative Histories of Sexually Transmitted Disease and HIV/AIDS in Africa: An Introduction." In *Histories of Sexually Transmitted Diseases and HIV/AIDS in Sub-Saharan Africa*. Edited by P. W. Setel, M. Lewis, and M. Lyons. Westport, Conn.: Greenwood, 1999. Pp. 1–15.

Setel, Philip, Milton Lewis, and Maryinez Lyons, eds. *Histories of Sexually Transmitted Diseases and HIV/AIDS in Sub-Saharan Africa*. Westport: Greenwood Press, 1999.

Shepherd, Lois. "Face-to-Face: A Call for Radical Responsibility in Place of Compassion." *St. John's Law Review* 77.3 (2003): 445–514.

Shire, C. "Men Don't Go to the Moon: Language, Space and Masculinities in Zimbabwe." In *Dislocating Masculinities: Comparative Ethnographies*. Edited by A. Cornwall and N. Lindisfarne. London: Routledge, 1994. Pp. 147–58.

Shisana O., N. Zungu-Dirwayi, and W. Shisana. "AIDS: A Threat to Human Security." Background paper. Harvard University Global Equity Initiative, 2002.

Shisana Olive, and Nompumelelo Zungu-Dirwayi. "Government's Changing Responses to HIV/AIDS." *Interfund Development Update* 4.3 (2003). Edited by David Everatt and Vincent Maphai.

Shorter, Aylward, and Edwin Onyancha, *The Church and AIDS in Africa: A Case Study of Nairobi City*. Nairobi: Paulines Publications, 1998.

Shutte, Augustine. *Ubuntu: An Ethic for a New South Africa*. Pietermaritzburg, South Africa: Cluster Publications, 2001.

Sitze, Adam. "Denialism." *The South Atlantic Quarterly* 103.4 (2004): 769–811.

Slote, Michael. *Morals from Motives*. Oxford: Oxford University Press, 2001.

Smith, Daniel J. "HIV/AIDS in Nigeria: The Challenges of a National Epidemic." In *Crafting the New Nigeria: Confronting the Challenges*. Edited by Robert I. Rotberg. Boulder and London: Lynne Rienner, 2004. Pp. 199–218.

Snow, Bill. "Vaccine Basics." In *AIDS Vaccine Handbook: Global Perspective*. Edited by Patricia Kahn. New York: AIDS Vaccine Advocacy Coalition, 2005. 25–30.

Sokolowski, Robert. *The God of Faith and Reason: Foundations of Christian Theology*. Notre Dame: University of Notre Dame Press, 1982.

South African Medical Research Council. *The Impact of HIV/AIDS on Adult Mortality in South Africa*. Research Report, September 2001.

Southern African Catholic Bishops' Conference. "A Message of Hope from the Catholic Bishops to the People of God in South Africa, Botswana and Swaziland." Pretoria, 2001.

Specter, Michael. "The Vaccine." *New Yorker*, February 3, 2003. Pp. 54–65.

Stephenson, Rob, Amy Ong Tsui, Sara Sulzbach, Phil Bardsley, Getachew Bekele, Tilahun Giday, Rehena Ahmed, Gopi Gopalkrishnan, and Bamikale Feyesitan. "Franchising Reproductive Health Services." *Health Services Research* 39.6 (2004): 2053–80.

Stiebert, Johanna. "Does the Hebrew Bible Have Anything to Tell Us about HIV/AIDS?" In *HIV/AIDS and the Curriculum: Methods of Integrating HIV/AIDS in Theological Programmes*. Edited by Musa W. Dube. Geneva: World Council of Churches, 2003.

Suess, Paulo. "*Mission Dei* and the Project of Jesus: The Poor and the 'Other' as Mediators of the Kingdom of God and Protagonists of the Churches." *International Review of Missions* 92 (2003): 550–59.

Sullivan, Lawrence. "Introduction." *Healing and Restoring: Health and Medicine in the World's Religious Traditions*. Edited by Lawrence Sullivan. New York and London: Macmillan, 1989. 1–8.

Tacket, C. O., and R. Edelman. "Ethical Issues Involving Volunteers in AIDS Vaccine Trials." *Journal of Infectious Diseases* 161 (1990).

Tangwa, Godfrey. "The HIV/AIDS Pandemic, African Traditional Values and the Search for a Vaccine in Africa." *Journal of Medicine and Philosophy* 27.2 (2002): 217–30.

Tanner, Kathryn. "The Care that Does Justice: Recent Writings in Feminist Ethics and Theology." *Journal of Religious Ethics* 24.1 (2001): 171–91.

Ter Haar, Gerrie. *Halfway to Paradise: African Christians in Europe*. Cardiff: Cardiff Academic Press, 1998.

———, ed. *Religious Communities in the Diaspora*. Nairobi: Acton, 2001.

Teresa, Mother. *Words to Love By*. Notre Dame: Ave Maria, 1983.

Thompson, T. J. "African Independent Churches in Britain: an Introductory Survey." In *New Religions and the New Europe*. Edited by R. Towler. Aarhus: Aarhus University Press, 1995. Pp. 224–31.

Tomlinson, John. *Globalization and Culture*. Chicago: The University of Chicago Press, 1999.

Treichler, P. A. *How to Have a Theory in an Epidemic: Cultural Chronicles of AIDS*. Durham: Duke University Press, 1999.

Trobisch, Walter. *The Collected Works of Walter Trobisch*. Downers Grove, Ill: InterVarsity, 1987.

Trouiller, Patrice, Piero Olliaro, Els Torreele, James Orbinski, Richard Laring, and Nathan Ford. "Drug Development for Neglected Diseases:

A Deficient Market and Public Health Policy Failure." *The Lancet* 359 (2002): 2188–94.

Tudor, Steven. *Compassion and Remorse: Acknowledging the Suffering Other.* Leuven: Peeters, 2001.

Twiss, Summer B. "History, Human Rights, and Globalization," *Journal of Religious Ethics* 32.1 (2004): 39–70.

U.S. National Intelligence Council (NIC). *The Next Wave of HIV/AIDS: Nigeria, Ethiopia, Russia, India, and China.* Washington, D.C., September 2002.

USCCB. *The Many Faces of AIDS: A Gospel Response. A Statement of the Administrative Board.* Washington, D.C.: USCC, 1987.

UNAIDS. *AIDS in Africa: Three Scenarios to 2005.* Geneva: UNAIDS, 2005.

UNAIDS and The World Bank. *AIDS, Poverty Reduction and Debt Relief: A Toolkit for Mainstreaming HIV/AIDS Programmes into Development Instruments.* Geneva: UNAIDS, 2001.

UNAIDS, UNFPA, and UNIFEM. *Women and HIV/AIDS: Confronting the Crisis.* Geneva and New York: UNAIDS, UNFPA, UNIFEM, 2004.

UNAIDS, UNICEF, and USAID. *Children on the Brink 2004: A Joint Report of New Orphan Estimates and a Framework for Action.* New York: United Nations Children's Fund, 2004.

United Nations Development Programme (UNDP). *Human Development Report 1992.* New York: Oxford University Press, 1992.

———. *Human Development Report 1998.* New York: Oxford University Press, 1998.

United Nations. *World Urbanization Prospectus: The 1996 Revision.* New York: United Nations, Department of Economic and Social Affairs, Population Division, 1998.

U.S. Catholic Bishop's Conference. *Called to Compassion and Responsibility: A Response to the HIV/AIDS Crisis.* Washington, D.C.: USCC Publishing Services, 1989.

———. *The Many Faces of AIDS: a Gospel Response.* Washington, D.C.: USCC Publishing Services, 1987.

Van Gelderen, C. J. "Insurance and Compensation in the Event of HIV Infection." *South African Medical Journal* 81.6 (1992): 33.

Villa-Vicencio, Charles. *A Theology of Reconstruction: Nation-Building and Human Rights.* Cambridge: Cambridge University Press, 1992.

Von Rad, Gerhard. "The Divine Likeness in the Old Testament." In *Theological Dictionary of the New Testament.* Edited by Gerhard Kittle, vol. 2. Grand Rapids: Eerdmans, 1964. 390–92.

Walker, Liz, Graeme Reid, and Morna Cornell. *Waiting to Happen: HIV/AIDS in South Africa: The Bigger Picture.* Boulder and London: Lynne Rienner, 2004.

Walrond, E. R. "Regional Policies in Relation to the HIV/AIDS Epidemic in the Commonwealth Caribbean." In *The Caribbean AIDS Epidemic.* Edited by G. Howe and A. Cobbley. Kingston: University of West Indies Press, 2000. 57–70.

Warren, Mitchell. "An Epidemic that Rages On." In *AIDS Vaccine Handbook: Global Perspective.* Edited by Patricia Kahn. New York: AIDS Vaccine Advocacy Coalition, 2005.

Watney, S. "Risk Groups or Risk Behaviors." In *AIDS in the World II: Global Dimensions, Social Roots, and Responses.* Edited by J. Mann and D. Tarantola. New York: Oxford University Press, 1996. Pp. 431–32.

Wei, Shang-Jin. "Risk and Reward of Embracing Globalization: The Governance Factor." *Journal of African Economies* 12. AERC Suppl. 1 (2003): 73–119.

Welker, Michael. "Creation and the Image of God: Their Understanding in Christian Tradition and the Biblical Grounds." *Journal of Ecumenical Studies* 34 (1997): 436–43.

Werbner, Richard. *Ritual Passage: Sacred Journey.* Washington, D.C.: Smithsonian Institution Press, 1989.

Wert, Newell J. "The Biblical and Theological Basis for Risking Compassion and Care for AIDS Patients." In *AIDS, Ethics and Religion: Embracing A World of Suffering.* Edited by Kenneth Overberg. Maryknoll, N.Y.: Orbis Books, 1994.

West, Gerald. "Reading the Bible in the Light of HIV/AIDS in South Africa." *Ecumenical Review* 55.4 (2003): 335–44.

Wheatley, Melvin E. "Open Letter to the United Methodist Rocky Mountain Conference." Denver, Colo., October 12, 1981.

Wilkin, Vincent. *The Image of God in Sex.* New York: Sheed & Ward, 1955.

Williams, Bernard. *Ethics and the Limits of Philosophy.* Cambridge, Mass.: Harvard University Press, 1985.

Wilmhurst, P. "Scientific Imperialism." *British Medical Journal* 314 (1997): 840–41.

Wilton, T. *EnGendering AIDS: Deconstructing Sex, Test and Epidemic.* London: Sage, 1997.

Winn, Phillip. "Personal Suspects and the Framing of Africa: Who's to Blame for AIDS?" *Mots Pluriels* 1.3 (1997). http://motspluriels.arts. uwa.edu.au/MP397pw.html.

Woodhill, William Joseph. *The Fellowship of Life: Virtue Ethics and Orthodox Christianity.* Washington D.C.: Georgetown University Press, 1996.

Woodward David, Nick Drager, Robert Beaglehole, and Debra A. Lipson. "Globalization and Health: A Framework for Analysis and Action." *Bulletin of the World Health Organization* 70 (2001): 875–80.

World Bank, *World Development Report,* 1995.

World Council of Churches. "Plan of Action: The Ecumenical Response to HIV/AIDS in Africa." *Global Consultation on the Ecumenical Response to the Challenge of HIV/AIDS.* Nairobi, November 25–28, 2001.

World Health Organization Advisory Committee on Health Research, 2002.

Yearly, Lee H. "Recent Work on Virtue." *Religious Studies Review* 16 (1990): 1–9.

Zuger, Abigail, Miles Zuger, and H. Stephen. "Physicians, AIDS, and Occupational Risk: Historic Traditions and Ethical Obligations." *Journal of the American Medical Association* 258.14 (1987): 1924–28.

Zulu, Eliya Msiyaphazi, F. Nii-Amoo Dodoo, and Alex Chika-Ezeh. "Sexual Risk-Taking in the Slums of Nairobi, Kenya 1993–98." *Population Studies* 56 (2002): 311–23.

Index

245